ASPECTS OF THE DEVELOPMENT OF COMPETENCE

**The Minnesota Symposia
on Child Psychology
Volume 14**

ASPECTS OF THE
DEVELOPMENT OF COMPETENCE

The Minnesota Symposia
on Child Psychology
Volume 14

EDITED BY
W. ANDREW COLLINS
University of Minnesota

LEA LAWRENCE ERLBAUM ASSOCIATES, PUBLISHERS
1981   Hillsdale, New Jersey

Lawrence Erlbaum Associates, Inc., Publishers
365 Broadway
Hillsdale, New Jersey 07642

Library of Congress Cataloging in Publication Data
Minnesota Symposium on Child Psychology, 14th,
 University of Minnesota, 1979
 Aspects of the development of competence.

 Papers from the conference sponsored by the Institute
of Child Development, University of Minnesota.
 "The Minnesota Symposia on Child Psychology, v. 14."
 Bibliography: p.
 Includes index.
 1. Performance in children—Congresses. 2. Cognition in children—Congresses. 3. Social interaction
in children—Congresses. I. Collins, W. Andrew,
1944-   II. Minnesota. University. Institute of
Child Development. III. Title.

 BF723.P365M56 1979   155.4'13   80-20568
 ISBN 0-89859-070-1

Printed in the United States of America

Contents

Preface

The Fourteenth Annual Minnesota Symposium on Child Psychology was held at the University of Minnesota, Minneapolis, October 18–20, 1979. As in each of the past twelve years, the Institute of Child Development convened six outstanding developmental scholars to present their current research within the programmatic perspective in which it was conceived. Although in several recent volumes, the six contributors have been drawn from the same sub-area of developmental study, the participants in the Fourteenth Symposium represent diverse foci. They are scholars in infant physiology, early perceptual processes, cognition, language development, social relations and personality—a sampling of the vigorous and varied activity in developmental psychology.

Nevertheless, despite the intentional diversity of the invited contributions, these six papers are similar in interesting and revealing ways. Uniformly, the authors focus on the child as an active participant in the cognitive and social transactions of typical experience; they go beyond the superficial invocation of "the active organism" (which one of them rightly calls the "slogan of cognitive [and developmental] psychology") to outline specific empirical and theoretical formulations that give substance to this view of the developing child. This commonality cuts across levels of analyses from the physiological to social and personality indicators. Although it was not the purpose, nor the achievement, of the Symposium to arrive at a synthesis across these different levels, with hindsight these six chapters appear to bring together representative problems and approaches that, over the long term, may be conducive to broad reflection on fundamental psychological and developmental processes.

In Chapter One, Frances Graham and her collaborators report investigations of the nature of control systems that are "presumed to affect the flow of information in cognition." In mature organisms the startle reflex has been found to be affected differently by transient and by sustained stimulation before a reflex stimulus is presented. Graham and her colleagues piece together evidence from a series of studies to indicate that, in the young infant, transient stimuli produce inhibitory responding, usually in the second month of life; but, according to the experimenters, the effect is relatively weak compared to the effect of transient stimuli on adults. Graham provides a detailed discussion of the physiological and neurochemical basis for inhibitory and facilitating responses and the probable maturational course of these neurophysiological correlates of cognitive control processes.

Marc Bornstein finds evidence in recent research of two kinds of perceptual organization near the beginning of life and discusses the relation of these organizational patterns to cognitive functioning in many domains. He argues that infants' abilities to respond to discriminably different stimuli as though they were the same indicates capacity for recognizing important perceptual similarities and that, within any given class or sensory domain, certain stimuli are especially salient to infants in the first six months of life. Bornstein argues that these perceptual organizations, added to other recognized congenitally organized behaviors such as grasping and rooting, stimulus seeking, and the ability to learn soon after birth, provide young human beings with the ability to perceive the world in organized ways very early on. They may also provide the important initial structures on the basis of which cognitive development proceeds.

In Chapter 3 Elissa Newport proposes that young deaf children's learning of American Sign Language is, like the language learning of hearing children, dependent on each child's internal analyses of morphemes that are acquired one by one. In contrast to the facilitative early organizational principles identified by Bornstein, language learning appears to require relatively laborious inductive effort over a period of several years, even though the environment for American Sign Language learners (particularly second- and later- generation signers) offers striking iconic and analogue possibilities that should make language learning a simpler process for them. Newport concludes that the similarity of processes apparently required for learning spoken languages, as well as this visual-gestural language, lies in the nature of the language learning mechanism itself.

These contributors' emphases on developmental regularities in cognitive functions is balanced by the analysis of differences in children's strategies presented by Michael Cole and Kenneth Traupman. The theme, as in much of Cole's writing about cross-cultural cognitive research, is the limitations of traditional performance measures for understanding the nature of cognitive capabilities. In Chapter 4, he and his collaborator report their analysis of detailed observations of a child identified by traditional procedures as learning disabled, concluding that in natural settings the child shows many adaptive task-achievement strategies. They urge a broader view of both assessment procedures and the nature of adaptive abilities themselves.

The sometimes deleterious effects of superfluous adult controls on children's interest in and performance on tasks is Mark Lepper's focus in Chapter 5. Lepper reviews his extensive research on the effects of extrinsic constraints on compliance and intrinsic motivation and proposes that the effectiveness of external pressure follows a "Minimal Sufficiency Principle," in which increased constraints beyond a level necessary for initial compliance or participation in many tasks undermines subsequent intrinsic control over behavior. As in other chapters, the role of children's constructive cognitive activity is central. In a final discussion, he notes the need to investigate the operation and effects of alternatives to the traditional emphasis on immediate reinforcement and punishment as means of socialization.

In her discussion of mastery motivation in Chapter 6, Susan Harter also addresses issues of external social forces and internalization in the development of a sense of competence. Departing from Robert White's seminal ideas about effectance, her emphasis has been more psychometric and differential than Lepper's; but like the research in earlier chapters, Harter's work concerns the nature of children's perceptions and concepts as bases for significant psychological responses. Much of her work to date has been devoted to issues of measurement of the mastery construct for children of different ages, and in her chapter she discusses implications of psychometrically sound methods for constructs and theories of mastery and competence.

Financial support for this fourteenth Minnesota Symposium was provided by Public Health Service Grant No. 1R13HD-10650 from the National Institute of Child Health and Human Development to the Institute of Child Development. In addition, part of the work of editing the papers was carried out while I was a Visiting Fellow at the Boys Town Center for the Study of Youth Development, Boys Town, Nebraska, and the provision of facilities there is gratefully acknowledged. The Symposium is carried out cooperatively by the faculty, staff, and students of the Institute of Child Development, whose efforts deserve the highest praise. Special acknowledgment is given to the Minnesota Symposium Committee composed of the following: Ryan Bliss; Mary Ann Chalkley; Helen Dickison; Wayne Duncan; Virginia Eaton; Elizabeth Haugen; Becky Jones; Daniel Keating; Judy List; Michael Livingston; Frank Manis; David Mitchell; Fred Morrison; Lynn Musser; Marion Perlmutter; and Mary Jo Ward. In addition, Catherine Meyer was an efficient and enterprising consultant and collaborator throughout this Symposium; and Julie Hamerski and, especially, Francie Schroeder contributed importantly to both the arrangements for the Symposium and the preparation of this volume.

Finally, the contributors themselves have been both extraordinarily stimulating intellectual collaborators and pleasant personal colleagues throughout the Symposium events and the editorial activities for Volume 14. Their talent and creativity in the study of children and development make the enterprise especially worthwhile.

W. ANDREW COLLINS
Minneapolis, Minnesota

ASPECTS OF THE DEVELOPMENT OF COMPETENCE

The Minnesota Symposia
on Child Psychology
Volume 14

1 Excitatory and Inhibitory Influences on Reflex Responsiveness

Frances K. Graham,
Barbara D. Strock
and
Bonnie L. Zeigler
University of Wisconsin, Madison

Control systems, presumed to affect the flow of information, play a central role in many cognitive theories (e.g., Kahneman, 1973; Neisser, 1967; Posner, 1975). The systems are variously delineated and named—alertness, arousal, activation, effort, attention, orienting, defense, and so on—but at least three distinctions appear to be important: (1) whether the control is automatic, preattentive, and nonselective; (2) whether it affects the selection of inputs to be enhanced; and (3) whether it affects the speed and vigor of outputs. In a recent paper, Graham (1979, b) suggested that the operation of these three kinds of control might be reflected by changes in response to a probe blink-eliciting stimulus.

Although blinking is an unconditioned brainstem reflex, it can, like any reflex, be modified via efferent projections from cortical as well as many other levels of the nervous system (e.g., Lundberg, 1966; Sauerland, Knauss, Nakamura, & Clemente, 1967). Thus, in theory, it is potentially able to reflect processes and mechanisms at all levels. In fact, psychologists in the early decades of this century used the method of unconditioned reflex modification to advantage for analysis of sensory processing (e.g., Cohen, Hilgard, & Wendt, 1933; Peak, 1933; Yerkes, 1905). The method was then abandoned for several decades in favor of the study of instrumentally or classically conditioned, learned responses, but it has recently been revived in a number of laboratories (e.g., Hoffman & Wible, 1969; Ison & Leonard, 1971; Thompson & Spencer, 1966). In the meantime, understanding the neuro-physiology of conditioned reflexes has advanced beyond knowledge of the associated behavioral phenomena.

1

THE STARTLE REFLEX AND ITS MEASUREMENT

The recent work on reflex modification has focused on the polysynaptic startle reflex. Landis and Hunt (1939), in an extensive cinemagraphic study, described the primary component of startle as an inflexibly patterned, flexor contraction beginning with the eyeblink and, in its full manifestation, progressing downward to involve the whole body. Landis and Hunt (1939) drew explicit attention to the fact that startle was not a directional response, involving movement "away from" a stimulus, because they found that the pattern was "in no way changed by the direction from which the stimulus comes [p. 31]." It cannot, therefore, be considered a "flight" reaction and may, as Graham (1979, b) suggested, be more appropriately described as an "interrupt" of ongoing activity.

The startle reaction is elicited by stimulation in any modality whose intensity increases sufficiently within a sufficiently short time. For acoustic stimuli delivered to the adult human or rat, a 90 dB rise within a 10–12 msec period must occur (Berg, 1973; Fleshler, 1965). The neuroanatomical structures responsible for organizing startle lie in the ventromedial reticular formation between the medulla and the pons at the level of the trapezoid body (Szabo & Hazafi, 1965). Gendelman and Davis (1979) have recently traced the pathway for acoustic startle from the cochlear nucleus through the nucleus reticularis pontis caudalis. At least in rats, the latter nucleus contains the largest cells found in the brainstem (Valverde, 1962). The final common path for the blink component also lies in the caudal portion of the pons, in the motor nucleus of the facial (seventh cranial) nerve.

Startle can be conveniently measured, in small mammals and birds, by the acceleration that the rapid flexor contraction imparts to a rigidly suspended chamber. The method could be easily adapted for study of the human infant, but appears not to have been used. Instead, human studies have employed direct or indirect methods of measuring the blink component. These have included recording the distance of lid movement, through potentiometric or photometric transducers, or the velocity of lid movement. Electromyographic (EMG) activity of the muscle that controls blink, orbicularis oculi, has also been recorded. An indirect method takes advantage of the fact that the electrooculogram shows distinctive changes during blinking. As far as has been determined, all of the methods yield similar findings.

Our laboratory has employed both the potentiometric and the electro-myographic methods. The former is the method that has been widely used in classical conditioning research. A thread attached to a small shoe connects the lid margin with a micropotentiometer mounted on a headset. The micropotentiometer converts distance of the lid movement to voltage changes and these are computer sampled once a msec for 250 msec following onset of the reflex-eliciting stimulus. The sensitivity of the system is such that it can detect movements as small as 33 micrometers and, with the sampling rate used, latencies to an accuracy of ± 1 msec.

The computer is programmed to score latency of the first detectable movement within a predetermined window and to score latency and size of the peak movement. The window is 20–120 msec for adults and 20–170 msec for infants, in each case determined from latency distributions so as to exclude less than 1% of movements that followed a reflex stimulus. The computer also rejects trials on which the lid is partially closed or is in movement at the time of stimulus delivery. (See Graham, Putnam, & Leavitt, 1975, for a more detailed description of the scoring criteria.)

Figure 1.1 shows a blink recorded from an infant subject and displayed on the computer oscilloscope. The blink displayed is characteristic of infant blinks in showing a rapid initial closure, a relatively long period during which the eye remains closed, and a relatively slow, often spasmodic opening. These features can be contrasted wtih the adult, potentiometrically recorded blink shown in the lower portion of Fig. 1.2.

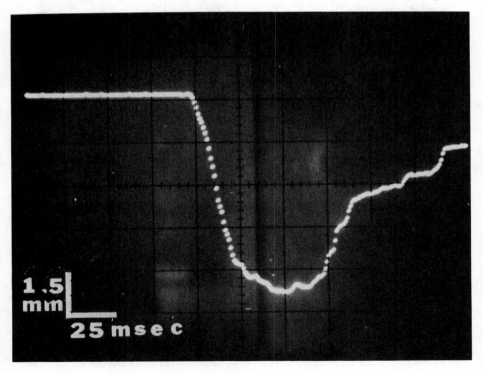

FIG. 1.1.   Computer-digitized (1/msec) infant blink, measured potentiometrically, and photographed from the oscilloscope display.

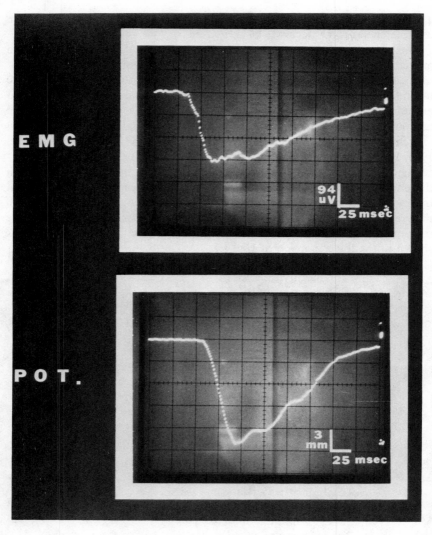

FIG. 1.2.   Computer-digitized (1/msec) adult blinks, simultaneously recorded
by electromyographic (*top*) and potentiometric (*bottom*) methods.

The upper portion of Fig. 1.2 shows the simultaneously recorded, integrated EMG for the same adult subject. We detect EMG activity by means of specifically designed, light-weight electrodes (Silverstein & Graham, 1978), having a total diameter of only 3 mm and a depth of approximately 1 mm. The electrodes are used in a bipolar configuration; this, in conjunction with their small size, makes it possible to detect only the activity from orbicularis oculi and to avoid recording activity from adjacent muscles. Fig. 1.2 illustrates

EMG activity beginning between 15 and 30 msec earlier than lid movement. The records came from a study of 12 adult subjects that showed a correlation, across subjects, of .91 between peak EMG and peak lid movement. Within-subject correlations, for 32 trials, ranged from .34 to .96, but only two subjects had coefficients less than .60.

Although eight of 12 infants tested also had within-subject correlations above .60, the between-subject correlation was low due to the variable sensitivity of potentiometric records. Infants were frequently restless during the application of two devices to the eyes, making it difficult to position the potentiometric device properly. The Silverstein electrodes are relatively easy to apply, however, and are clearly preferable whenever movement could disturb headset positioning.

STARTLE MODIFICATION
IN MATURE ORGANISMS

The procedure for modifying a startle reflex, however measured, involves variations in a simple two-stimulus paradigm (Fig. 1.3). On control trials, the reflex-eliciting stimulus is presented alone. On experimental trials, the reflex-eliciting probe is preceded by another stimulus. The first stimulus is called a conditioning stimulus or, because the effects are unlearned and the stimulus should be distinguished from the CS in Pavlovian conditioning, a preconditioning stimulus. In our work and most of the behavioral work on startle reflex modification, preconditioning stimuli are too weak to elicit the reflex itself. However, in neurological and neurophysiological work, conditioning stimuli are often identical to the reflex-eliciting stimuli. In either case, responses to the probe stimuli presented alone are compared with responses to the preconditioned probe. Characteristics of the prestimuli and of the experimental design are varied in order to activate different control systems.

Inhibition by Transient Prestimulation

A system capable of profoundly inhibiting reflex response is activated by any transient change in stimulation that shortly precedes the reflex-eliciting stimulus. The change may be a stimulus onset, offset, or qualitative change and need last no longer than 10–20 msec (e.g., Stitt, Hoffman, Marsh, & Boskoff, 1974). The effect has been demonstrated with acoustic, visual, and tactual stimulation (e.g., Buckland, Buckland, Jamieson, & Ison, 1969; Ison & Leonard, 1971; Stitt, Hoffman, Marsh, & Schwartz, 1976), although in human subjects the inhibition produced by visual and tactual prestimuli may be preceded by a brief period of facilitation (Graham, in press). Further, the modality of the conditioning stimulus need not be the same as the modality of the reflex-eliciting stimulus. An effect is produced even by stimuli at threshold

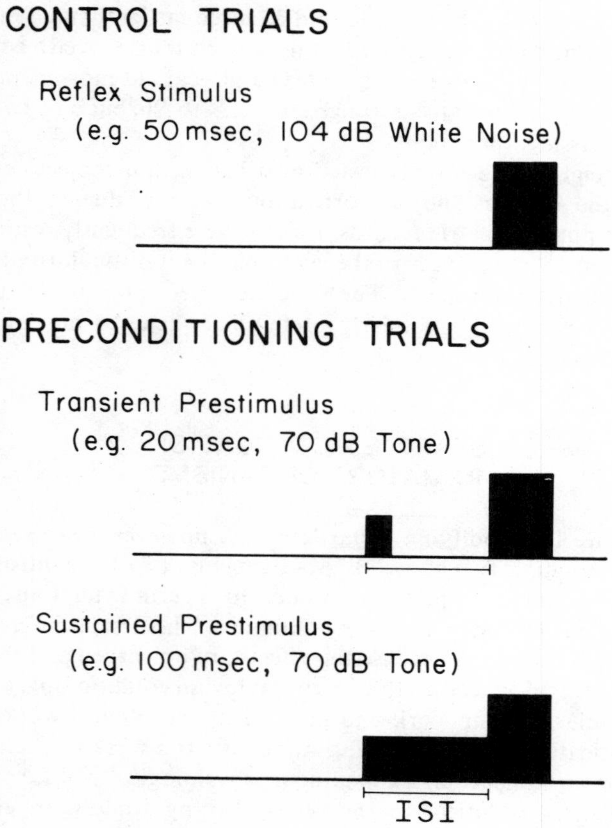

FIG. 1.3.   Two-stimulus paradigm used in reflex modification (preconditioning) studies. Horizontal scale = time; vertical scale = stimulus intensity.

intensity, but is greater with more intense prestimuli (Hoffman & Wible, 1970; Reiter & Ison, 1977). Intensity of the reflex-eliciting stimulus does not affect the amount of inhibition, however. Although an intense reflex stimulus elicits a large response and a weak reflex stimulus a small response, a given conditioning stimulus at a given lead interval will reduce both responses by the same amount (e.g., Stitt, Hoffman, & Marsh, 1976).

With acoustic prestimulation of moderate intensity, the inhibitory effect begins within approximately 16 msec and lasts for approximately 300 msec. The peak inhibition usually occurs between 60 and 120 msec in human adult subjects (e.g., Graham & Murray, 1977), but very similar functions have been seen in a variety of species. To give some idea of the effect in individual subjects during individual trials, Fig. 1.4 illustrates three trials of one subject.

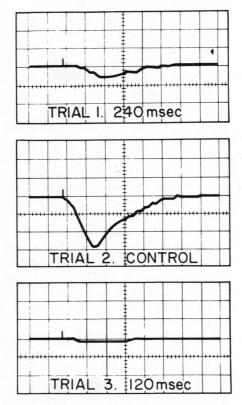

FIG. 1.4.   First three trials of adult subject from Graham and Murray (1977, Exp. 1). Horizontal scale unit = 25 msec; vertical scale unit = .85 mm of lid movement (potentiometric method). Copyright © 1975, The Society for Psychophysiological Research. Reprinted with permission of the publisher from Graham, F. K. The more or less startling effects of weak prestimulation. *Psychophysiology,* 1975, *12,* 238–248, Fig. 6.

On Trial 1, a 20-msec, 70 dB tone was delivered 240 msec before a white noise reflex-eliciting stimulus. Illustrating the unlearned nature of the effect, the blink was clearly inhibited by comparison with response to the reflex stimulus presented alone on Trial 2. On Trial 3, when the conditioning stimulus was presented at a more nearly optimal interval, blinking was almost completely suppressed.

This powerful effect is not due to a number of well-known mechanisms for producing inhibition, including learning, sensory masking, and the protective ear reflexes (e.g., Ison & Ash, 1977; Ison, Reiter, & Warren, 1979). Nor, because it is undiminished in REM and non-REM sleep, can it be ascribed to the neurophysiological mechanism producing reflex suppression in sleep

(Silverstein, Graham, & Calloway, 1980). Recently reported work from our laboratory also indicates that the preconditioning effect operates independently of the inhibitory loop producing a silent period in EMG (Graham, 1979a). Not surprisingly,the effect does not require cortex (Davis & Gendelman, 1977); more unexpectedly, it also survives cerebellar lesions (Leitner, Powers, & Hoffman, 1979) and fairly extensive lesions of reticular nuclei in the vicinity of the area in which startle is organized (Hammond, 1973). Although reticular lesions reduced the unconditioned reflex, they did not affect the inhibitory preconditioning. A recent report from Hoffman's laboratory (Leitner et al., 1979) does implicate midbrain structures, specifically nucleus cuneiformis of the lateral tegmentum. These cells receive multimodal inputs and project to pontis caudalis, the area described by Gendelman and Davis (1979) as part of the pathway for acoustic startle.

Thus, a profound, widespread inhibition of flexor activity can be produced within a few msec of a stimulus change in any modality. The effect is apparently abolished by midbrain tegmental lesions, but is unaffected by well-known mechanisms for inhibiting reflexes during sleep or during motor activity. Although it has not previously been suggested, the underlying mechanism may well be—or must, at least, include—presynaptic inhibition, whose characteristics closely parallel those of the behavioral phenomenon. Presynaptic inhibition, resulting from partial depolarization of flexor reflex afferents (FRAs), was first observed to follow conditioning stimulation of muscle and cutaneous afferents (e.g., Eccles, 1964; Eccles, Kostyuk, & Schmidt, 1962). Later work has shown that acoustic and visual stimuli are also effective in producing partial depolarization of FRAs (Mallart, 1965; Wright & Barnes, 1972). In fact, Mallart (1965) suggested that: "there is a system for a general presynaptic inhibition of the sensory input which can be activated by any kind of sensory stimulation evoking the general flexion reflex [p. 720]." A more limited description of his findings would be that presynaptic inhibition of the FRAs could be activated by any kind of sensory stimulation.

Presynaptic inhibition resembles the preconditioned inhibition of startle in other respects as well. It is notable for having a more profound effect and a much longer duration, in excess of 200 msec, than other inhibitory effects obtained at the spinal level (e.g., Thompson, 1967). It is also independent of duration of the conditioning stimulus (Wright & Barnes, 1972). Two additional findings reported by Wright and Barnes are particularly pertinent: (1) large diameter, rapidly conducting fibers appeared to mediate the effect; and (2) preconditioning by an acoustic stimulus required intact inferior colliculi. As in the case of inhibitory conditioning of behavioral startle, partial depolarization of FRAs by acoustic conditioning stimuli can be obtained in the absence of cerebellum or of any structures rostral to the intercollicular level.

Eccles et al. (1962), in an attempt to explain the widespread presynaptic inhibition of FRAs, suggested that it "provides the first stage in what we may term 'perceptual attention', whereby powerful sensory inputs with an implication of urgency can suppress all concurrent trivial inputs into the central nervous system [p. 277]." This is very similar to the idea proposed by Graham (1975) to account for inhibitory preconditioning of behavioral startle—namely, that it reflected "a wired-in negative feedback which reduces the distraction produced by reflexes such as startle, and thus protects what has been called preattentive stimulus processing [p. 246]." It is known that a stimulus can be detected rapidly, but it takes a few hundred msec to recognize that it is a particular change. Massaro has shown, with a backward masking paradigm, that even recognition of simple sounds is disrupted if a second change occurs within approximately 250 msec (e.g., Massaro, 1975). Similarly, Ross, Ferreira, and Ross (1974) found that a stimulus, interposed in the CS–UCS interval after acquisition of a conditioned response, disrupted a conditioned discrimination, but had no effect on simple conditioning. Simple conditioning requires only that the CS be detected, not that it be recognized or discriminated.

Facilitation by Sustained Prestimulation

Sustained prestimuli do not have the same effect as transient stimuli. Note that in Fig. 1.3, the illustrated transient and sustained preconditioners have the same onset characteristics, i.e., rise time and peak voltage. However, because sustained stimulation lasts longer, it will deliver more total energy and its loudness will be much greater. In the example, the transient stimulus is only about 40 dB above sensation level although its steady-state intensity is 70 dB. Thus, a sustained stimulus has two aspects—the transient change at its onset and a steady-state portion as it is prolonged. The effect due to prolongation alone can be isolated only by obtaining the difference between the effects of a sustained and transient stimulus.

Fig. 1.5 summarizes findings from a published study by Graham and Murray (1977) in which both sustained and transient conditioning stimuli were used. There were three experiments of nine subjects each, two using 70 dB and one using 60 dB conditioning tones. The lead interval from onset of tone prestimulus to onset of reflex-eliciting noise (i.e., stimulus onset asynchrony) is shown on the abscissa; change in blink size is on the ordinate. Inhibition was particularly strong at the 120-msec interval and occurred in all 27 subjects. A more important point is that inhibition was just as marked with the transient 20-msec prestimulus as it was when prestimulation was sustained throughout the interval. This is notable because a 10 dB increase in transient intensity produced significantly more inhibition. In contrast, increasing steady-state loudness by as much as 30 dB tended to produce less inhibition.

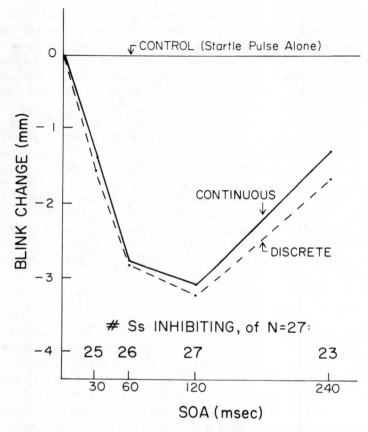

FIG. 1.5. Reduction in peak blink magnitude below control magnitude as a function of 70 dB, 20-msec transient (discrete) or sustained (continuous) tone prestimulation leading a reflex-eliciting stimulus (104 dB, 50-msec white noise) by stimulus onset asynchronies (SOA) of 30–240 msec. Mean for three experiments of nine adult subjects each, reported in Graham & Murray (1977).

The facilitating effects of sustained prestimulation are evident only in lessened inhibition, or in reduced latency, at such short conditioning intervals. However, as intervals are lengthened, the inhibitory effect of stimulus onset decays and the facilitating effects of sustained stimulation become apparent both in increases in blink size and in faster latencies.

Fig. 1.6 illustrates the results of several experiments examining the effects of sustained preconditioning tones 800–2000 msec in duration on the magnitude of reflex blinking in adult subjects. At the shortest lead interval, blink did not differ significantly from control level; when the conditioning tone was present for 2 seconds, however, blink magnitude was augmented

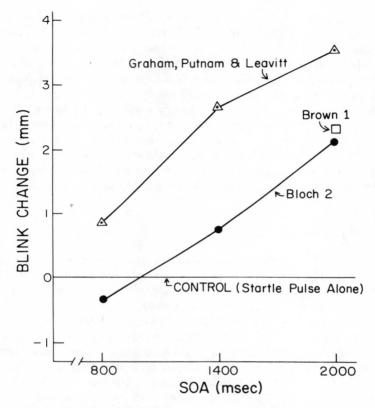

FIG. 1.6.   Peak blink magnitude change as a function of duration (SOA) of 70 dB sustained prestimuli leading 104 dB, 50-msec white noise. Data from Bloch (1972, Exp. 2), Brown (1975, Exp. 1), and Graham et al. (1975). Copyright © 1975, The Society for Psychophysiological Research. Reprinted with permission of the publisher from Graham, F. K. The more or less startling effects of weak prestimulation. *Psychophysiology,* 1975, *12,* 238–248, Fig. 8.

above control level. This effect was significant in each of the three experiments shown.

Like the inhibitory effect, facilitation is seen with cross-modal as well as intramodal stimulation. With nonhuman subjects, the effect of sustained prestimulation is evident even after hours of stimulation (Hoffman, Marsh, & Stein, 1969), but in human subjects, it was not found after 20 sec (Putnam, 1975). It appears that, in the human, persistent monotonous stimulation either loses its activating effect relatively quickly or is inhibited by higher-level mechanisms. Starr and Livingston (1963) found that the response to sustained acoustic stimuli became progressively shortened at higher levels of the nervous system and, in cortex, produced negative potentials.

As would be expected of an intensity-dependent system, startle facilitation also varies with prestimulus intensity when stimulus duration is held constant (Hoffman & Searle, 1965; Ison & Hammond, 1971; Ison & Leonard, 1971; Ison, McAdam, & Hammond, 1973; Putnam, 1975; Stitt et al., 1976). Up to moderate intensity levels, facilitation is increased. At higher levels, at least when conditioning and probe stimuli are in the same modality, reduced response has been seen. This might be interpreted as a U-shaped activation function, although it is difficult to ensure the absence of masking or fatigue effects with same modality stimulation. In any case, the findings are in keeping with the conclusion that, up to some intensity level, an intensity-dependent, cross-modally activated system serves to enhance a motor reflex and the facilitation is nonselective with regard to sensory channel.

Orienting–Attentional Effects

Thus, two independent effects on reflex response depend on the characteristics of prior stimulation and its temporal relationship to the probe stimulus. A third effect can be seen if the conditioning stimulus is attention directing. When prestimulation directs attention towards the reflex-eliciting probe, the reflex is facilitated; when it directs attention away from the probe, the reflex is inhibited. Manipulations that have been used to enlist attention include lead-interval variation, introducing a novel lead stimulus, and using the lead stimulus as a warning signal to discriminate some aspect of the probe stimulus (Bohlin & Graham, 1977; Bohlin, Graham, Silverstein, & Hackley, 1979; Graham, 1975). The effect of these manipulations is monitored during the interstimulus interval by measuring heart-rate activity. They all produce significant cardiac deceleration, which is assumed to reflect an orienting–attentional process (Graham & Clifton, 1966; Lacey, 1959); they also produce a facilitated reflex. If the lead stimulus is a warning signal to discriminate stimulation in a sensory channel other than that of the probe, however, a reduced reflex occurs (Putnam & Meiss, 1980; Silverstein & Graham, 1979). 1979).

The attentional effect is not discussed further here, because we do not yet have developmental data with respect to it. However, the capacity of the paradigm to reflect selective attention is one of its most attractive features. Some of the manipulations producing attention are clearly applicable to the young infant; Anthony and Putnam (1980) have successfully used the task manipulation with young children.

In summary, research on the mature organism has shown that the flexor startle reflex is differentially modified by conditioning stimulation. The conceptual framework was summarized in a recent review of evidence that heart-rate changes, as well as startle reflexes, vary as a function of sensory and central processes (Graham, 1979b).

CARDIAC AND STARTLE REFLEXES
IN THE EARLY DEVELOPMENT OF RODENTS

The question addressed in this chapter is whether or not the same reflex modification effects are present in early infancy—specifically, whether transient stimulation produces inhibiting effects and sustained stimulation, facilitating effects. A popular generalization has been the idea that facilitatory influences dominate inhibitory influences in the young organism, because the later-developing higher structures were viewed as serving to modulate the excesses of the earlier-developing lower structures. This is clearly an oversimplification. Reticular formation, for example, is the classical locus of an arousal or activating system. But, although it develops relatively early, its myelination is incomplete into the second decade of life (Yakovlev & Lecours, 1967). Further, its connections to many parts of the brain are inhibitory as well as facilitatory (e.g., Magoun, 1963). However, the generalization may prove to be correct for the neurochemical systems determining activity level (e.g., Fibiger, Lytle, & Campbell, 1970; Ray & Nagy, 1978; Williams, Hamilton, & Carlton, 1975) and the control of cardiovascular function (Assali, Brinkman, Woods, Dandavino, & Nuwayhid, 1977; Rogers & Richmond, 1978). In both cases, excitatory, noradrenergic effects are dominant in the immediate postnatal period and are subsequently modulated as concentrations of substances indexing cholinergic activity increase (Ray & Nagy, 1978).

Research relating physiological and behavioral development in rodents is particularly relevant to present concerns. The third week of postnatal life in the rodent is characterized as a period of intense maturation. Massive proliferation of synaptic connections within cortex (Aghajanian & Bloom, 1967) and between cortical and brainstem structures (Hicks & D'Amato, 1975) is paralleled by changes in brain chemistry and the development of sensitivity to substances that block cholinergic and serotonergic inhibitory expressions (e.g., Campbell, Lytle, & Fibiger, 1969; Mabry & Campbell, 1974; Ray & Nagy, 1978).

During the same period, there is a marked change in the phasic heart-rate response to stimulation, and preconditioning stimuli begin to acquire some ability to inhibit the startle reflex. Recent research from Byron Campbell's laboratory (Haroutunian & Campbell, 1979) has shown that there are differences in the heart-rate response of 15- and 20-day-old rat pups to moderately intense auditory and visual stimuli. In Fig. 1.7, heart rate during a

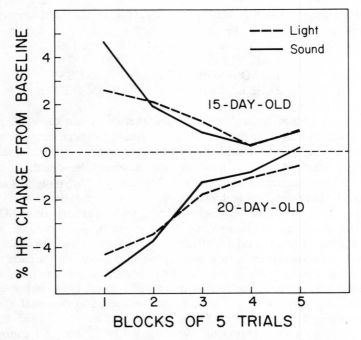

FIG. 1.7.   Heart-rate response of infant rats to 30-sec, moderately intense, visual and auditory stimuli. Data from Haroutunian and Campbell (1979), redrawn with permission of the authors.

30-sec stimulation period is expressed as percent change from a 5-sec period just prior to stimulation, and is plotted as a function of five-trial blocks. It is evident that heart-rate changes were accelerative at 15 days and shifted to deceleration at 20 days.

This developmental change is, of course, similar to the shift seen in human infants between the second and third months of life. Although it is difficult to make between-species comparisons of maturational stages, heart-rate change is only one of a number of qualitative changes in behavior and electro-physiological activity that suggest that around 2 to 3 months of age in humans, there is also a shift from primarily subcortical to predominantly cortical control (Berg & Berg, 1979; Bronson, 1974; Emde & Robinson, in press; Karmel & Maisel, 1975; Parmelee & Sigman, 1976; Salapatek, 1975).

Several other studies have found that rat pups in the third week of life also show heart-rate decelerations to startling or electric shock stimulations that earlier had no effect or elicited heart-rate accelerations (Beattie, 1977; Chalmers & Levine, 1974; Hofer & Reiser, 1969). In Beattie's research, for example, a 104 dB, 30-msec tone had no effect on heart rate on days 12 and 13, but elicited a decrease of more than 40 beats on day 14. The same stimulus produced only a small biphasic response of deceleration–acceleration by day 24–25 and a 12-beat acceleration in adult animals. The adult response was similar to the response obtained in other laboratories to startle-eliciting stimuli (Chalmers & Hoffman, 1973; Chalmers, Hohf, & Levine, 1974).

Two of the studies showed that on the day heart-rate deceleration appeared, it became possible for the first time to elicit the somatic startle response reliably (Beattie, 1977; Hofer & Reiser, 1969). Beattie also found that the startle response could be inhibited with a transient prepulse of 80 dB. However, inhibition amounted to only about 30%, considerably less than the approximately 60% commonly reported for adult animals. The inhibition did not increase significantly over the 10-day period that did produce a change in the heart-rate response.

A recent study by Parisi and Ison (1979) has also reported an inhibitory conditioning effect on startle, beginning on day 13 at the same time that the control reflex developed. Inhibition increased significantly over a 7–8 day period in this case, but it is difficult to interpret the change because magnitude of the control reflex increased simultaneously. As noted earlier, preconditioned reduction of reflex size remains constant in adult animals when control reflex size varies as a function of eliciting stimulus intensity; i.e., the magnitude of inhibition is not a constant proportion or percentage of the control reflex, but a constant difference. This may not be true when control reflex size varies as a function of nervous sytem maturation and/or body weight, however. Weight is an important consideration when startle is measured by the force exerted to accelerate a rigid chamber.

CARDIAC AND STARTLE REFLEXES IN EARLY HUMAN DEVELOPMENT

The work with rodents indicates that deceleratory heart-rate responses and inhibitory preconditioning of startle appear during a period of rapid development of neurochemical systems related to inhibition and of proliferation of intrinsic and extrinsic cortical connections. We have examined preconditioning effects on both heart rate and the startle blink during a period of human infancy that might be expected to show a similar developmental pattern, i.e., the period beginning at 6 to 9 postnatal weeks.

Unconditioned and Spontaneous Blinking

In the human, as well as the rat, the primary component of startle, including blink and body flexion, is apparently not fully developed in the first few weeks of life. Wagner (1938) proposed the general term "body jerk" to describe all infant behavior characterized by a sudden jerk or tensing of the trunk, plus limb movement, regardless of the type of eliciting stimulation or specific directional response pattern. Landis and Hunt (1939) and Hunt (1939) took exception to this view and proposed that there were two identifiable response patterns in the jerky behavior in infants. The first pattern was the Moro reflex, typified by extension of the torso and limbs; this response, present at birth, generally began to weaken by the sixth week of life. The second response showed the flexion movements characteristic of adult startle. Although it appeared sometime during the first 6 weeks, it was dominated by the stronger Moro reflex. Landis and Hunt emphasized that these were two different responses, probably mediated by different mechanisms. The delayed appearance of the primary flexion component is of interest because it is this component that is sensitive to transient stimulus intensity.

Low rates of spontaneous blinking also suggest that the underlying mechanisms are not fully functional early in life. Zametkin, Stevens, and Pittman (1979) reported rates of fewer than one blink per minute before 2 months of age, in comparison to an adult rate of about 15 per minute. Confirming these results, our data show that spontaneous blinks occur only 3–4 times per minute in infants 6, 9, and 24 weeks of age, and 10 times per minute in college-age adults.

A paucity of spontaneous blinks has particular significance in light of the finding that such blinks are mediated almost entirely by large motoneurons (Graham, 1979a). It has been known for at least a century that there are two types of muscle fibers—pale fibers producing rapid, phasic movement and red fibers capable of maintained, tonic contractions. More recent work (e.g., Granit, 1972) shows that the two types of muscle fiber are innervated by congruent motoneurons. Large, rapidly conducting neurons, with short time constants and brief afterhyperpolarizations, innervate the pale muscle fibers. These motoneurons fire at a high rate to repetitive, brief stimulation, but do not maintain firing to a sustained input. In contrast, small, slowly conducting motoneurons, capable of sustained firing, innervate the red muscle fibers. Both types of muscle fiber are found in orbicularis oculi and, because they are anatomically segregated (e.g., Gray, 1973), their activity can be recorded separately with bipolar configurations of the Silverstein electrodes.

In three adult experiments (Graham, 1979a), reflex stimulation produced EMG activity at the sites of both pale and red muscle, but spontaneous blinking was restricted almost entirely to the pale fibers. The pattern was characteristic of 35 of 36 subjects studied, and did not depend on the relative size of reflex and spontaneous blinks, measured potentiometrically. Even when spontaneous blinks were larger than reflex blinks, activity was present at the lid margin where pale fibers are found and was virtually absent in the red muscle surrounding the eye. Therefore, whereas reflex blinking involves both pale and red fibers of orbicularis oculi, adult spontaneous blinking primarily involves pale, fast fibers and the associated large, fast motoneurons.

Experimental Procedures for Preconditioning Studies

A major problem in infant research is the difficulty of maintaining subjects in a defined state. The data described here, unless otherwise specified, were based only on trials in which the infant was rated as awake and alert. Because the studies were not specifically concerned with secular effects such as habituation, testing was interrupted if the state became unacceptable and was resumed if the infant returned to the desired state.

Stimulation was delivered through earphones to the subject, who was restrained in an infant seat within a large soundproof chamber (Model 404–A IAC). A rater remained with the infant, while parents and the experimenter were in an adjacent equipment room where they could view the infant on a television monitor. Equipment, procedures, and rating methods were generally similar to those described in previous publications (e.g., Brown, Leavitt, & Graham, 1977; Graham & Jackson, 1970).

The problem of changing state necessitated a design employing no more than three conditions—one control and two preconditioning treatments. Infants were tested for up to 16 trials per condition when possible, and were included if at least two trials per condition were acceptable. The average number of trials completed per condition was 7.0 in the studies described here. Presentation order was such that three-trial blocks contained one trial of each type and the number of intervening conditions was equalized over a 21-trial sequence. Condition presented on the first trial was balanced across subjects. Minimum intertrial intervals ranged from 25–40 seconds, sufficiently long to allow physiological changes to return to a steady state.

Most of the findings discussed come from four experiments with infants and four companion experiments with adults. There were 12 subjects per experiment and, in the infant groups, half were 6 weeks and half 9 weeks of age, ± 3 days. To equate roughly for the number of trials actually completed by infants, adults were scheduled for only 8 trials per condition. The subjects listened to acoustic preconditioning and startle stimuli through earphones and their blinks were detected by the potentiometric method. Both lid movement and heart-rate activity were recorded continuously on a Beckman polygraph, while computer-digitized samples were stored on tape. The computer also controlled stimulus delivery and timing.

Three types of experiments were conducted: In two studies, we tested for the effects of transient prestimulation; in one, for the effects of sustained prestimulation; and in one, for the effect of sustained prestimulation and for the effect of its transient offset.

The control condition in all experiments was a 50-msec burst of white noise. For the *transient* experiments, the experimental conditions of two studies also included a 25-msec, 1000 Hz tone presented prior to the startle-eliciting noise burst. The prestimulation preceded the startle pulse by 75 or 175 msec in one experiment, and by 225 or 275 msec in a second experiment. The duration of the prepulse, 25 msec, was selected on the basis of pilot work with infants from which we concluded that a 20-msec prestimulus was not effective in producing the desired preconditioning effects, although 25- and 30-msec prestimuli were found to be equally effective. The "offset" condition of the third type of experiment was the termination of a 4-sec sustained tone, which preceded the startle pulse by 200 msec.

For the *sustained* experiments, each subject also received two types of prestimulation in addition to the control trials. In one experiment, the prestimulus was a 1000 Hz tone sustained for either 1 or 2 sec and terminated at onset of the startle pulse. In the other experiment, the tone was sustained for 4 sec; its offset was either coincident with startle-stimulus onset, for analysis of sustained effects, or as previously described, 200 msec earlier, for analysis of transient offset effects.

In both infant and adult sustained experiments, startle-stimulus intensity was 109 dB and prestimulus intensity 75 dB sound pressure level (SPL). These levels were 5 dB higher than we had used in earlier adult experiments, but the increases were necessary to obtain reliable blinking from infants. It should be noted that, with a 50-msec duration, the white noise burst sounds like a click and is well below the 140 dB safety level recommended by the Department of Labor Occupational Safety and Health Administration. In transient infant experiments, startle-pulse intensity remained at 109 dB, but prepulse intensity was 84 dB or, in two earlier studies, 79 dB (Brown, Putnam, Strock, & Graham, 1975). Prepulse intensity was raised to these levels in an effort to increase the inhibitory effect. For the transient adult experiments, we retained the 70 dB prepulse and 104 dB startle pulse used in Graham and Murray (1977), because an 84 dB stimulus, although a powerful inhibitor in adults, may also elicit unconditioned blinking.

Blink Modification

Fig. 1.8 illustrates the effects of transient prestimulation for the experiments just described using 79 dB and 84 dB prepulses with 6- and 9-week-old infants, and for two later studies in which 84 dB prepulses were presented to older infants. Differences between peak blink magnitude on control and prestimulation trials are expressed as percent of control magnitude, rather than absolute difference, because EMG was used with the older infants and the potentiometric method with the other groups. The greater activity of the older infants necessitated the shift in recording method.

As expected, adult blinking was significantly inhibited by 70 dB stimulation at each of the four lead intervals. Inhibition was also significant following offset of the sustained stimulus (not shown). In contrast, blinking in 6- and 9-

pathetic development, because skin conductance responses, mediated by a branch of the sympathetic system that employs acetylcholine as its transmitter, are difficult to elicit in newborns (Berg & Berg, 1979; Crowell, Davis, Chun, & Spellacy, 1965).

In addition, although major cardiovascular control centers are located in the medulla, which is relatively mature at birth, supramedullary centers, including the hypothalamus and motor cortex, exert considerable control over cardiovascular activity (Cohen & MacDonald, 1974). Thus, there may be increasing probability of decelerative cardiac response as maturation proceeds rostrally and as cardiovascular response comes under the predominantly parasympathetic control characteristic of normal adult function.

Because autonomic and somatic systems interact, it may also be useful to consider reflex behavior in terms of the maturity of the cardiovascular system. It was noted earlier that Beattie's (1977) animals did not show any increase of inhibitory preconditioning over the 10-day period that did see a return to an accelerative cardiac response. Because there is no indication of a lessening of deceleration in the human response over the 4-month period studied, it may be that full maturation of the inhibitory effect on the reflex blink should not be expected before the cardiac response begins to reverse.

Heart Rate Preconditioning

Although conditioning of the heart-rate response has received little attention, one study has reported that inhibitory preconditioning occurs in the adult rat (Chalmers & Hoffman, 1973) and another study has found that it occurs in the human newborn (Burke & Crook, 1975). Our results demonstrate not only inhibitory, but also facilitatory, effects of preconditioning stimuli on the human heart-rate response to a startle stimulus. Effects of transient prestimuli for 6–9 week-old infants and for adults are illustrated in Fig. 1.11. The abscissa indicates seconds post startle stimulus onset whereas the ordinate scales heart-rate differences from the control curve—i.e., the response on control trials was subtracted from the response on preconditioning trials so that values above zero indicate accelerated heart rate. In both groups, transient prestimuli produced significantly decelerated difference responses at the longer lead intervals. In infants, the preconditioned response was only less of an acceleration, but in adults, heart rate on the initial second was significantly below baseline.

Transient preconditioning also had a significant effect on heart-rate responses of the 24-week-old infants (not shown). Algebraically, the change was in the opposite direction from that of 6–9 week-old infants and adults— i.e., the response was a lesser deceleration. Thus, at all ages, the effect of prestimuli was to reduce the magnitude of the control response, whether the control response was accelerative or decelerative.

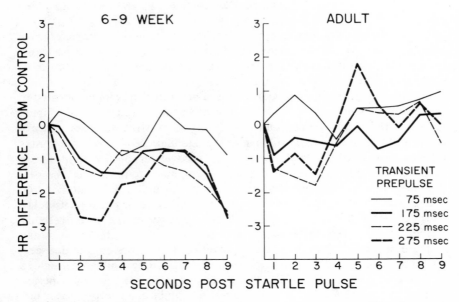

FIG. 1.11. Differences between mean heart-rate response on unconditioned control and transient preconditioned trials as a function of age and of lead-interval variation from 75–275 msec.

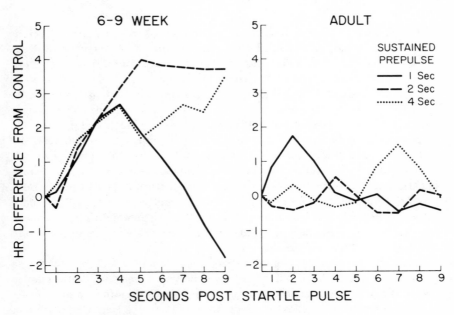

FIG. 1.12. Differences between mean heart-rate response on unconditioned control and sustained preconditioning trials as a function of age and lead intervals (prestimulus duration) varying from 1–4 sec.

Fig. 1.12 shows analogous data for the effects of sustained prestimuli. The acceleration present in the unconditioned control response was markedly increased by preconditioning in 6–9 week-old infant subjects, but preconditioning produced only a slight and nonsignificant increase in adults. The infant effects were significant with 2 and 4 sec sustained stimuli; no adult effects were significant.

The difference between transient and sustained effects can be seen more clearly in Fig. 1.13. The sustained prestimulation curves are the mean of the 1, 2, and 4 sec conditions and the transient curves are the mean of the four short-

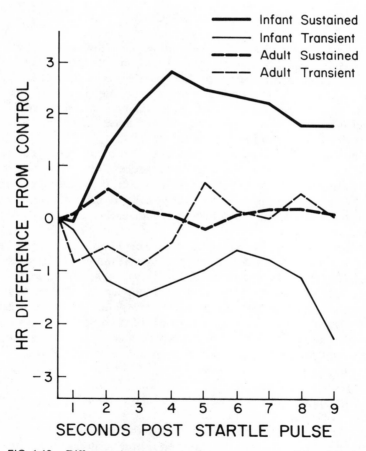

FIG. 1.13.   Differences between heart-rate response on unconditioned (control) and preconditioned trials as a function of age and nature of preconditioning stimuli. Transient preconditioning curves, mean of four short-interval conditions; sustained preconditioning curves, mean of three long-interval conditions.

interval conditions. Note that the facilitatory effect was relatively larger than the inhibitory effect in infants, whereas the reverse was true in adults. Two further differences are also evident: Effects began slightly earlier, or changed more rapidly, in adults, and they lasted longer in infants.

If preconditioned heart-rate responses are expressed as percent of control values rather than differences, to compensate for the dissimilarity in resting levels of infant and adult heart rate, infants still show a much more facilitated response than adults, whereas the initially greater inhibition in adults in increased.

IMPLICATIONS

What are the implications of these findings and how are they related to neurophysiological development during the 4-month period studied? We began the research in an effort to determine whether three phasic control systems, identified in the adult and presumably important in information processing, were functional in the young infant. The reflex-modification techniques we used were originally developed in our laboratory because of their obvious suitability for work with infants.

We have not yet investigated, in the infant, the preconditioning control that is associated with an *orienting-attentional* process, but we have discovered that orienting is an extremely strong response during the period of study. At least, that is how we would interpret the fact that large cardiac decelerations are elicited by a startle stimulus that, both earlier and later, elicits an accelerative response.

A similar finding has been reported for the cardiac response to presumably emotional situations—the visual cliff, a looming stimulus, and the presence of strangers (Campos, 1976; Hruska & Yonas, 1972; Waters, Matas, & Sroufe, 1975). Campos suggests that onset of a decelerative reaction indicates orienting or attention to a stimulus whose potential threat is not yet cognitively appreciated, and that the shift back to acceleration may only occur when implications of the situation are better recognized. A recognized threat would presumably activate the accelerative defensive reflex.

To interpret the decelerative response, even to startling stimuli, as an orienting-attentional response seems reasonable. Campos (1976) documented this interpretation with systematic behavioral observation. We have not done so, but our casual observations are consistent with the interpretation—i.e., our infants do seem to orient behaviorally to the startle stimulus. Obviously, the interpretation would be strengthened if other criteria of orienting were demonstrated, such as habituation and dishabituation to a stimulus change that was not an increase in intensity (Graham, 1979b). We have not yet seen the return to an accelerative response in the infant. This may happen when brief clicks become less novel or interesting so that they do not elicit orienting and, therefore, large decelerations no longer obscure small accelerative startle responses.

In any case, in terms of the physiological development that underlies or is necessary for the increasing strength of cardiac orienting evident after 2 months of age, it appears that nothing is necessary that is not present at birth. Decelerative responses can be obtained in the first few days of life, in both rodents (Ashida, 1972) and human infants, although they are difficult to elicit (Berg & Berg, 1979; Clifton, 1974). Further, Graham, Leavitt, Strock, and Brown (1978) reported decelerative responses to sensory stimuli in a 3- to 6-week old anencephalic infant. The fact that the infant also showed rapid habituation of the response and dishabituation to a change of speech syllables is especially notable because the normal infant does not show such behavior for several more weeks. Work by Buchwald and collaborators (Buchwald, 1975; Buchwald & Brown, 1973; Norman, Buchwald, & Villablanca, 1977) has shown that similarly impressive abilities are present in the adult cat after decerebration. The cat brainstem was capable not only of supporting behavioral acoustic startle and orienting reflexes, but of habituation of these reflexes and of acquisition of conditioned discriminations between different sine wave frequencies. As a result of studies of animals lesioned at several brain levels, Buchwald and Brown (1973) concluded that habituation became increasingly easy to observe with progressive deletions of higher levels. Precocious performance was also observed by Bignall and Schramm (1974) in research with decerebrate kittens; for example, climbing behavior and prey killing emerged far earlier than in normal kittens. The point important for understanding development is that the brainstem not only has unexpected competence that may be masked by higher structures, but immature higher structures may also serve to slow the apparent course of development.

How they do so is a question for which there is no very precise answer. Buchwald and Brown (1973) suggested that the intact cat shows behavior that is erratic because it is correlated with constantly fluctuating arousal levels. It is also possible to think in terms of complex structures having more noise, in the sense of unpredictability, and, especially, of there being greater noise in pathways composed of structures that differ in maturity.

Despite the evidence that even newborn rats and human infants can show orienting responses, there is a very striking subsequent change in the probability and degree of cardiac deceleration. This may well be due, as indicated earlier, to maturation of cholinergic systems and connections between cholinergic inhibitory forebrain areas and medullary areas. That cardiac deceleration is an unusually strong response for a period of time following this change is not surprising. It is a common phenomenon in development that emergent abilities dominant behavior for a time. Again, there is insufficient knowledge to describe very precisely what happens, but it is compatible with the uneven course of maturation in the nervous system. Although brain maturation proceeds in a generally rostral direction, it does not do so in a sweeping fashion. Some tracts myelinate ahead of others in the same cross section of brain (Gilles, Dooling, & Fulchiero, 1976; Yakovlev & Lecours, 1967); even adjacent cells in the same nucleus may mature at different rates (Anokhin, 1964). Thus, as one system incorporates new elements, for a time, these elements may be relatively unopposed by a complementary system that has not yet matured to the same degree, but will eventually provide a more even balance.

In our investigations, we have shown that *sustained intensity* does precondition the reflex blink by 6–9 weeks of life. The effect is a relatively strong and prolonged facilitation whose onset is delayed by comparison with adults. The neural locus of this effect might be presumed to lie in reticular formation, given the well-known activating properties of this structure (e.g., Magoun, 1963). However, Davis and Gendelman (1977), in the only lesion study that specifically examines facilitatory preconditioning effects on startle, found that facilitation disappeared after decerebration—i.e., after complete separation of forebrain from midbrain. The study may not be definitive because it was done on acute preparations (rat) and employed background stimulation rather than a discrete trials procedure. Nonetheless, our data suggest that, whatever structures mediate the effect, the pathway is longer and/or less mature than the pathway required for the unconditioned response.

Because conditioned and unconditioned responses employ the same peripheral input and output paths, effects of immaturity in these pathways are estimated by differences in the latencies of adult and infant unconditioned reflexes. There was no observable difference in the latencies of cardiac responses, at least as measured in 1-sec periods (Fig. 1.10); and the differences in blink reflexes amounted to no more than 12 msec measured by EMG (Fig. 1.14). It is interesting that there was virtually no latency difference between adults and infants during sleep. On the assumption that the waking state requires a higher level of organization, this may be another example of the slowing of activity that can be imposed by higher levels. Clearly then, immaturity in paths common to the unconditioned and preconditioned reflexes could not account for a 2–3-sec delay in onset of facilitatory preconditioning effects or, even, for a 100–200-msec delay in onset of inhibitory preconditioning.

The existence of such central delays in unlearned effects of one stimulus on the response to another suggests that efforts to establish learned associations and memories need to take this into account. In fact, Lipsitt (1963) suggested a number of years ago that some of the problems in demonstrating infant learning stemmed from using time relationships based on adult research. Later work in Lipsitt's laboratory (Little, 1971) showed that conditioned responses could be acquired by 10–30 days of age if intervals were 1500 msec, but not less, in contrast to an optimal interval of 250–500 msec for the adult (Gormezano & Moore, 1969).

ONSET LATENCY (msec) OF
ACOUSTIC STARTLE REFLEX (EMG)

STATE	INFANT 6–9 wk	INFANT 24 wk	ADULT 18–22 yr
Waking	65.8	62.9	54.4
Sleep			
REM–active	52.1		47.8
NREM–quiet	64.4		63.4

FIG. 1.14.   Latency of blink, measured by integrated EMG, as a function of state and age. Infant means from unpublished data; adult means from unpublished data and from Silverstein et al. (1980).

Our investigations have also shown that *transient stimuli* produce inhibitory preconditioning by 6–9 weeks of life, but the effect is relatively weak compared to the effect in adults. Although transient stimuli have not been tested at conditioning intervals longer then 275 msec, except for a 2000-msec interval, they did not produce significant inhibition either at 275 or at 2000 msec intervals. Further, in the 16- and 24-week-old infants, the only change was in the direction of greater inhibition at shorter intervals. Thus, it is unlikely that we have missed a point at which young infants would be as markedly inhibited as adults. The same cannot be claimed for the facilitating effect because infants showed greater facilitation than adults with a 4-sec stimulus and the optimal interval may be still longer.

It is also unlikely that the inhibitory effect was weak because prestimuli might have elicited strong orienting responses. Although orienting elicited by prestimuli can facilitate blinking in adults, if the prestimuli are presented at long lead intervals, there is no evidence that orienting has an effect at short intervals. If it does, the effect must be slight, because substantial inhibition has been obtained at short intervals in situations where prestimuli did elicit orienting (Graham et al., 1975).

Another factor that can probably be excluded is infant–adult differences in auditory sensitivity, at least to sustained auditory stimuli, because the 75 dB sustained tones were equally effective in infants and adults. If the sensory system does contribute to the weak inhibitory effect, it would have to be by virtue of less adequate processing of transient stimuli. Studies of brainstem evoked potentials to transient stimuli have estimated infant thresholds within 10–17 dB of adult thresholds (Hecox, 1975; Lieberman, Sohmer, & Szabo, 1973), so that a 14 dB difference in preconditioning stimulus intensity should compensate for any difference. It is worth noting, however, that the potentials evoked from inferior colliculi do not reach adult latency values before 1 year of age or later (Hecox, 1975; Salamy & McKean, 1976). Because inferior colliculi were necessary for inhibitory preconditioning of spinal reflexes (Wright & Barnes, 1972), immaturity at this level could be important. However, all that is known is that conduction times to inferior colliculi are longer in infants by 2 or 3 msec. Unless the impulses transmitted were also less effective, immaturity in the primary auditory path would be inadequate to explain either the weak preconditioning or the long delays we have obtained.

What, then, does account for the weak inhibition? One possibility is that this is another example of immature higher structures interfering with a relatively low-level effect. Another possibility is that inhibition depends on fast, transient-sensitive, short–time-constant neurons, and that these mature later than slow, temporally integrating neurons.

Graham and Murray (1977) suggested on the basis of the behavioral data from adults, that inhibitory preconditioning did depend, primarily, on the activity of neurons with short time constants and facilitatory preconditioning depended on the activity of long–time-constant neurons. They were led to this hypothesis by two findings that could not easily be otherwise explained: first, the evidence that inhibition was increased by an increase in transient intensity but was not affected by a much larger increase in steady-state loudness; second, that the two manipulations, changing onset intensity and changing duration, had opposed effects on reflex latency and reflex magnitude.

Subsequent work with Silverstein and Hackley (described in Graham, 1979a) has shown that transient and sustained prestimuli do have the predicted differential effects on the fast and slow motoneurons that activate orbicularis oculi, transient stimuli producing relatively greater inhibition of large motoneurons and sustained stimuli, relatively greater facilitation of small motoneurons.

The distinction between large, fast-conducting neurons that have a short time constant and fire only briefly to sustained inputs and small, slowly conducting neurons that show sustained firing to sustained inputs can be seen throughout the nervous system. Evarts (1965) has shown that the differences associated with large and small motoneurons hold not only for bulbospinal neurons, but also for cortical pyramidal cells. Size-associated differences have also been identified in afferent systems, as in the X and Y cells of the visual system (MacLeod, 1978). Although fast and slow (or large and small) neurons represent the extremes, and intermediate types have been identified within both motor and sensory systems, differences associated with size appear to be pervasive in the nervous system. To cite Lüscher, Ruenzel, Fetz, and Henneman (1979), size-associated differences may constitute one of the few "general rules of organization [p. 1161]."

Do fast and slow neurons mature at different rates? There is some evidence that they do. Muscles of newborn mammals are all of the slow type and differentiate into fast and slow only postnatally (e.g., Denny-Brown, 1929; Jacobson, 1970). As noted earlier, muscle fibers are innervated by congruent motoneurons and, further, muscle type is determined by neuron type. Cross-union studies show that mechanical and biochemical characteristics of the muscle are reversed if the nerve type is reversed (Jacobson, 1970). Although the muscle-innervating alpha motoneurons thus show a small–large order of maturation, gamma neurons, which are still smaller, mature later than either type of alpha neuron (Skoglund, 1966). However, gamma and alpha motoneurons belong to different systems, gammas controlling the sensory receptor rather than muscle tension. Granit (1972) points out that neuron size and conduction velocity as indicators of control characteristics are valid for comparisons within but not between different systems.

Additionally, there is evidence for differential maturation of sensory neurons. Several studies indicate that the transient–sensitive, large Y cells reach maturity in the lateral geniculate at a later date than the sustained, small X cells (Daniels, Pettigrew, & Norman, 1978; Hickey, 1977; Norman, Pettigrew, & Daniels, 1977). The relation between these results and the earlier finding that specific system projections to visual cortex were functional later than nonspecific system projections (e.g., Rose & Ellingson, 1970) is not clear. Although specific systems generally have a more rapidly conducting path than nonspecific systems, they presumably include both large and small neurons. However, such general changes as increasing nerve diameter, decreasing duration of afterhyperpolarization (Skoglund, 1966), and relatively late development of axosomatic synapses (Purpura, 1971) would presumably all lead to activity more like that of the transient–sensitive fast cell.

These findings are, of course, too fragmented to be conclusive. With the explosion of research in developmental neurophysiology over the last decade, we can hope that more definitive answers will shortly be forthcoming.

In summary, then, our studies of infants between 2 and 6 months of age suggest that this is a period during which cardiac orienting and facilitatory preconditioning by sustained stimuli are pronounced, but inhibitory preconditioning by transient stimuli remains weak. The latter fact is surprising, because it would seem reasonable to expect early maturation of a midbrain phenomenon that involves the whole flexor musculature, is responsive to multimodal inputs, and is robust in rat, rabbit, pigeon, and human adult. That such a phenomenon matures relatively late suggests that it may be a relatively late phylogenetic innovation and that it is not necessary for the maintenance of vital infant functions. As noted earlier, Graham (1979b) described it as part of a preattentive mechanism and Eccles et al. (1962) described the similar presynaptic inhibition of FRAs as the "first stage" of "perceptual attention [p. 277]."

It is not necessary to assume that a first stage or preprocess develop before the later stage unless the subsequent stage could not take place otherwise.

Presumably, this is not the case with the processing of sensory inputs. As long as inputs can be transmitted through the nervous system by slowly conducting, long–time-constant neurons, it would not be necessary to engage a special mechanism that: (1) could detect the first signs of stimulus change; (2) could conduct this information rapidly to higher centers; and (3) could simultaneously attenuate low-level lines to flexor motor outputs. Thus, it should be possible for orienting–attentional processes to be brought into operation by activity in slowly transmitting paths before rapidly transmitting paths become available. This poses the interesting question of whether the characteristics of information-processing in infants owe more to the immatury of preattentive processes than to the state of maturity of processes usually considered to be more advanced.

ACKNOWLEDGMENTS

This work was supported by The William T. Grant Foundation, Public Health Service grant HD01490, and by a Research Scientist award K3–MH21762. In addition to the many collaborators whose work is cited in the text, special appreciation is expressed to Lois E. Putnam and James W. Brown for the extensive pilot work that made the present studies possible, and to Susan K. Cogan and Alexis R. Itkin for their contributions in the conduct and analysis of studies.

REFERENCES

Aghajanian, G. K., & Bloom, F. E. The formation of synaptic junctions in developing rat brain: A quantitative electron microscopic study. *Brain Research,* 1967, *6,* 716–727.

Anokhin, P. K. Systemogenesis as a general regulator of brain development. *Progress in Brain Research,* 1964, *9,* 54–86.

Anthony, B. J., & Putnam, L. E. Startle and cardiac indices of developmental differences in anticipatory attention. *Psychophysiology,* 1980, *17,* 324. (Abstract)

Ashida, S. Developmental changes in basal and evoked heart rate in neonatal rats. *Journal of Comparative and Physiological Psychology,* 1972, *78,* 368–374.

Assali, N. S., Brinkman, C. R., Woods, J. R., Dandavino, A., & Nuwayhid, B. Development of neurohumoral control of fetal, neonatal, and adult cardiovascular function. *American Journal of Obstetrics and Gynecology,* 1977, *129,* 748–759.

Beattie, M. S. *The effects of neonatal isocortical ablations on acoustic startle response plasticity: An ontogenetic study in the rat.* Unpublished doctoral thesis, Ohio State University, 1977.

Berg, K. M. *Elicitation of acoustic startle in the human.* Unpublished doctoral thesis, University of Wisconsin, 1973.

Berg, W. K., & Berg, K. M. Psychophysiological development in infancy: State, sensory function, and attention. In J. Osofsky (Ed.), *Handbook of infant development.* New York: Wiley, 1979.

Berg, W. K., Clarkson, M. G., & Silverstein, L. D. Inhibition of infants' reflex blinks by near-threshold auditory stimuli. *Psychophysiology,* 1979, *16,* 191. (Abstract)

Bignall, K. E., & Schramm, L. Behavior of chronically decerebrated kittens. *Experimental Neurology,* 1974, *42,* 519–531.

Bloch, R. M. *Inhibition and facilitation effects of a prepulse on the human blink response to a startle pulse.* Unpublished doctoral thesis, University of Wisconsin, 1972.

Bohlin, G., & Graham, F. K. Cardiac deceleration and reflex blink facilitation. *Psychophysiology,* 1977, *14,* 423–430.

Bohlin, G., Graham, F. K., Silverstein, L. D., & Hackley, S. A. *Cardiac orienting and startle blink modification in novel and signal situations.* Unpublished data, 1979.

Bronson, G. The postnatal growth of visual capacity. *Child Development,* 1974, *45,* 873–890.

Brown, J. W. *Contingent negative variation and cardiac orienting preceding startle modification.* Unpublished doctoral thesis, University of Wisconsin, 1975.

Brown, J. W., Leavitt, L. A., & Graham, F. K. Response to auditory stimuli in 6- and 9-week-old infants. *Developmental Psychobiology,* 1977, *10,* 255–266.

Brown, J. W., Putnam, L. E., Strock, B. D., & Graham, F. K. *Blink reflex inhibition in 6- and 9-week old infants.* Unpublished data, 1975.

Buchwald, J. S. Brainstem substrates of sensory information processing and adaptive behavior. In N. A. Buchwald & M. A. B. Brazier (Eds.), *Brain mechanisms in mental retardation.* New York: Academic Press, 1975.

Buchwald, J. S., & Brown, K. A. Subcortical mechanisms of behavioral plasticity. In J. D. Maser (Ed.), *Efferent organization and the integration of behavior.* New York: Academic Press, 1973.

Buckland, G., Buckland, J., Jamieson, C., & Ison, J. R. Inhibition of startle response to acoustic stimulation produced by visual prestimulation. *Journal of Comparative and Physiological Psychology,* 1969, *67,* 493–496.

Burke, P. M., & Crook, C. K. *The effect of an antecedent tone on cardiac response to a sudden auditory stimulus in the human newborn.* Unpublished manuscript, February 1975.

Campbell, B. A., Lytle, L. D., & Fibiger, H. C. Ontogeny of adrenergic arousal and cholinergic inhibitory mechanisms in the rat. *Science,* 1969, *166,* 637–638.

Campos, J. J. Heart rate: A sensitive tool for the study of emotional development in the infant. In L. Lipsitt (Ed.), *Developmental psychobiology: The significance of infancy.* Hillsdale, N.J.: Lawrence Erlbaum Associates, 1976.

Chalmers, D. V., & Hoffman, H. S. Cardiac and startle responses to acoustic stimuli in the rat. *Physiological Psychology,* 1973, *1,* 74–76.

Chalmers, D. V., Hohf, J. C., & Levine, S. The effects of prior aversive stimulation on the behavioral and physiological responses to intense acoustic stimuli in the rat. *Physiology and Behavior,* 1974, *12,* 711–717.

Chalmers, D. V., & Levine, S. The development of heart rate responses to weak and strong shock in the preweaning rat. *Developmental Psychobiology,* 1974, *7,* 519–527.

Clifton, R. K. Cardiac conditioning and orienting in the infant. In P. Obrist, A. H. Black, J. Brener, & L. DiCara (Eds.), *Cardiovascular psychophysiology: Current issues in response mechanisms, biofeedback, and methodology.* Chicago: Aldine, 1974.

Cohen, D. H., & MacDonald, R. L. A selective review of central neural pathways involved in cardiovascular control. In P. A. Obrist, A H. Black, J. Brener, & L. V. DiCara (Eds.), *Cardiovascular psychophysiology: Current issues in response mechanisms, biofeedback, and methodology.* Chicago: Aldine, 1974.

Cohen, L. H., Hilgard, E. R., & Wendt, G. R. Sensitivity to light in a case of hysterical blindness studied by reinforcement–inhibition and conditioning methods. *Yale Journal of Biological Medicine,* 1933, *6,* 61–67.

Crowell, D. H., Davis, C. M., Chun, B. J., & Spellacy, F. J. Galvanic skin reflex in newborn humans. *Science,* 1965, *148,* 1108–1111.

Daniels, J. D., Pettigrew, J. D., & Norman, J. L. Development of single-neuron responses in kitten's lateral geniculate nucleus. *Journal of Neurophysiology,* 1978, *41,* 1373–1393.

Davis, M., & Gendelman, P. M. Plasticity of the acoustic startle response in the acutely decerebrate rat. *Journal of Comparative and Physiological Psychology,* 1977, *91,* 549–563.

Denny-Brown, D. The histological features of striped muscle in relation to its functional activity. *Proceedings of the Royal Society,* 1929, *104B,* 371–411.

Eccles, J. C. *The physiology of the synapses.* Berlin, Göttingen, Heidelberg: Springer-Verlag, 1964.

Eccles, J. C., Kostyuk, P. G., & Schmidt, R. F. Presynaptic inhibition of the central actions of flexor reflex afferents. *Journal of Physiology,* 1962, *161,* 258–281.

Emde, R. N., & Robinson, J. The first two months: Recent research in developmental psychobiology and the changing view of the newborn. In J. Noshpitz & J. Call (Eds.), *Basic handbook of child psychiatry.* New York: Basic Books, in press.

Evarts, E. V. Relation of discharge frequency to conduction velocity in pyramidal tract neurons. *Journal of Neurophysiology,* 1965, *28,* 216–228.

Fibiger, H. C., Lytle, L. D., & Campbell, B. A. Cholinergic modulation of adrenergic arousal in the developing rat. *Journal of Comparative and Physiological Psychology,* 1970, *72,* 384–389.

Fleshler, M. Adequate acoustic stimulus for startle reaction in the rat. *Journal of Comparative and Physiological Psychology,* 1965, *60,* 200–207.

Gendelman, D. S., & Davis, M. The primary acoustic startle circuit in the rat. *Society for Neuroscience Abstracts,* 1979, *5,* 494. (Abstract)

Gilles, F. H., Dooling, E., & Fulchiero, A. Sequence of myelination in the human fetus. *Transactions of the American Neurological Association,* 1976, *101,* 1–3.

Gormezano, I., & Moore, J. W. Classical conditioning. In M. H. Marx (Ed.), *Learning: Processes.* New York: Macmillan, 1969.

Graham, F. K. The more or less startling effects of weak prestimulation. *Psychophysiology,* 1975, *12,* 238–248.

Graham, F. K. *Programming the human blink: Biassed activity in fast and slow motor units.* Presidential address to the Division of Physiological and Comparative Psychology, American Psychological Association, New York, September 1979.(a)

Graham, F. K. Distinguishing among orienting, defense, and startle reflexes. In H. D. Kimmel, E. H. van Olst, & J. F. Orlebeke (Eds.), *The orienting reflex in humans.* An international conference sponsored by the Scientific Affairs Division of the North Atlantic Treaty Organization. Hillsdale, N.J.: Lawrence Erlbaum Associates, 1979. (b)

Graham, F. K. Control of reflex blink excitability. In R. F. Thompson, L. H. Hicks, & V. B. Shvyrkov (Eds.), *Neural mechanisms of goal-directed behavior and learning.* New York: Academic Press, in press.

Graham, F. K., & Clifton, R. K. Heart rate change as a component of the orienting response. *Psychological Bulletin,* 1966, *65,* 305–320.

Graham, F. K., & Jackson, J. C. Arousal systems and infant heart rate responses. In L. P. Lipsitt & H. W. Reese (Eds.), *Advances in child development and behavior* (Vol. 5). New York: Academic Press, 1970.

Graham, F. K., Leavitt, L. A., Strock, B. D., & Brown, J. W. Precocious cardiac orienting in a human, anencephalic infant. *Science,* 1978, *199,* 322–324.

Graham, F. K., & Murray, G. M. Discordant effects of weak prestimulation on magnitude and latency of the reflex blink. *Physiological Psychology,* 1977, *5,* 108–114.

Graham, F. K., Putnam, L. E., & Leavitt, L. A. Lead stimulation effects on human cardiac orienting and blink reflexes. *Journal of Experimental Psychology: Human Perception and Performance,* 1975, *1,* 161–169.

Granit, R. *Mechanisms regulating the discharge of motoneurons.* Springfield, Ill.: Charles C. Thomas, 1972.

Gray, H. *Anatomy of the human body.* (29th American ed.) C. M. Goss (Ed.). Philadelphia: Lea and Fibiger, 1973.

Hammond, G. R. Lesions of pontine and medullary reticular formation and prestimulus inhibition of the acoustic startle reaction in rats. *Physiology and Behavior,* 1973, *8,* 535–537.

Haroutunian, V., & Campbell, B. A. *The emergence and habituation of the orienting response in the rat.* Paper presented at the meeting of the International Society for Developmental Psychobiology, Atlanta, November 1979.

Hecox, K. Electrophysiological correlates of human auditory development. In L. B. Cohen & P. Salapatek (Eds.). *Infant perception: From sensation to cognition* (Vol. 2). New York: Academic Press, 1975.

Hickey, T. L. Postnatal development of the human lateral geniculate nucleus: Relationship to a critical period for the visual system. *Science,* 1977, *198,* 836–838.

Hicks, S. P., & D'Amato, C. J. Motor–sensory cortex–corticospinal system and developing locomotion and placing in rats. *American Journal of Anatomy,* 1975, *143,* 1–42.

Hofer, M. A., & Reiser, M. F. The development of cardiac rate regulation in preweanling rats. *Psychosomatic Medicine,* 1969, *31,* 372–388.

Hoffman, H. S., Marsh, R. R., & Stein, N. Persistence of background acoustic stimulation in controlling startle. *Journal of Comparative and Physiological Psychology,* 1969, *68,* 280–283.

Hoffman, H. S., & Searle, J. L. Acoustic variables in the modification of startle reaction in the rat. *Journal of Comparative and Physiological Psychology,* 1965, *60,* 53–58.

Hoffman, H. S., & Wible, B. L. Temporal parameters in startle facilitation by steady background signals. *Journal of the Acoustical Society of America,* 1969, *45,* 7–12.

Hoffman, H. S., & Wible, B. L. Role of weak signals in acoustic startle. *Journal of the Acoustical Society of America,* 1970, *47,* 489–497.

Hruska, K., & Yonas, A. Developmental changes in cardiac responses to the optical stimulus of impending collision. *Psychophysiology,* 1972, *9,* 272. (Abstract)

Hunt, W. A. "Body jerk" as a concept in describing infant behavior. *Journal of Genetic Psychology,* 1939, *55,* 215–220.

Ison, J. R., & Ash, B. Effects of experience on stimulus-produced reflex inhibition in the human. *Bulletin of the Psychonomic Society,* 1977, *10,* 467–468.

Ison, J. R., & Hammond, G. R. Modification of the startle reflex in the rat by changes in the auditory and visual environments. *Journal of Comparative and Physiological Psychology,* 1971, *75,* 435–452.

Ison, J. R., & Leonard, D. W. Effects of auditory stimuli on the amplitude of the nictitating membrane reflex of the rabbit (Oryctolagus Coniculus). *Journal of Comparative and Physiological Psychology,* 1971, *75,* 157–164.

Ison, J. R., McAdam, D. W., & Hammond, G. R. Latency and amplitude changes in the acoustic startle reflex of the rat produced by variation in auditory prestimulation. *Physiology and Behavior,* 1973, *10,* 1035–1039.

Ison, J. R., Reiter, L. A., & Warren, M. P. Modulation of the acoustic startle reflex in humans in the absence of anticipatory changes in the middle ear reflex. *Journal of Experimental Psychology: Human Perception and Performance,* 1979, *4,* 639–642.

Jacobson, M. *Developmental neurobiology.* New York: Holt, Rinehart & Winston, 1970.

Kahneman, D. *Attention and effort.* Englewood Cliffs, N.J.: Prentice-Hall, 1973.

Karmel, B. Z., & Maisel, E. B. A neuronal model for infant visual attention. In L. B. Cohen & P. Salapatek (Eds.), *Infant perception: From sensation to cognition* (Vol. 1). New York: Academic Press, 1975.

Lacey, J. I. Psychophysiological approaches to the evaluation of psychotherapeutic process and outcome. In E. A. Rubinstein & M. B. Parloff (Eds.), *Research in psychotherapy.* Washington, D.C.: American Psychological Association, 1959.

Landis, C., & Hunt, W. A. *The startle pattern.* New York: Farrar and Rinehart, 1939.

Leitner, D. S., Powers, A. S., & Hoffman, H. S. *The neural system for the inhibition of startle.* Manuscript submitted for publication, 1979.

Lieberman, A., Sohmer, H., & Szabo, G. Cochlear audiometry (electrocochleography) during the neonatal period. *Developmental Medicine and Child Neurology,* 1973, *15,* 8–13.

Lipsitt, L. P. Learning in the first year of life. In L. P. Lipsitt & C. C. Spiker (Eds.), *Advances in child development and behavior* (Vol. 1). New York: Academic Press, 1963.

Little, A. H. *Eyelid conditioning in the human infant as a function of the ISI.* Paper presented at the meeting of the Society for Research in Child Development, Minneapolis, 1971.

Lundberg, A. Integration in the reflex pathway. In R. Granit (Ed.), *Muscular afferents and motor control.* Proceedings of 1st Nobel Symposium, Södergarn, Sweden, 1965. New York: Wiley, 1966.

Lüscher, H. R., Ruenzel, P., Fetz, E., & Henneman, E. Postsynaptic population potentials recorded from ventral roots perfused with isotonic sucrose: Connections of groups Ia and II spindle afferent fibers with large populations of motoneurons. *Journal of Neurophysiology,* 1979, *42,* 1146–1164.

Mabry, P. D., & Campbell, B. A. Ontongeny of serotonergic inhibition of behavioral arousal in the rat.. *Journal of Comparative and Physiological Psychology,* 1974, *86,* 193–201.

MacLeod, D. I. A. Visual sensitivity. In M. R. Rosenzweig & L. W. Porter (Eds.), *Annual review of psychology* (Vol. 29). Palo Alto, Calif.: Annual Reviews, 1978.

Magoun, H. W. *The waking brain.* Springfield, Ill.: Charles C. Thomas, 1963.

Mallart, A. Heterosegmental and heterosensory presynaptic inhibition. *Nature,* 1965, *206,* 719–720.

Marsh, R. R., Hoffman, H. S., & Stitt, C. L. Reflex inhibition audiometry. *Acta Otolaryngologica,* 1978, *85,* 336–341.

Massaro, D. W. Backward recognition masking. *Journal of the Acoustical Society of America,* 1975, *58,* 1059–1065.

Neisser, U. *Cognitive psychology.* Englewood Cliffs, N.J.: Prentice-Hall, 1967.

Norman, J. L., Pettigrew, J. D., & Daniels, J. D. Early development of X-cells in kitten lateral geniculate nucleus. *Science,* 1977, *198,* 202–204.

Norman, R. J., Buchwald, J. S., & Villablanca, J. R. Classical conditioning with auditory discrimination of the eye blink in decerebrate cats. *Science,* 1977, *196,* 551–553.

Obrist, P. A., Lawler, J. E., Howard, J. L., Smithson, K. W., Martin, P. L., & Manning, J. Sympathetic influences on cardiac rate and contractility during acute stress in humans. *Psychophysiology,* 1974, *11,* 405–427.

Obrist, P. A., Wood, D. M., & Perez-Reyes, M. Heart rate during conditioning in humans: Effects of UCS intensity, vagal blockade and adrenergic block of vasomotor activity. *Journal of Experimental Psychology,* 1965, *70,* 32–42.

Parisi, T., & Ison, J. R. Development of the acoustic startle response in the rat: Ontogenetic changes in the magnitude of inhibition by prepulse stimulation. *Developmental Psychobiology,* 1979, *12,* 219–230.

Parmelee, A. H., Jr., & Sigman, M. Development of visual behavior and neurological organization in pre-term and full-term infants. In A. D. Pick (Ed.), *Minnesota symposium on child psychology* (Vol. 10). Minneapolis: University of Minnesota Press, 1976.

Peak, H. Reflex and voluntary reactions of the eyelid. *Journal of General Psychology,* 1933, *8,* 130–156.

Posner, M. I. Psychobiology of attention. In M. S. Gazzaniga & C. Blakemore (Eds.), *Handbook of psychobiology.* New York: Academic Press, 1975.

Purpura, D. P. Synaptogenesis in mammalian cortex: Problems and perspectives. In M. B. Sterman, D. J. McGinty, & A. M. Adinolfi (Eds.), *Brain development and behavior.* New York: Academic press, 1971.

Putnam, L. E. *The human startle reaction: Mechanisms of modification by background acoustic stimulation.* Unpublished doctoral dissertation, University of Wisconsin, 1975.

Putnam, L. E., & Meiss, D. A. Reflex inhibition during HR deceleration: Selective attention or motor interference? *Psychophysiology,* 1980, *17,* 324. (Abstract)

Ray, D., & Nagy, Z. M. Emerging cholinergic mechanisms and ontogeny of response inhibition in the mouse. *Journal of Comparative and Physiological Psychology,* 1978, *92,* 335–349.

Reiter, L. A., & Ison, J. R. Inhibition of the human eyeblink reflex: An evaluation of the sensitivity of the Wendt–Yerkes method for threshold detection. *Journal of Experimental Psychology: Human Perception and Performance,* 1977, *3,* 325–336.

Rogers, M. C., & Richmond, J. B. The autonomic nervous system. In U. Stave (Ed.), *Perinatal physiology.* New York: Plenum Medical Book, 1978.

Rose, G. H., & Ellingson, R. J. Ontogenesis of evoked potentials. In W. A. Himwich (Ed.), *Developmental neurobiology.* Springfield, Ill.: Charles C. Thomas, 1970.

Ross, L. E., Ferreira, M. C., & Ross, S. M. Backward masking of conditioned stimuli: Effects on differential and single-cue classical conditioning performance. *Journal of Experimental Psychology,* 1974, *103,* 603–613.

Salamy, A., & McKean, C. M. Postnatal development of human brainstem potentials during the first year of life. *Electroencephalography and Clinical Neurophysiology,* 1976, *40,* 418–426.

Salapatek, P. Pattern perception in early infancy. In L. B. Cohen & P. Salapatek (Eds.), *Infant perception: From sensation to cognition* (Vol. 1). New York: Academic Press, 1975.

Sauerland, E. K., Knauss, T., Nakamura, Y., & Clemente, C. D. Inhibition of monosynaptic and polysynaptic reflexes and muscle tone by electrical stimulation of the cerebral cortex. *Experimental Neurology,* 1967, *17,* 159–171.

Silverstein, L. D., & Graham, F. K. Eyeblink EMG: A miniature eyelid electrode for recording from orbicularis oculi. *Psychophysiology,* 1978, *15,* 377–379.

Silverstein, L. D., & Graham, F. K. Selective attention effects of reflex activity. *Psychophysiology,* 1979, *16,* 202. (Abstract)

Silverstein, L. D., Graham, F. K., & Calloway, J. M. Preconditioning and excitability of the human orbicularis oculi reflex as a function of state. *Electroencephalography and Clinical Neurophysiology,* 1980, *48,* 406–417.

Skoglund, S. Muscle afferents and motor control in the kitten. In R. Granit (Ed.), *Muscle afferents and motor control.* Proceedings of 1st Nobel Symposium, Södergarn, Sweden, 1965. New York: Wiley, 1966.

Starr, A., & Livingston, R. B. Long-lasting nervous system responses to prolonged sound stimulation in waking cats. *Journal of Neurophysiology,* 1963, *26,* 416–431.

Stitt, C. L., Hoffman, H. S., & Marsh, R. R. Interaction versus independence of startle-modification processes in the rat. *Journal of Experimental Psychology: Animal Behavior Processes,* 1976, *2,* 260–265.

Stitt, C. L., Hoffman, H. S., Marsh, R., & Boskoff, K. J. Modification of the rat's startle reaction by an antecedent change in the acoustic environment. *Journal of Comparative and Physiological Psychology,* 1974, *86,* 826–836.

Stitt, C. L., Hoffman, H. S., Marsh, R. R., & Schwartz, G. M. Modification of the pigeon's visual startle reaction by the sensory environment. *Journal of Comparative and Physiological Psychology,* 1976, *90,* 601–619.

Szabo, I., & Hazafi, K. Elicitability of the acoustic startle reaction after brain stem lesions. *Acta Physiologica, Academy of Science of Hungary,* 1965, *27,* 155–165.

Thompson, R. F. *Foundations of physiological psychology.* New York: Harper and Row, 1967.

Thompson, R. F., & Spencer, W. A. Habituation: A model phenomenon for the study of neuronal substrates of behavior. *Psychological Review,* 1966, *173,* 16–43.

Valverde, F. Reticular formation of the albino rat's brain stem cytoarchitecture and corticofugal connections. *Journal of Comparative Neurology,* 1962, *119,* 25–49.

Wagner, I. F. The body jerk of the neonate. *Journal of Genetic Psychology,* 1938, *52,* 65–77.

Waters, E., Matas, L., & Sroufe, L. A. Infants' reactions to an approaching stranger: Description, validation, and functional significance of wariness. *Child Development,* 1975, *46,* 348–356.

Williams, J. M., Hamilton, L. W., & Carlton, P. L. Ontogenetic dissociation of two classes of habituation. *Journal of Comparative and Physiological Psychology,* 1975, *89,* 733–737.

Wright, C. G., & Barnes, C. D. Audio-spinal reflex responses in decerebrate and chloralose anesthetized cats. *Brain Research,* 1972, *36,* 307–331.

Yakovlev, P. I., & Lecours, A. R. The myelogenetic cycles of regional maturation of the brain. In A. Minkowski (Ed.), *Regional development of the brain in early life.* Philadelphia: F. A. Davis, 1967.

Yerkes, R. M. The sense of hearing in frogs. *Journal of Comparative Neurology and Psychology,* 1905, *15,* 279–304.

Zametkin, A. J., Stevens, J. R., & Pittman, R. Ontogeny of spontaneous blinking and of habituation of the blink reflex. *Annals of Neurology,* 1979, *5,* 453–457.

2 Two Kinds of Perceptual Organization Near the Beginning of Life

Marc H. Bornstein
New York University

PROLOGUE: A PHILOSOPHICAL QUERY

In the second edition of *An Essay Concerning Human Understanding,* John Locke (1690/1961, p. 114) recounts an epistolary exchange with his friend, that "very ingenious and studious promoter of real knowledge" William Molyneux. Molyneux had been provoked by Locke's first edition to ponder the role of experience in thought, and he wrote to Locke asking whether a man born blind, but experienced in touch, and suddenly given the gift of sight as an adult, could distinguish a cube from a globe by vision alone. Molyneux himself reasoned in the negative; being a fellow empiricist, Locke concurred that "the blind man, at first sight, would not be able with certainty to say which was the globe, which the cube, whilst he only saw them, though he could unerringly name them by his touch."

Molyneux's query was framed in terms limited to the literal exchange of equivalent information among the senses; in actuality, Molyneux was asking about the origins of perceptual knowledge and the role of experience in the acquisition of such knowledge. This being the case, it would have been equally reasonable for Molyneux to have cast his question in terms of infant development. Indeed, Locke inserted this "acute and judicious" proposer's question amidst his dissertation on the origins of ideas, and ever since it has been a typical and continuing activity among philosophers to speculate about the origins of knowledge.

In almost linear descent, philosophers with an interest in epistemology and psychologists with interests in perception and development have put Molyneux's question in the following form: Assuming environmental flux and variety, how does the infant come to organize and make sense of the perceptual world? Despite a long tradition of nativism, among whose adherents are counted Kant, Hering, and Mach, classical opinion about perceptual understanding near the beginning of life has come down to us in the influential form of two empiricist epigrams. Locke himself is reputed to have described the mind of the infant as a "tabula rasa," and James characterized the infant's world as "a blooming, buzzing confusion." The implication of both these statements is that much of the organization children and adults perceive in the world derives from extensive experience in it. Yet, even the staunchest nurturists, including Locke (1690/1961), have had to concede to the newborn infant something in the way of a sensory sense: "I doubt not but *children,* by the exercise of their senses about objects that affect them *in the womb,* receive some *few* ideas, before they are born...[p. 112]."

In this chapter, I examine data that give evidence for some of the ways human beings begin to perceive order and structure in the world in which they develop. Even though it may not have occurred to Molyneux to frame his philosophical speculation in terms of infant development, and in spite of long-standing opinion of great experimental psychologists (since Helmholtz) that experimentation with human infants may be "infeasible," two decades of infant research have yielded good evidence that human infants possess incipient perceptual knowledge. With this, they begin to bring order to flux and complexity in the physical world. Is perception an acceptable site to search for the origins of knowledge? I believe, as Locke did (1690/1961), that it is: "Perception is the first operation of all our intellectual faculties, and the inlet of all knowledge in our minds [p. 117]."

INTRODUCTION

Properties of the physical world are complex and constantly in flux. By contrast, our perceptions are characterized by a critical degree of organization that replaces physical variety and instability with psychological unity and coherence. However, it has often been thought that physical variety and instability in the material world must be especially problematic for infants, before they have had much experience or formal tuition. How does the infant perceiver organize and make sense of the world?

In this chapter, I suggest that infants, too, perceive structure and organization. To support this view, I pursue four lines of argument: First, I suggest that two kinds of *perceptual organization* contribute especially to psychological unity and coherence. One is equivalence classification, or the categorization and equivalent treatment of discriminably different stimuli based on their perceptual similarity. The other is prototypicality, or the perceptual salience and cognitive advantage of select stimuli from different equivalence classes or sensory domains. Equivalence classification and prototypicality reflect the fact that perception does not mirror physics: Not every different physical stimulus is perceived or responded to as different, nor is every different stimulus equal in status. I discuss the structure and function of equivalence classification and prototypicality in perception.

Second, I recount evidence that these *two kinds of perceptual organization exist and function near the beginning of life.* For this argument, I draw particularly from my own studies on color vision and pattern vision; findings in these domains may stand as prototypical of this category of investigation. Further, perceptual organizations like categorization and typicality frequently reflect biological structure and function; in the course of this chapter, I allude to brain structures and operations that support this interpretation.

My third argument is a *comparative* one. Equivalence classification and prototypicality can be found in a wide variety of animal species, and this phylogenetic perspective throws light on the adaptive and functional nature of these two kinds of perceptual organization.

Finally, I discuss *developmental continuity* in equivalence classification and prototypicality. Specifically, I draw parallels between their appearance in infancy and at least partially analogous behaviors identifiable in maturity. Further, I discuss the utility and meaning of these two kinds of perceptual organization in development.

TWO KINDS OF PERCEPTUAL ORGANIZATION: STRUCTURE AND FUNCTION

Equivalence Classification

Perception involves the act of categorization.—J. S. Bruner, 1957, p. 123.

By equivalence class, I mean a set of discriminable, nonidentical stimuli that are treated as equivalent based on their relative perceptual similarity. This relation is at least as old as David Hume's (1748/1955) observation that: "I have found that such an object has always been attended with such an effect, and I foresee that other objects which are in appearance similar will be attended with similar effects [p. 48]."

The following behavioral experiment with monkeys helps to illustrate equivalence classification and concretize Hume's observation. Sandell, Gross, and Bornstein (1979) trained monkeys to press a key illuminated with one or another wavelength. In extinction, we showed the animals the training wavelength and four others surrounding it. As shown in Fig. 2.1A, one animal produced a triangularly symmetric generalization gradient giving monotonically fewer responses to test stimuli (559 nm, 579 nm, 609 nm, and 623 nm) increasingly physically different from its training stimulus (582nm). However, a second animal trained at a different point in the spectrum (497 nm) produced an asymmetric generalization gradient in extinction, giving a similarly high

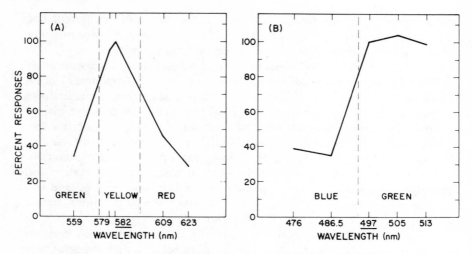

FIG. 2.1.   Symmetric and asymmetric wavelength generalization in monkeys; the asymmetric generalization illustrates "equivalence classification." Generalization is expressed as a percentage of responses to the training stimulus (underlined). Boundaries between human color names are indicated by dashed vertical lines. (A) Green to yellow (573 nm) and yellow to red (596 nm). (B) Blue to green (494 nm). (After Sandell, Gross, & Bornstein, 1979, Experiments 4 and 1, respectively.)

number of responses to two test stimuli (505 nm and 513 nm) and a similarly low number of responses to two others (476 nm and 486.5 nm) (Fig. 2.1B). Since physical variation among test stimuli is relatively similar in the two situations, what explains the difference in behavior—especially the second animal's equivalent treatment of different wavelengths?

The two situations actually contrast in the following way: The first animal, trained on yellow (582 nm), generalized only to another yellow (579 nm), but not to green (559 nm) or to red (609 nm and 623 nm). The second animal, trained on green (497 nm), generalized to two other greens (505 nm and 513 nm), but not to two blues (476 nm and 486.5 nm). That is, the second animal treated equivalently three greens that have been independently demonstrated to be mutually discriminable in the monkey (DeValois, 1973). (Indeed, for this animal, the training stimulus, 497 nm, was actually physically closer to one of the blues, 486.5 nm, than to one of the greens, 513 nm.) In short, psychological similarity among wavelengths—their shared hue quality— rather than physical difference underlay generalization in monkeys. Hues exemplify equivalence classes.

Equivalence classes have been thought to play a significant role in cognition. Classification helps to organize experience. It also allows perceivers to recognize familiar information and to assimilate new information, thereby rendering the unfamiliar familiar; moreover, assimilation to extant categories is quick and less effortful than is construction of new categories. In turn, the organization of information enhances retention and governs its later accessibility in thought. Categorical structures give meaning to incoming stimulation, familiar and unfamiliar alike. Finally, the rudiments of higher mental processes, like conceptual abilities, may be found in decisions related to categorization.

Equivalence classification is one type of perceptual organization. To understand the significance of organization as a general perceptual process and its efficacy as a principle of perception, look at Fig. 2.2. Initially, the field appears to be an unstructured, unfocused disarray of elements. Shortly,

FIG. 2.2. An unorganized disarray of elements is eventually organized into the picture of a "Horse and Rider." (After Street, 1931. Copyright Teachers College Press. Used by permission.)

however, an organization emerges that gives structure to the array and focuses attention. Even though energy impinging at the end organ is not changed, perception is changed. An organized, structured, and meaningful configuration in this "Street" figure—a horse and rider—is now apparent.

Equivalence classes have been conceived to be structured in two dimensions. A "vertical" dimension describes levels of abstractness and inclusiveness. A class may be part of a larger domain (which itself may be subordinate to yet an even larger one); likewise, a class may be superordinate to subordinate classes. I am concerned in this chapter principally with a middle level of classification (e.g., "red"); higher levels are more abstract and perceptually meaningful in a different way (e.g., "color"), and lower levels often encompass too fine distinctions (e.g., "maroon"). The second dimension of classification is on the "horizontal" and describes which stimuli are included in the class. The boundaries around natural classes (like "red") are not well defined; for example, vermilion, burgundy, fuchsia, mauve, coral, and cardinal are borderline reds. Similarity is therefore a defining aspect of equivalence classification, but similarity must be qualified. All entities are logically similar *in some way,* though not all are coclassified; equivalence classification reflects the particular ways in which certain entities are perceptually similar (e.g., Wertheimer, 1923/1958). This consideration of stimulus status in a class suggests a second kind of perceptual organization.

Prototypicality

The problem of stimulus selection arises from the fact that there is a greater array of stimulation potentially available to an organism at any given moment than the organism can take in, remember, or respond to.—E. E. Maccoby, 1969, p. 68.

By prototypicality, I mean the quality of a single stimulus or select few stimuli in a given class *or* in a sensory domain to stand out in relief as preferred and cognitively salient. Many instances of an equivalence class or a sensory domain may be independent and discriminable from one another, though they are not all equal in status. Prototypes are first among equals, so to speak (Rosch, 1978). (This use of the term prototype does not connote the stimulus that shares the most features with other members of the class.)

Prototypes may appear in equivalence classes, such as hues, as shown in Fig. 2.3A. When they do, they are by definition focal, meaning they are often central, clear, simple, and representative; thus, "ruby" matches our idea of "red" better than "fuchsia," a red with blue in it, or "vermilion," a red with yellow in it. The latter two are near-boundary reds. Stimuli nearer to a boundary between classes are typically less clear and embody the class less essentially than focal stimuli in that they are usually complex combinations of

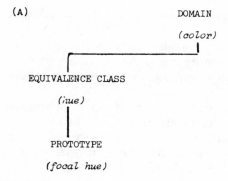

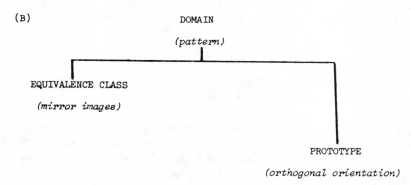

FIG. 2.3.   Two relationships of a prototype to a sensory domain. (A) A prototype may be a member of an equivalence class that is part of a domain. (B) A prototype may appear directly in a domain.

the parent category and its neighbor.[1] Evidence for the special nature of the prototype in a class can be found simply by looking back to Fig. 2.1B. Even though the animal in this study was trained on the green 497 nm, it actually gave more generalization responses to 505 nm; this color is farther from the blue–green boundary, and its dominant wavelength falls closer to the spectral site of focal green (i.e., green with the least blue or yellow in it; Boynton, 1975). (The "peak shift" of spontaneous generalization towards the center or

[1]The similarity between "lesser" members of an equivalence class and the prototype is not symmetrical; i.e., members compare with the prototype, not vice versa (Rosch, 1975a; Tversky, 1977).

prototype of a category is characteristic of a wide variety of animals that see color; Bornstein, 1974.)

Prototypes can also appear in sensory domains; that is, prototypes are not always necessarily members of a similarity group. An example is shown in Fig. 2.3B: The vertical and horizontal orthogonals may represent orientation prototypically.

Prototypes have also been thought to serve a series of important functions in perception, though obviously not every prototype has actually to serve every function. Prototypes are salient, and they attract attention to themselves and to their class or to their domain. Because prototypes are often simple structurally or psychologically, they are easily encoded and are remembered best. Because prototypes are often particularly clear, they may also represent categories or domains. Where prototypes are members of an equivalence class, they function in two additional ways. First, the "fuzzy" boundary structure of natural categories practically dictates that prototypes act as reference points from which the category membership of other instances is judged. Second, prototypes help to differentiate categories by maximizing distinctions among structures most of whose other members are less distinctive.

TWO KINDS OF PERCEPTUAL ORGANIZATION NEAR THE BEGINNING OF LIFE

Though much is known about the structure and function of equivalence classification and prototypicality in mature cognition, relatively little is understood about their initial stages or their development. We have known for some time that the senses are relatively well developed at birth and that infants sense physical stimulation: Babies see, hear, smell, taste, and feel (Cohen & Salapatek, 1975; Kessen, Haith, & Salapatek, 1970). These abilities have been gauged principally from evidence that infants discriminate *between* domains of physical stimulation. The subject matter with which I am concerned here draws on the baby's tendency to discriminate degrees and perceptually to select *within* sensory domains. I wish to propose a view, based on recent research chiefly in vision and audition, that human infants naturally perceive rudimentary organization within select dimensions of sensation in a manner similar to adults. Specifically, infants tend to group discriminable stimuli within certain domains into equivalence classes, and they tend to select (or *be selected by*) one or a small set of stimuli within a domain or category as prototypical of it.

How can we assess equivalence classification and prototypicality in infancy? Each type of perceptual organization warrants two key experiments. For equivalence classification, one would want to show *generalization* among stimuli—that is, to demonstrate that infants perceive or treat a group of stimuli as relatively similar or equivalent to one another. Then (to transcend the trivial case in which all stimuli are identical), one might also want to show *discrimination* among the same stimuli—that is, to demonstrate that infants can perceive members of an equivalence class to be nonidentical. (I assume that nonidentical stimuli that are not discriminated would naturally be coclassified.) For prototypicality, one would want to show *preference*—that is, to demonstrate that infants choose, for example, to look longer at one stimulus (or a select few stimuli). One would also want to show a *processing* advantage—that is, to demonstrate that infants encode, remember, or utilize the same stimulus (or stimuli) to advantage in information processing. (These are criteria for categorization and typicality that might apply in infant perception; they are not necessarily the ones to adopt with adults.) Most of the studies I now turn to were conducted to these ends with infants 2–5 months of age.

Equivalence Classification

Colors. Color-normal (trichromatic) adults organize the wavelength spectrum into an orderly and regular array of hues. In it, we commonly identify four basic, qualitatively distinctive categories: blue, green, yellow, and red (Boynton, 1975). This basic four-fold categorization of the spectrum is linguistically, psychologically, and biologically meaningful (for a review of arguments, see Bornstein, 1973, 1975a). Soon after young children learn the names for colors, they, too, linguistically partition the spectrum in this way. Historically, psychologists (e.g., Beare, 1963; Graham, 1965), psycholinguists (e.g, Brown & Lenneberg, 1954; Kopp & Lane, 1968), anthropologists (e.g., Carroll, 1966; Ray, 1952, 1953; Whorf, 1952), and philosophers (e.g., Quine, 1969) have favored the view that the child's initial spectral divisions are arbitrarily derived and that they develop out of differential training.

Against this setting, Bornstein, Kessen, and Weiskopf (1976) examined whether the infant's perception of physical variation in the wavelength spectrum were random or organized into correlate psychological categories of hue, as it is for adults. Four-month-olds were divided into three kinds of groups—six boundary groups, two category groups, and a control—each of which was habituated to a different spectral light. Following habituation, the babies in the boundary and category groups were probed for their recognition of the old habituation light and for their discrimination of two new spectral lights that were equally displaced in physical terms (i.e., nanometers) from the habituation stimulus. For the boundary groups, the new test lights were selected so that one was from the same adult hue category as the habituation light and the other was from a different, adjacent hue category (e.g., if the habituation stimulus was blue, one test stimulus was blue and one was green). For the category groups, the two new test lights were selected from the same adult hue category. If infants were simply sensate beings tied to physical differences among wavelengths—if they failed to perceive psychological organization in the spectrum as adults do—babies in boundary groups ought to have discriminated the two new stimuli equally. They did not. Like the monkey referred to earlier, babies in the boundary groups showed asymmetric generalization (of habituation) to the two new stimuli. Fig. 2.4A shows an example: These babies persistently treated as similar the habituation wavelength (480 nm) and the test wavelength (450 nm) from the same adult hue category (i.e., they generalized habituation from one blue to another), and they selectively treated as different the wavelength (510 nm) from the different hue category (i.e., they dishabituated to green). Babies in the category groups generalized habituation to both new wavelengths, treating both similar to the habituation stimulus. For example, Fig. 2.4B shows that babies who were habituated to blue (450 nm) generalized among three blues (430 nm, 450 nm, and 470 nm). Although two test lights in every group were "new," only ones of different hues were sufficiently "novel" to elicit infant dishabituation. Control-group infants were shown only the habituation

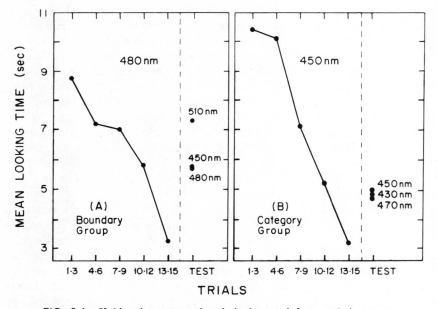

FIG. 2.4. Habituation to wavelength in human infants and, in a test following habituation, generalization of habituation and dishabituation. Transition from habituation to test is indicated by the dashed vertical line. (A) A boundary group; here one new test wavelength is from the same category as the habituation wavelength and one from another category across a category boundary between them. (B) A category group; here both new test wavelengths are from the same category as the habituation wavelength. (After Bornstein, Kessen, & Weiskopf, 1976, Study 1.)

wavelength; like category-group babies, they maintained a low level of looking throughout their "test."

Several boundary and category groups were seen in this study, and their data spanned the visible spectrum. Fig. 2.5 compares equivalence classes of hue and regions of probable interhue transition for two developmental levels. The infant data summarize the category and boundary groups seen in the habituation study just described (Bornstein eι al., 1976, Figure 4). The adult data are wavelengths that according to Boynton and Gordon (1965), adults name with the single-hue term indicated more than 70% of the time. Clearly, infants and adults partition the spectrum in a similar fashion. We concluded that young babies perceive psychological organization in the wavelength spectrum far in advance of extensive experience or formal language training and that babies respect similar hue categories and boundaries as established in adults. A related study found some evidence of similar classification among 3-month-olds (Bornstein, 1976a).

In Fig. 2.5, equivalence classes of hue are depicted as discrete. However, it would be incorrect to conclude from this summary depiction that infants (or adults) do not discriminate among the wavelengths that they group into equivalence classes. To demonstrate the infant's competence at discriminating among members of a hue class, I compared rates of habituation in two groups of babies, one shown the same blue (476 nm) on every trial, and the other shown a variety of six blues (455 nm, 470 nm, 476 nm, 480 nm, 484 nm, and 490 nm) selected within the boundaries of the infant's blue category (as

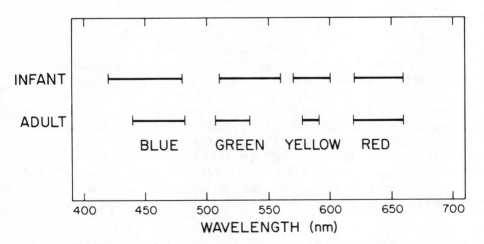

FIG. 2.5.   Equivalence classes of hue in the infant and the adult. The infant data summarize the results of Bornstein, Kessen, and Weiskopf (1976). The adult data are from Boynton and Gordon (1965); they represent regions of the wavelength spectrum that adults name exclusively blue, green, yellow, *or* red 70% or more of the time.

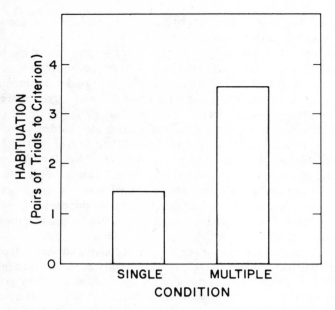

FIG. 2.6. Infants habituate faster to the re-presentation of the same wavelength (single condition) than to the presentation of a series of wavelengths from one hue class (multiple condition). Rate is measured in pairs of trials to a constant habituation criterion (looking on two consecutive trials ≤ 80% of looking on the first three trials). A trial was equal to the duration of an infant's first look.

determined in Bornstein et al., 1976). If the wavelengths in a class were indiscriminable for infants, the two groups ought to habituate equally quickly; if the wavelengths are only similar, habituation to variety ought to be somewhat slower than habituation to identity (Fantz, 1964; McCall & Kagan, 1967). Fig. 2.6 shows that infants reached a fixed habituation criterion with repetition of a single blue (1.4 pairs of trials) significantly faster than they reached the same criterion with the multiple blue series (3.5 pairs of trials).[2]

Still, discriminability within a hue category is not as good as discriminability between hue categories. Several sources of evidence support this conclusion. First, Fagan (1974) found that 4-month-olds look longer at checkerboards constructed of two different hues (e.g., red and green) than at checkerboards constructed of two samples of the same hue (e.g., two reds). Second, our

---

[2]Stern (1977) has observed that a mother will often use within-category variability (of word, stress, sound, pitch, intensity, or timing) effectively to maintain her infant's attention and interest. "The repetition run provides the mother with the means to create themes and variations. Most repetitive runs do not repeat the unit exactly, and some variation is progressively introduced, such as 'Hello... Helloooo... Helllooooo![p. 95]" According to Stern, over half of such runs, vocal and nonverbal, involve variation.

original categorization study showed dishabituation between but not within categories. Finally, I found that infants take twice as long to habituate to a variety of hues (7.4 pairs of trials when shown blues, greens, yellows, and reds) than to variety within a hue (3.5 pairs in multiple blue condition above).

Equivalence classifications of hue in humans (as well as in monkeys) may reflect to some degree the organism's ability to discriminate among wavelengths. Primate discriminability of wavelength is nonmonotonic (i.e., in some spectral regions it is acute, but in others it is poor), and where discrimination is poor, organisms tend to generalize, whereas they tend to differentiate where discrimination is acute. In the case of wavelength and hue, discrimination and generalization (or equivalence classification) approximately correlate in an inversely related fashion (Bornstein, 1978a; A. A. Wright, 1972; W. D. Wright, 1947).

It is interesting to note in this connection the correspondence between behavioral wavelength discrimination in humans and in Old World monkeys (like the macaques in Sandell et al., 1979) on the one hand, and, on the other, the discrimination characteristics of color-specific cells identified in the primate lateral geniculate nucleus (LGN). Although not the last visual area where analysis of chromatic input takes place, LGN recordings suggest that a remarkably close relationship exists between the tuning curves for color-sensitive cells and behavioral discrimination of wavelength (DeValois, 1973; DeValois & DeValois, 1975).

In summary, human infants, like human adults (and monkeys), partition the photic spectrum into equivalence classes of hue that group discriminably different wavelengths by their apparent perceptual similarity. This perceptual grouping is related (in some degree) to the organism's native ability to discriminate along the wavelength continuum.

Recall for a moment Molyneux's question to Locke. Two hundred seventy years later, Gregory and Wallace (1963) described the visual discriminations of a man blinded at about 9 months of age whose sight was restored in adulthood. Immediately afterward, the man could correctly identify color numerals on isochromatic plates that are typically used to test for color deficiencies. These numerals are constructed of small circles each of a different variant of a hue. This man then gave evidence of equivalence classification in the absence of extensive experience.

Patterns. Ernst Mach (1885/1959) observed at the beginning of this century that "adults ... do not readily notice a change from left to right [p. 110]," and psychological research since has confirmed that human adults frequently perceive a stimulus and its reflection 180° around the vertical axis (its left–right or lateral mirror image) to be especially similar (Gross & Bornstein, 1978; Olson & Attneave, 1970; Pomerantz, Sager, & Stoever, 1977; Wolff, 1971). Children notoriously treat as equivalent left–right versions of a pattern (Davidson, 1935; Orton, 1937; Rudel & Teuber, 1963), as does a wide variety of other animal species, even though virtually all visual vertebrates are otherwise highly sensitive to orientation change (for a review, see Bradshaw, Bradley, & Patterson, 1976, or Corballis & Beale, 1976). In short, mirror-image patterns are perceptually similar and are sometimes treated psychologically as equivalent. Therefore, mirror images constitute a second equivalence class in vision.

In this context, Bornstein, Gross, and Wolf (1978) investigated the perception of mirror images by human infants. In one experiment, infants were habituated to a line tilted 45° right from vertical; they were then tested with the same oblique, a vertical line, and an oblique tilted 45° left from vertical. Fig. 2.7 shows the test phase following habituation. Babies dishabituated to the vertical relative to the right 45° tilt (an angular displacement of 45°), but they failed to dishabituate to the left 45° tilt (a displacement of 90°). That is, babies treated left–right mirror-image obliques equivalently. In order to determine whether infants simply confuse all obliques—the "oblique effect" (Appelle, 1972)—or actually perceive lateral mirror images as similar, two further experiments were conducted. In the first of these, babies were

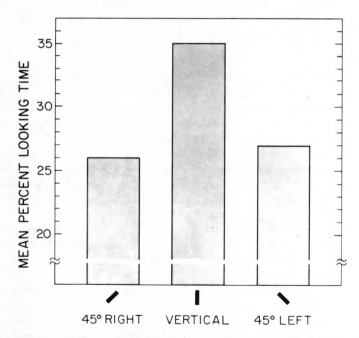

FIG. 2.7. Following habituation to a 45°-right oblique, infants generalize habituation to the habituation stimulus and to its mirror image (a 45°-left oblique), but they dishabituate to a different orientation of the same stimulus. (After Bornstein, Gross, & Wolf, 1978, Experiment II. Copyright Elsevier Sequoia S. A. Used by permission.)

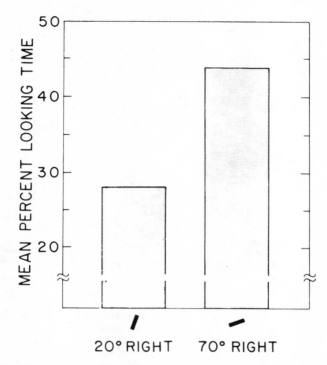

FIG. 2.8. At the end of habituation to a 20°–right oblique, infants dishabituate to a test 70°–right oblique. (After Bornstein, Gross, & Wolf, 1978, Experiment III. Copyright Elsevier Sequoia S. A. Used by permission.)

habituated to a line tilted 20° right from vertical and were immediately tested with a line tilted 70° to the right of vertical. As shown in Fig. 2.8, the babies dishabituated, thereby demonstrating that they can discriminate among at least some nonmirror-image obliques (differing by 50°).

In the second follow-up experiment, patterns other than obliques were studied. This time, the fact that habituation to repetition of the same stimulus is faster and more complete than is habituation to varied stimulation was used to assess infant discrimination of 90° versus 180° (lateral mirror-image) rotations of geometric patterns. Four groups of babies experienced different stimulus presentation conditions. One group was shown a standard stimulus (⊏) on successive trials; two other groups saw the standard stimulus on approximately 50% of the trials intermixed with presentations of one or another 90° rotation of the standard (⊓ and ⊔, respectively); the fourth group was shown the standard stimulus intermixed over trials with its lateral mirror image (⊐). Babies in all four groups saw the standard stimulus in the same trial position; only the context in which the standard appeared varied. This design facilitated intergroup comparison. To compare habituation in the four

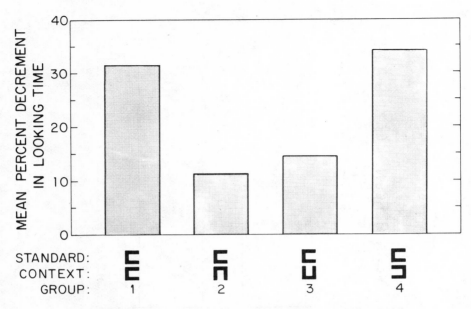

FIG. 2.9. Infants show large and equivalent decrements in looking time between the beginning and end of habituation to the repetition of a single standard stimulus (Group 1) and to the intermixing over trials of a standard and its lateral mirror image (Group 4). Infants decline less when the standard and its orthogonal rotations are intermixed (Groups 2 or 3). The standard stimulus and the context stimulus shown to each group are indicated on the abscissa. (After Bornstein, Gross, & Wolf, 1978, Experiment IV. Copyright Elsevier Sequoia S. A. Used by permission.)

groups, we measured the amounts that babies declined in looking from the first three standard stimulus trials to the last three standard stimulus trials in the series. Fig. 2.9 shows that the group shown the standard stimulus on each trial and the group shown the standard intermixed with its lateral mirror image both decreased significant amounts in looking; moreover, decrements in the two were equivalent. By contrast, neither of the groups shown the standard and its orthogonal rotations showed a reliable decrement. Further, the standard and mirror-image groups declined reliably more than the 90°-rotation groups. In an additional experiment (Bornstein et al., 1978), we found that babies also perceive vertical mirror images as similar, though vertical pairs proved to be less similar than lateral ones.

These results, like the previous ones with obliques, indicate that young infants perceive mirror-image pairs of patterns as equivalent. Of course, infants might still discriminate between mirror images. McGurk (1974), for example, found that older babies could discriminate vertical mirror images, and Hendrickson and Muehl (1962) and Jeffrey (1958) have trained older children, who, under like circumstances, confuse lateral mirror images, to discriminate between them.

Equivalence classification of hue is associated with an identifiable biological substrate. It is again interesting to note, therefore, that representations of the visual world in the two striate cortices form mirror images and that in prestriate cortex adjacent retinotopic maps tend also to be mirror images of one another (Kaas, 1978).

A second type of pattern to which the notion of equivalence classification in infancy may be applicable is facial expression. Darwin (1872/1915) suggested that certain expressions might be universally produced and recognized. Intriguingly, there is more than suggestive evidence that infants, who can discriminate among certain facial expressions (e.g., Young-Browne, Rosenfeld, & Horowitz, 1977), generalize across faces with the same expression (LeBarbera, Izard, Vietze, & Parisi, 1976). Fagan's (1979) studies also show that infants generalize among discriminable faces with the same pose.

Other Senses, Other Classes.   Young children and adults perceive and respond to physical variation in domains other than vision in ways that yield equivalence classes. Among the most celebrated in contemporary psychology is the "categorical" perception of phonemes in speech, i.e., the perceptual grouping and equivalent treatment of formant differences that cue voicing and place of articulation (Aslin & Pisoni, 1980; Liberman, Cooper, Shankweiler, & Studdert-Kennedy, 1967). Although adults seem to partition these dimensions discretely, psycholinguists have repeatedly demonstrated that adults can discriminate within categories (for a summary, see Bornstein, 1979). Extensive research with infants by Eimas (e.g., 1975) and others (also summarized in Bornstein, 1979) has shown similar equivalence classification near the beginning of life. Not all auditory equivalence classes in adults are subunits of speech, however; Cutting and Rosner (1974), for example, demonstrated equivalence classification of select nonspeech, musical sounds, in this case cued by rise time. These same investigators also found that 2-month-olds classify similar variations in rise time as equivalent (Jusczyk, Rosner, Cutting, Foard, & Smith, 1977). (It is important to note that within-category discrimination both for speech and nonspeech sounds has not been demonstrated in infants as it has been in adults. Auditory studies with infants, like those with adults, necessarily involve successive discriminations that are considerably impoverished by the time error.)

In gustation and somesthesis, there is reason to believe that humans of all ages (as well as other species) perceptually organize select physical variation into equivalence classes. Theory is more confused here, and conclusive data are sorely lacking. First, consider taste. According to McBurney and Gent

(1979), the psychophysical evidence is compelling that "four taste qualities together exhaust the qualities of taste experience [p. 151]." These primaries are sweet, salty, sour, and bitter. Human newborns discriminate among categories of gustatory stimuli, for example by showing pleasure to sweets (sucking, intake, increased heart rate, positive gustofacial reflex) and displeasure to bitters (Engen, Lipsitt, & Peck, 1974; Jacobs, Smutz, & DuBose, 1977; Lipsitt, 1977; Steiner, 1977). Though babies respond differentially within a taste class, e.g., of sugars (Desor, Maller, & Greene, 1977; Engen et al., 1974; Nowlis & Kessen, 1976), they give evidence of less discrimination within taste qualities than between them (Jacobs et al., 1977). It is in this light interesting that nerve fibers in the monkey chorda tympani, which are sensitive principally to a single taste stimulus (e.g., sugar), not only "discriminate" within tastes (e.g., the sweets of sucrose and fructose) by the vigor of their response, but seem in some cases to respond better to multiple testants of the same quality (e.g., sweet) than to testants of other taste qualities (Frank, 1977). There is suggestive evidence, therefore, that infants (like adults) organize tastes perceptually and do so on the basis of identifiable neural mechanisms. Second, consider touch. The universe of surface sensations has been partitioned into major qualities, two of which are cold and heat. Pertinently, Crudden (1937) found that infants are differentially sensitive to warm and cold, yet Usol'tsev and Terekhova (1958) showed broad generalization gradients over degrees of thermal stimulation (cited in Kessen et al., 1970).

In summary, human infants give ample evidence that they perceive as similar and treat as equivalent discriminable stimuli drawn from select dimensions within different sensory domains. I have already hinted at some of the values equivalence classification might serve in perception and cognition, but I defer specific discussion about function until after a consideration of data that show prototypicality in infant perception.

Prototypicality

The number of discriminable stimuli in an equivalence class or in a sensory domain can be very large; for example, an estimated 7,295,000 colors construct the psychological color solid (Nickerson & Newhall, 1943). Yet, not all stimuli in a class or domain necessarily hold equal status; rather, one or a select few may be psychologically salient. They are usually preferred, processed with facility, remembered more durably, relied upon more frequently in discrimination, and, when appropriate, may be referred to in establishing category membership. These stimuli are prototypical of their class or domain. Again I focus at the outset on prototypicality among colors; prototypes in pattern vision and in other senses, such as gustation and audition, are explored after.

Colors. Do infants prefer some colors over others? Do these stimuli meet the functional criteria of prototypes just enumerated?

Most colors consist of two hues in a mixture, even if one of the two dominates; however, select colors yield nearly a single percept (Boynton, 1975). Long ago, Newton (1671–1672) recognized their status as "Original and simple"; they are prototypes. More recently, Berlin and Kay (1969) have found that peoples from a wide variety of societies agree quite closely that certain chromatic stimuli—Berlin and Kay called them "focal" colors—constitute a narrowly defined set of the best examples of different basic color names; that is, focal colors are universally the best representatives of hue categories. Numerous psychological studies among young children and adults have also revealed that focal colors possess many other properties of prototypes; they tend to be preferred, remembered, and most frequently used in discrimination, and they serve as referents in judgments of category membership (for summary discussions, see Bornstein, 1973, 1975a, 1978a, or Rosch, 1975a, 1978).

To ascertain first whether human infants would especially prefer proto-typical colors, I showed five groups of babies a variety of monochromatic lights selected to span the visible spectrum and to exemplify prototypical colors as well as a variety of other in-between colors (Bornstein, 1975c). Four wavelengths (460 nm, 520 nm, 580 nm, and 630 nm) represented good examples of the hue categories of blue, green, yellow, and red, respectively; four others (430 nm, 490 nm, 560 nm, and 600 nm) were combinations of these basic hues, respectively, violet, blue–green, green–yellow, and yellow–red. Four groups saw different subsets of all possible pairings of prototypical colors and color mixtures in a paired-comparisons design; one additional group saw the eight colors in a single-stimulus design. Infants showed a consistent pattern of differential attention regardless of experimental treatment: Fig. 2.10 shows that babies looked reliably longer at prototypes than at mixtures containing them, even though not all prototypes are preferred to all mixtures. Apparently there exists—even in infancy—a preference hierarchy for hue (Bornstein, 1978a).

Reviews of other infant and adult studies of color preference confirm the strong dichotomous preference for prototypical colors over mixtures (Bornstein, 1975b, 1978a). Further, when adults were asked to rate the pleasantness of spectral lights shown to infants as part of the infant preference study just

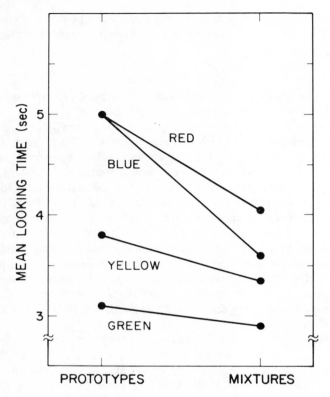

FIG. 2.10. Infants prefer chromatic prototypes to surrounding mixtures. From a paired-comparisons design. (After Bornstein, 1975c. Copyright Academic Press, Inc. Used by permission.)

cited, they gave ratings that significantly closely paralleled the infants' pattern of differential attention (Fig. 2.11).

Not only are prototypes aesthetically affective for infants, they tend to be cognitively effective. In three experiments, I found that prototypical colors function in infant perception in ways that one would expect extrapolating from adult cognitive data. In the first experiment, I found that infants habituate to prototypical colors faster than they do to chromatic mixtures. Habituation rate in infants has been hypothesized to be a partial analog of encodability in adults (e.g., Cohen, DeLoache, & Strauss, 1979), and adults are known to learn and to identify prototypical colors faster than other colors (Beare, 1963; Heider, 1972; Rosch, 1978). Fig. 2.12, for example, shows results of a study in which Bornstein and Monroe (1981) found that, *ceteris paribus,* adults will identify chromatic prototypes (centers of color categories) significantly faster than mixtures (boundaries between them). In the infant

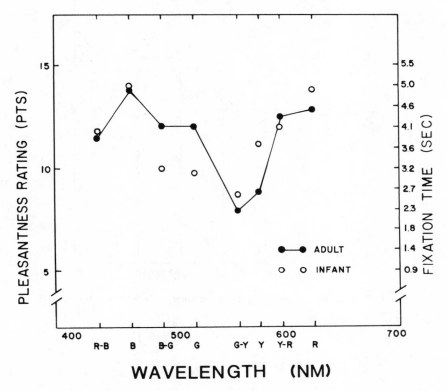

FIG. 2.11. Infant preferences for wavelengths correlate with adult pleasantness ratings of the same wavelengths. Letters B (blue), G (green), Y (yellow), and R (red) indicate the apparent hue of the wavelength. The two ordinate scales have been adjusted by a double linear-regression technique so as to be equivalent. (After Bornstein, 1975c. Copyright Academic Press, Inc. Used by permission.)

habituation study, two groups were habituated with prototypes (one saw blue, 476 nm, and the other saw red, the complement of 493 nm), and two other groups were habituated with chromatic mixtures (one saw blue–green, 490 nm, and the other saw yellow–red, 603 nm). Habituation rate was assessed by deriving the slope of a linear-regression fit to each child's looking-time data. Rates of habituation in the prototype groups were statistically equal as were habituation rates in the mixture groups. As Fig. 2.13 shows, however, the average slope of habituation to chromatic prototypes (–.75) was significantly steeper than that to chromatic mixtures (–.54). This result is further supported by habituation data from the category study cited earlier (Bornstein et al., 1976); slope of habituation in that study increased with

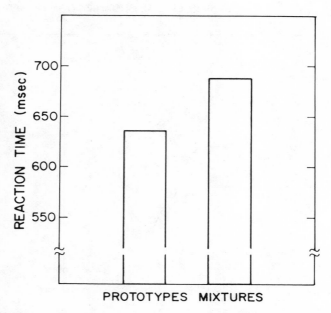

FIG. 2.12. Adults classify chromatic prototypes faster than chromatic mixtures.

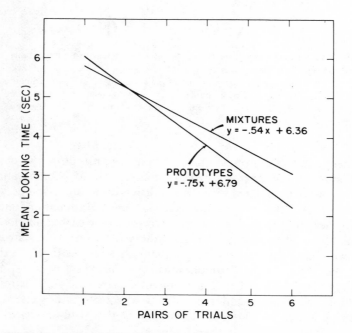

FIG. 2.13. Infants habituate faster to chromatic prototypes than to chromatic mixtures. Habituation functions are mean least-squares fits.

proximity of the habituation wavelength to a category center (Bornstein, 1978a).[3]

Another supposed advantage for adults in the perception of prototypes is that they are remembered better (Bornstein, 1976b; Heider, 1972; Rosch, 1975b, 1978). In a second experiment, I found that infants, too, recognize prototypical colors after a delay better than they do color mixtures. Four groups of infants participated: Two were habituated to prototypes (blue or red, as above) and two to mixtures (blue–green or yellow–red, as above as well). After habituation, a variety of other colors was shown, but prototype and mixture groups were matched for this interference. Subsequently, the babies were retested for their recognition of the habituation prototype or mixture, as appropriate. Presumably, a low level of looking on the retest would indicate the infants' long-term recognition of the color, whereas recovery to the habituation stimulus in the retest would indicate forgetting. On the retest, the two prototype groups did not differ from one another, nor did the two mixture groups differ from each other. As Fig. 2.14 shows, only the groups habituated to chromatic mixtures recovered looking reliably from the end of habituation to the retest. The prototype groups did not dishabituate reliably. Indeed, on the retest itself, babies in the mixture groups looked reliably more than those habituated to prototypes. Both groups recovered equally to a neutral, control pattern, however. Thus, even though prototype and mixture groups habituated to the same degree and experienced equivalent interference, babies remembered prototypical colors better than color mixtures.

Prototypes, which are psychologically salient, are habituated to faster and recognized better. In the last experiment, I found that infants use prototypes qualitatively to differentiate among hue classes. Following habituation to a stimulus, discrimination may be based on qualitative or quantitative change away from the stimulus. These two theoretical possibilities are illustrated in Fig. 2.15. Many discrimination experiments show the quantitative result, namely a correlation between the amount of stimulus change and the amount of response change (for reviews, see Cohen et al., 1979; Cohen & Gelber, 1975; Kessen et al., 1970). Fig. 2.15A illustrates this line of reasoning: After habituation to a short wavelength, infants would be expected to recover looking, as measured by more dishabituation, in the degree to which test wavelengths differ physically from the habituation wavelength, i.e., to recover more to a long wavelength than to a middle wavelength. Alternatively, infants who see categories of hue in the spectrum might be expected to respond to qualitative differences among prototypes of those categories. Fig.

---

[3]Jeffrey (1968) has theorized that habituation of attention (orienting) to different cues ought to occur at rates directly related to the relative salience of those cues—the most salient is attended to first and most, and it is habituated to first, etc. Miller (1972) has previously provided evidence from 4-month-olds that, indeed, habituation to components of a pattern takes place in the order that infants initially express interest in them (but, see Lasky, 1979). The habituation data presented here are consonant with this serial-habituation interpretation.

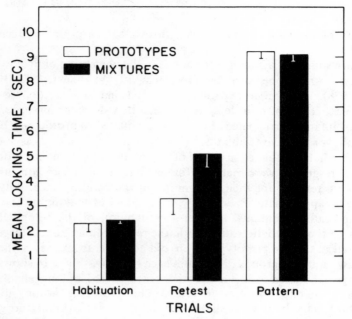

FIG. 2.14. Infants who were habituated to chromatic mixtures dishabituate on a delayed retest; they forget. Infants who were habituated to chromatic prototypes remain habituated on the retest; they remember. Both groups dishabituate on test trials when a neutral pattern is shown . (SEM is shown.)

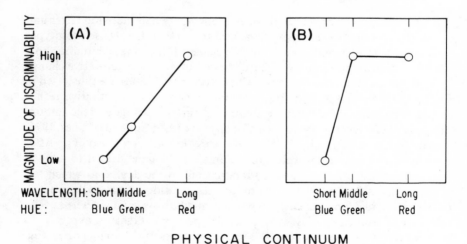

FIG. 2.15. Two possible patterns of discriminability among physically different, psychologically prototypical hues. Short wavelengths, blue in hue, are the standard against which comparison is made. (A) Response magnitude is a monotonic (and linear) function of the physical or quantitative differences among stimuli. (B) Response magnitude is a simple function of qualitative differences among stimuli.

2.15B illustrates this possibility: Habituated to blue, babies would give equivalent dishabituation to other test hues (green or red) independent of wavelength. In the experiment, one group of infants was habituated with blue and was tested with the same blue and with green and red; a second group was habituated with red, and was tested with the same red and with green and blue. For both groups, one of the two new test stimuli was physically (i.e., quantitatively) close, and one was distant from the habituation stimulus; for both groups also, the two new test hues were equivalently different from the habituation hue psychologically (i.e., qualitatively). Fig. 2.16 shows combined results for the two groups; response patterns for the two did not differ from one another statistically. Babies generalized habituation on the retest trials (they showed a nonsignificant increase); but, contrary to the linear or monotonic prediction, they dishabituated equivalently to the two new test stimuli. In other words, infants used prototypes effectively to anchor qualitative distinctions among hue categories.

Humans of all ages see and respond to selected colors as prototypical. It is interesting that the special nature of these same colors may be related directly to the sensitivity of neural tissue in the visual system. In this connection, I have previously shown (Bornstein, 1973) that the wavelengths to which types of cells in the LGN respond maximally (DeValois, 1973) correspond closely

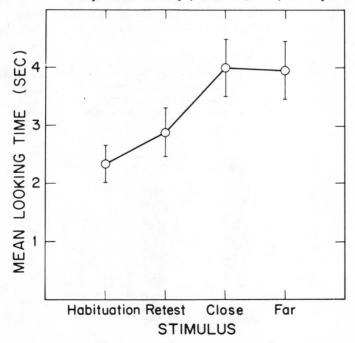

FIG. 2.16. Infants generalize habituation on retest of the habituation prototype, but they discriminate qualitatively, i.e., equally, change to close and far test hue prototypes. (SEM is shown.)

with wavelengths that represent cross-culturally agreed upon foci of color identifications (Berlin & Kay, 1969)—namely, the chromatic prototypes.

Once again, I have concentrated on prototypes in color vision.[4] But prototypes have also emerged in the study of other dimensions of vision.

Patterns.   Do infants prefer some patterns to others? Do these patterns function like prototypes in infant perception?

Both children and adults tend to see the vertical and horizontal as the principal dimensions of visual space (e.g., Appelle, 1972; Bornstein, 1978b; Braine, 1978; Gibson, 1966; Howard & Templeton, 1966; Olson, 1970). The orthogonals are perceptually visible, differentiable, and stable next to the obliques; they are also psychologically salient, identified more rapidly, and remembered better; finally, they frequently serve as referents in judging lines and angles of orientation (Olson & Attneave, 1970; Pick, Yonas & Rieser, 1979; Rosch, 1975a, 1978; Wertheimer, 1923/1958). Gibson (1934, 1937) even found a "peak shift" in human judgments of orientation: He showed that tilted forms are often perceived and reproduced upright and that lines tilted up to 10° off axis are consistently "normalized" in the direction of vertical or horizontal. In short, vertical and horizontal are psychologically primary and function as our anchoring frames of spatial reference.

To ascertain whether infants would especially prefer the principal orthogonals, I displayed to babies square-wave gratings aligned horizontally,

---

[4]Another psychological dimension of color, saturation, may harbor prototypes. Infants prefer higher levels of saturation (Fig. 2.i) (Bornstein, 1978b, Experiment I). Intriguingly, adults find that saturated values are canonical "reference points" in judging colors (Harkness, 1973; Rosch, 1975a), and children and adults alike typically recode and remember colors as more saturated (Bartleson, 1960; Gilbert, 1894).

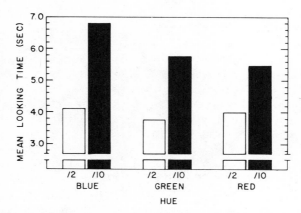

FIG. i.   Infants prefer higher saturations (/10) to lower saturations (/2) of different hues. (After Bornstein, 1978b, Experiment I. Copyright Academic Press, Inc. Used by permission.)

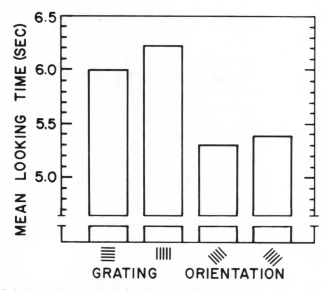

FIG. 2.17.   Infants prefer horizontal and vertical grating orientations equally and more than oblique ones. (After Bornstein, 1978b, Experiment II. Copyright Academic Press, Inc. Used by permission.)

vertically, 45° to the left of vertical, or 45° to the right for fixed durations. As shown in Fig. 2.17, babies looked at orthogonal gratings equally (confirming McKenzie & Day, 1971, and Moffett, 1969) and reliably more than at otherwise identical oblique ones, a preference consistent with other reports of an oblique effect in infants (Leehey, Moskowitz-Cook, Brill, & Held, 1975).

Prototypicality includes more than preference; it implies rapid habituation, better recognition, and better discriminability. Not all of the pertinent studies in orientation perception have been conducted with infants. However, some investigators have found that vertical and horizontal possess demonstrative salience for the neonate, even on the first day of life (e.g., Kessen, Salapatek, & Haith, 1972).

These results suggest that orientation perception is endogenously anisotropic, and the findings are again interesting in light of the claim that the salience of orthogonality may be related to the neurophysiological wiring of the visual system. Mansfield (1974), Pettigrew, Nikara, and Bishop (1968), and Leventhal and Hirsch (1977) have found in monkeys and in cats that orientation selectivity of striate cortex cells mediating foveal vision over-represents the principal meridians. (However, it is important to note that other investigators—e.g., Hubel & Wiesel, 1968, and Schiller, Finlay, & Volman, 1976—have disputed any such anisotropy.) In man, cortex for central vision is also thought to be most densely populated with cells sensitive to the orthogonals (Bouma & Andriessen, 1968; Marg, Adams, & Rutkin, 1968); certainly, horizontal and vertical gratings (moving or stationary) elicit greater amplitude cortical evoked potentials than do oblique gratings (Freeman & Thibos, 1973; Maffei & Campbell, 1970; Yoshida, Iwahara, & Nagamura, 1975).

Orthogonals represent prototypical orientations, but they are not the only pattern prototypes. Though there is no agreed-upon metric of form (Zusne, 1970), adults tend to see and to identify as prototypical certain other characteristics of patterns. One is symmetry, the equivalent reflection of parts of a pattern or configuration about an axis. It has been recognized for some time that adults and older children prefer symmetry (Aristotle, 1908; Arnheim, 1974; Darwin, 1871/1913; Mowatt, 1940; Paraskevopoulos, 1968; Szilagyi & Baird, 1977); psychological research in the last century has repeatedly demonstrated that symmetrical stimuli are also consistently

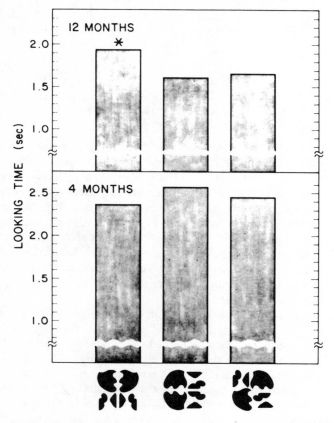

FIG. 2.18. Four-month-olds prefer vertically symmetrical, horizontally symmetrical, and asymmetrical stimuli equally, but 12-month-olds prefer vertical ones (as indicated by the asterisk) to the other two. Samples of the stimuli are shown on the abscissa.

detected faster, remembered better, and discriminated more accurately than asymmetrical ones over a wide age range (Attneave, 1957a, 1968; Boswell, 1976; Garner, 1978; Julesz, 1971; Koffka, 1935; Mach, 1885/1959; Rosch, 1973, 1978). In short, symmetrical patterns are "good patterns" (Garner, 1970).

To ascertain whether infants prefer symmetry and whether they process it more efficiently than asymmetry, Bornstein, Ferdinandsen, and Gross (1979) brought a group of 4-month-olds to the laboratory on three occasions. Once the babies saw a vertically symmetrical pattern, once a horizontally symmetrical one, and once an asymmetrical one; all patterns were constructed of the same elements, and all were shown for fixed durations that permitted continuous viewing. Preference was assessed by comparing the amounts of time the infants looked at each pattern initially. These babies showed no statistically reliable preference when stimuli were presented singly. Fig. 2.18 shows the results of a follow-up cross-sectional experiment using a paired-comparisons design. Choice is perhaps a more sensitive measure of preference. This study confirmed the lack of preference at 4 months, but it revealed that a reliable preference for vertical symmetry emerges by 1 year of age.

In the original symmetry study, we also analyzed processing of three types of symmetry among the 4-month babies by comparing rates and amounts of habituation to each. Fig. 2.19 shows that babies habituate to vertically symmetrical patterns faster than to horizontally symmetrical or asymmetrical ones, but the rates of habituation to horizontal and asymmetrical patterns do not differ. Fig. 2.20 shows that between the beginning and end of the habituation period babies decline most to vertical symmetry and less, by equal amounts, to horizontal symmetry and asymmetry.

These results raise two questions about the advantage for symmetry in infant perception. First, do infants at all see the structure or "good form" in horizontal symmetry, but simply not process it like they do vertical symmetry? Fisher, Ferdinandsen, and Bornstein (1980) investigated this question by assessing the young infant's ability to discriminate among vertically symmetrical, horizontally symmetrical, and asymmetrical forms. We found that babies who were habituated with verticals discriminated change to horizontals and asymmetricals (and vice versa), but that comparable babies failed to discriminate among horizontals and asymmetricals or among asymmetricals. In answer to the first question, the data seem to indicate that *vertical* symmetry (and not symmetry per se) is a prototypical characteristic of pattern organization near the beginning of life.

The second question concerns the limits under which vertical symmetry has an advantage in perception. Adult observers efficiently process vertically symmetrical patterns only when they are separated about the vertical meridian by less than 4° of visual angle (Bruce & Morgan, 1975; Corballis & Roldan, 1974). Infants show a similarly narrow region over which they

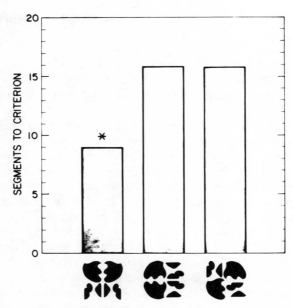

FIG. 2.19. Infants habituate faster to vertically symmetrical stimuli (as indicated by the asterisk) than to either horizontally symmetrical or asymmetrical stimuli, to which they habituate at the same rate. Rate is measured by the number of temporal segments prior to reaching a constant habituation criterion (looking in three consecutive 10-sec segments ≤ 50% of looking on the first three segments).

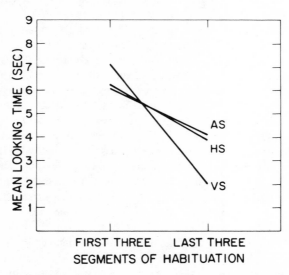

FIG. 2.20. Between the beginning and end of habituation, infants decline in looking more to vertically symmetrical (VS) than to horizontally symmetrical (HS) or asymmetrical (AS) stimuli, to which they decline equivalently. (Examples of the stimuli are shown in Fig. 2.18.)

demonstrate a similar efficiency in processing vertical symmetry. Fig. 2.21 shows that babies habituate significantly faster to vertically symmetrical patterns narrowly aligned about the vertical meridian (0°–2.5°) than to patterns separated by 5° or more. (Babies shown the contiguous displays also habituate reliably more than those shown discontiguous ones.) Babies shown the discontiguous patterns behave like babies habituated to unstructured, asymmetrical patterns (even when they are constituted of the same elements).

Rapid detection of a vertically symmetrical pattern has a suggestive basis in anatomy. Assuming that symmetry is recognized by matching across the midline of the stimulus (e.g., Bruce & Morgan, 1975), we might expect matching to be facilitated when meridional separation is less than 2°-3° because pattern parts fixated centrally and separated by only 1° or 2° of

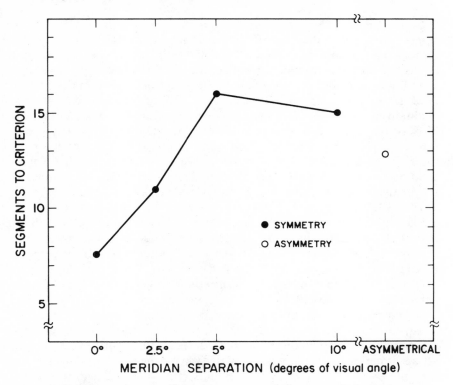

FIG. 2.21. Infants habituate faster to a vertically symmetrical stimulus contiguous or nearly contiguous at the vertical meridian (0°–2.5°) than the same stimulus separated by more than 5° of visual angle. Rate is measured by the number of temporal segments prior to reaching a constant criterion (looking in three consecutive 10-sec segments ≤ 50% of looking on the first three segments). The asymmetrical stimulus was constructed of the same elements as the symmetrical stimulus.

visual angle project to both cerebral hemispheres, whereas pattern parts fixated centrally but separated by more project cross-laterally first to the separate hemispheres (Blakemore, 1969; Stone, Leicester, & Sherman, 1973). Matching parts that fall within the central vertical strip of retina would therefore be expected to be more efficient than matching parts that fall outside it.

Orthogonality and symmetry are two characteristics of visual patterns that may be prototypical. Gestalt psychology suggests that there are others in "good form," e.g., continuation. Thus Rosch (1973, 1978) found that adults in different societies process "good forms" more efficiently than their deformations, just as Bower (1966) had shown earlier that 2-month-olds see a simple form, though interrupted, as a continued "good form."

Other Senses, Other Prototypes. Studies of prototypicality in mature perception can point the way to finding early developmental parallels in other senses—for example, hearing and taste. Concerning audition, infants and adults are similarly "frequency bound" in that both selectively orient to stimuli less than 4000 Hz, the region of the frequency spectrum that carries information about speech (Eisenberg, 1976). Infants, too, discriminate qualitatively among at least some "phonemes" (Eimas, 1975), like they do hues. As for gustation, newborns (1–3 days) and infants (20–28 weeks) prefer sucrose and fructose more than glucose and lactose, and they generally prefer higher concentrations of these sweets. Their hedonics parallel young children's stated preferences (e.g., for sweets) and adults' intake and ratings of the relative sweetness of the same stimuli (Desor et al., 1977; Desor, Maller, & Turner, 1973; Engen et al., 1974; Moscowitz, 1971; Nowlis & Kessen, 1976; Stellar, 1977). Again it is interesting to note in this connection that recordings from the chorda tympani in both hamsters (*Mesocricetus auratus*) and squirrel monkeys (*Saimiri sciureus*) show that different taste fibers respond best to one of the four basic tastes and that these fibers respond more to particular stimuli and to higher concentrations of their appropriate stimulus (Frank, 1977; Nowlis, 1978).

In summary, certain stimuli are special in infancy (as well as in adulthood)—perhaps because of their special biological status—and because they are special, they help infants to organize the perceptual world. These stimuli attract attention to themselves and, in this way, to the classes or domains that they represent. They encourage in infants efficient and rapid processing, augment their discriminative powers, and may enhance memory.

Summary

Infants near the beginning of life do not perceive all physical stimuli in a sensory domain as equally different from one another in psychological terms; rather, they treat some as equivalent based on the perceptual similarity of the stimuli. Nor do infants regard all stimuli in a class or domain as holding the same status; rather, they perceive some to be prototypical, and they prefer them, process them faster, remember them better, and use them efficaciously in judging class membership as well as in qualitative differentiation among classes. Infants categorize and typify colors and patterns as well as sounds and tastes. Indeed, the data suggest that parallel sorts of structures with parallel functions may be at work regardless of the sense; it would appear that the structure of sensory systems provides a basis, and their function a handy explanation, for at least some of the classification and prototypicality effects first displayed so very near to the beginning of life. We ought therefore to admit the possibility that equivalence classification and prototypicality, so pervasive in adult perception and cognition and in adult language and social behavior, already exist in a chrysalis state in infancy.

One further point ought to be made before I pursue the third argument of this chapter. Equivalence classification and prototypicality are two kinds of perceptual organization, though they are not the only two. Other kinds of perceptual organization have been assessed in young babies. For example, Demany, McKenzie, and Vurpillot (1977) recently found that 2- to 3-month-olds discriminated temporal forms of auditory stimulation from regular pulsations and from other temporal forms of the same mean acoustic density. These babies tended to group successive sounds into perceptual units or configurations—that is, to perceive rhythm. Although I have concentrated on equivalence classification and prototypicality as two forms of perceptual organization, I have not intended this discussion to be exclusive or exhaustive.

A COMPARATIVE VIEW: ONTOGENY AND PHYLOGENY OF PERCEPTUAL ORGANIZATION

Even a brief consideration of equivalence classification and prototypicality in species other than man throws additional light on their nature. Equivalence classification and prototypicality are widespread among animals. They are also species specific (in the sense that their precise manifestation may vary from species to species). Further, they are adaptive and functional in similar ways for different species. A brief review of these two types of perceptual organization in a select few invertebrate and vertebrate species exemplifies these characteristics.

Several organisms that see color have been shown behaviorally to partition the spectrum into equivalence classes of "hue" (see Table 2.1). Data for the honeybee, pigeon, and monkey, together with those for human infants and adults, are compared graphically in Fig. 2.22. All of these organisms categorize hue, though their visible spectra differ, and they partition the spectrum in different locations. For each species, psychophysical research has

TABLE 2.1
Cross-Species Comparisons of Select Equivalence Classes

Investigator(s)	(Date)	Common Name	Generic Name
		"HUES"	
von Frisch	(1950)	Honeybee	*Apis mellifera*
Wright & Cumming	(1971)	Pigeon	*Columba livia*
Sandell et al.	(1979)	Monkey	*Macaca fascicularis* and *M. mulatta*
Bornstein et al.	(1976)	Infant	*Infans tyrannus*
Boynton & Gordon	(1965)	Adult	*Homo sapiens*
		"MIRROR IMAGES"	
Sutherland	(1957)	Octopus	*Octopus vulgaris*
Mackintosh & Sutherland	(1963)	Goldfish	*Carassius auratus*
Van Hof	(1965)	Rabbit	*Oryctolagus domesticus*
Lashley	(1938)	Rat	*Rattus rattus*
Parriss	(1964)	Cat	*Felis domesticus*
Warren	(1969)	Cat	*Felis domesticus*
Riopelle et al.	(1964)	Monkey	*Macaca mulatta*
Nissen & McCulloch	(1937)	Chimpanzee	*Pan troglodytes*
Bornstein et al.	(1978)	Infant	*Infans tyrannus*
Appelle	(1972)	Adult	*Homo sapiens*
		"PHONEMES"	
Kuhl & Miller	(1975)	Chinchilla	*Chinchilla laniger*
Morse & Snowdon	(1975)	Monkey	*Macaca mulatta*
Waters & Wilson	(1976)	Monkey	*Macaca mulatta*
Sinnott et al.	(1976)	Monkey	*Macaca mulatta*
Eimas	(1975)	Infant	*Infans tyrannus*
Liberman et al.	(1967)	Adult	*Homo sapiens*

shown that wavelength discriminability is reciprocally related (at least to a first approximation) to hue categorization (Bornstein, 1979). For a wide variety of animals, too, "mirror images" represent similar stimuli (Appelle, 1972; Bradshaw et al., 1976; Corballis & Beale, 1976) (Table 2.1). Further, data from chinchillas and monkeys support the view that "phonemes" are also perceived by more than a single species (Table 2.1). Finally, comparative studies of taste (Dethier, 1978; Nowlis, 1978) show that categorization is the prevalent mode of perception, but what are coclassified vary among species. The butterfly (*Pieris repae L.*) distinguishes sodium from potassium—it has a different receptor for each—but the blowfly (*Phormia regina*) has only one receptor and classifies the two tastes together.

Research in animal behavior shows conclusively that many species perceive "prototypes." For example, many organisms prefer particular stimulus values in a class or domain, as shown in studies of selective attention, problem solving, and conditioning (Mackintosh, 1974). On the wavelength continuum, asymmetric generalization ("peak shifts") towards a focal hue in the

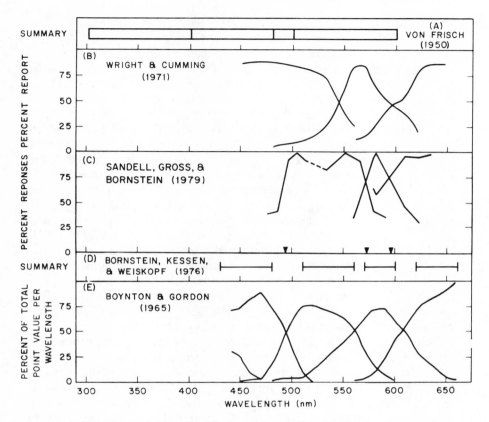

FIG. 2.22. Equivalence classifications of hue as a function of wavelength for several species. (A) Classification by landings on novel-color sugar-dishes in the *honeybee*. (B) Classification by matching-to-sample of probe wavelengths in the *pigeon*. (C) Classification by generalization to novel wavelengths in extinction in the *monkey*. (The dotted line is an interpolation. Arrows indicate cross-over points of adult human color-naming functions from the same study.) (D) Classification by generalization of habituation to new wavelengths in the *human infant*. (E) Classification by color naming in the *human adult*. (Left to right: blue, green, yellow, and red. The increasing function at very short wavelengths is for red.)

category is common following training at a peripheral value (Bornstein, 1974). Von Frisch (1950) observed this in bees, Blough (1961) in pigeons, Ganz (1962) previously in monkeys, and Tomie and Thomas (1974) in humans. Among different spatial orientations, horizontal and vertical are principal not only for humans but for a host of infrahuman species. They show a clear perceptual advantage in the octopus, goldfish, rabbit, rat, squirrel, cat, and chimpanzee (summarized by Appelle, 1972, under the "oblique effect"), as well as in the monkey (Bauer, Owens, Thomas,

MacDonald, & Held, 1978; Boltz, Harwerth, & Smith, 1979). Likewise, preference for sugar (the "sweet tooth") or specific sugars is, according to Pfaffmann (1977) and Dethier (1978), very common in the series.

Thus, equivalence classification and prototypicality are widespread among different animal species, though their exact manifestations may be specific to the particular species. These are my first two points. It is of interest that such species differences occur because either the tuning curves of individual units or ensembles of units in different species may play a role in designating which stimuli will be responded to as similar (i.e., the quality and breadth of equivalence classification) and what may be the "best stimulus" (i.e., the prototype). In this way, neural characteristics may define the perceptual window through which organisms experience and organize their world; therefore, perceptual organization is related to perceptual ecology and evolutionary demand. The significance of species specificity in sensation and perception has elsewhere been poetically described by von Uexküll (1934).

The phylogenetic ubiquity of perceptual organization suggests that it is a valuable mode of adaptation towards disambiguating and filtering environmental stimulation. At a minimum, equivalence classifications conserve invariance where the rule of life is perceptual change; in this connection, Sokal (1974) has reminded us that "classificatory ability must have been a component of fitness in biological evolution [p. 1115]." Prototypicality, on the other hand, provides discernible landmarks within and between perceptual domains. These are ready bases for detection and rapid processing of salient information in the perceptual environment regardless of organism. In this light, it is interesting that dimensions that are organized for one species tend to be organized for others also. Bruner (1957) argued that categories in general may be hierarchically ordered in terms of "accessibility", and he explicitly wrote about the meaningfulness of such a hierarchy in comparative terms:

... the cost of close looks is generally too high under the conditions of speed, risk, and limited capacity imposed upon organisms by their environment or their constitutions. The ability to use minimal cues quickly in categorizing the events of the environment is what gives the organism its lead time in adjusting to events [p. 142].

It is likely, therefore, that perceptual organizations would be similar and similarly adaptive and functional for different species.

Phylogenetic comparison quickly renders the remarkable types of perceptual organization I have described in humans, and particularly in human infants, unremarkable; rather, they seem to be normal and expected. This kind of comparison shows us quite distinctly that all organisms must make sense of their world and that they begin to do so—indeed, they go quite a far distance—in the absence of language and culture. In this sense, infrahumans are akin to the very young of our own species.

DEVELOPMENTAL CONTINUITY:
UTILITY AND MEANING

Perception and Cognition

Both equivalence classification and prototypicality have consequences for the growth of cognition that are independent of development and that would be useful at any age; others are intimately related to developmental stage, and they seem especially useful in infancy and early childhood. Independent of an organism's developmental status, equivalence classification might help to structure experience in two important ways. First, classification simplifies the potential complex of quantitative information available at the sensory surface and reduces it instead to usable qualitative chunks of information (Miller, 1956). Second, classification guarantees generalization over select variations of organismic and environmental fluctuation, thereby providing for perceptual constancy in the context of natural variation. According to Hochberg (1978), understanding how we perceive stability and constancy despite physical flux is "one of the major problems of classical perceptual research [p. 1218]." Equivalence classification helps towards that understanding. It would be adaptive in object identification and recognition, for example, for organisms to generalize over changes in wavelength (or illumination or context) to extract a constancy of hue (Bornstein, 1979; Cornsweet, 1978). Along similar lines, Gross and Bornstein (1978) proposed that the perceptual equivalence of mirror images may reflect an economical mode of visual processing because in the natural world there are virtually no mirror images except for the two sides or profiles of the same face or body *or* an object and its silhouette. Therefore, when mirror images occur in nature, they are almost always aspects of the same object, and it would be more adaptive to treat them equivalently—not to discriminate them. Likewise, one could argue that language has evolved to take advantage of natural classifications because it would be adaptive to disregard speaker variation in favor of phonemic invariance. The many-to-one reduction characteristic of equivalence classification is thus of inestimable value to perceptual analysis, ensuring the perceptual clarity of a class at the same time that it throws into relief contrasts between classes. Both consequences are assets in stimulus identification (Garner, 1966). Finally, organization facilitates encoding and enhances recognition and recall (Miller, 1956; Wiseman & Neisser, 1974).

Organization for the *infant* organism may have especial significance. First, organized information tends to emerge out of the general perceptual noise in which it is embedded—like figure from ground (Rubin, 1915/1958). Therefore, organized information attracts attention to itself and in this way to select perceptual dimensions among many that are available in the ambience. As a consequence, the young may be sensitized first to organized dimensions; in discussing the human infant's perception of "phonemes", Marler (1976) has drawn the following ethological parallel: This organization "would focus the infant's attention on the appropriate class of external stimuli for social responsiveness, much as the auditory templates of some birds are thought to restrict responsiveness to members of their own species [p. 327]."

Organization is also valuable to the young because it may facilitate various aspects of encoding and memory. Equivalence classification helps the young begin to make sense of the world because each stimulus is not new. Because babies possess "perceptual knowledge", they "recognize" stimuli they may not have actually experienced previously. This advantage represents a true cognitive headstart. Events are not experienced as unique, but neither are memories exact; either would be fantastically disruptive to cognitive development, as they were to the cognitive functioning of Luria's (1965/1968) mnemonist, S. The first time one experiences a "Street" figure, one witnesses how organization can emerge from disarray, and one observes then that organization can structure perception, attract attention to itself, and afford meaning. To these three perceptual principles, it is possible to add a fourth: Once energy impinging at the senses is perceptually organized, its organization is long lasting. Look back to Fig. 2.2. Notice this time that the "Horse and Rider" are more immediately evident. The implications of these several characteristics for early development are transparent because organization— whether innate or acquired—brings the organism from undifferentiated, chaotic sensation to integrated, lasting perceptual understanding.

Last, it is conceivable that equivalence classification in infancy foreruns the child's developing ability to form concepts. That is, in the essence of equivalence classification, we can perhaps detect the *Anlage* of abstraction processes. In a study that builds on the infant's classification of hue, I habituated babies to a variety of colors from three hue classes (e.g., blues, greens, and yellows), omitting from the habituation series exposure to the fourth basic hue (in the example case, red). After reaching a habituation criterion, the babies were tested with the novel hue (red) and an achromatic pattern. Fig. 2.23 shows that babies declined in looking from the beginning of habituation (exposure to the initial color) to a habituation criterion and that they remained low on postcriterion trials. Following such variegated experience, babies generalized habituation to the novel color, but they dishabituated to a neutral, control pattern, thereby demonstrating in infants James's (1890) dictum that "we can mean *color* without meaning any particular color [p. 460]." Babies of different ages seem ready to form concepts in other domains as well (e.g., Cohen & Strauss, 1979; Fagan, 1979). Out of equivalence classification may also spring simple conceptual behavior in young children (Anglin, 1977; Brown, 1973; Bruner, Goodnow, & Austin, 1956; Bruner, Olver, & Greenfield, 1966; Faulkender, Wright, & Waldron, 1974), class inclusion (Inhelder & Piaget, 1964; Wohlwill, 1968), and finally, general conceptual and classificatory behavior (Bourne, 1966; Posner, 1973). In summary, we might say that equivalence classification *in infancy*

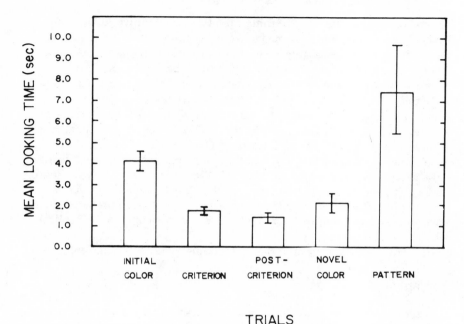

FIG. 2.23.   Infants show a concept of color. They habituate over a color series (initial color through post–criterion) and maintain habituation on novel-color test trials, but they dishabituate to a neutral, control pattern. (SEM is shown.)

exemplifies the ethological concept of "forward reference", when a behavior that appears early acquires increasing meaning later in development.

Prototypicality also carries consequences for cognition that are independent of development and others that specifically enhance it. Prototypes especially engage attention, and insofar as they represent a class or domain prototypes draw attention to that class or domain and clarify and differentiate it from others. Further, attention gates subsequent processes, such as perceived importance, action, and memory (Odom, 1972; Odom & Guzman, 1972). One can therefore easily reconcile on perceptual grounds why we have selected color primaries to signal and control traffic, and one can just as easily imagine that the fact that particularly important stimuli are vertically symmetrical—for example, parents and progeny, and predators and prey— contributes to the unique status of vertical symmetry. Certain sweets, among the entire variety of chemicals, may be preferred (even near the beginning of life) for other equally adaptive reasons.

Other properties of prototypicality seem to be specific to developmental status. For example, prototypes describe the antecedents of logical search in perceptual exploration (Wright & Vlietstra, 1975). Further, the role of salient stimuli or dimensions in governing attention in cognitive judgment is, as Piaget (1961/1969) has shown, far from insignificant. Finally, prototypes naturally forerun mental representations at the developmental stage when "iconic" modes of thought are presumed to be basic (Bruner, 1964).

Prototypes and equivalence classifications doubtlessly interact developmentally. Some equivalence classes (e.g., hues) may be defined in terms of prototypical members, or, more constructively, categories may actually form around prototypes (Anglin, 1977; Posner, 1973; Rosch, 1973). Salient critical stimuli can facilitate concept learning (Hull, 1920; Posner, 1973), and pretraining on the prototype of a set of related patterns can hasten learning new variations of the set (Attneave, 1957b). Finally, prototypes invoke analogy (perhaps extension) to social psychological phenomena, such as early stereotyping (Cantor & Mischel, 1979), and they may even provide a strong basis of aesthetic response (Bornstein, 1978b; Bornstein et al., 1981; Braine, 1978).

In all this, I have said only that perception "teaches" cognition.

Perception and Langauge

Perceptual organizations of the types discussed here are key facets of, to borrow Kessen and Nelson's (1978) enviable formulation, "what the child brings to language." Although language production is a year or more away, equivalence classification and prototypicality lay foundations for language behavior in the child within the first 6 months; moreover, many of the principles of language production utilize characteristics of classification and prototypicality and may, therefore, already be second nature to the toddler. Because linguistic comprehension far precedes production, we ought first to examine the role of perceptual organization there.

I suspect that at least two sorts of organization that I have discussed play nontrivial roles in language learning. In a specific way, natural categorizations of voicing and place of articulation doubtlessly potentiate in the child selective attention to that class of environmental sounds associated with language, and they ready the child to hear differences among particular instances of speech and to disregard variability within classes of speech sounds. As Eimas (1978) has said: "Undoubtedly the acquisition of language would be seriously extended, and perhaps impossible, if it were necessary for the human infant to learn the special nature of speech and its manner of processing [p. 371]." In a more general way, the infant's sensitivity to the temporal structure of rhythmic patterning foretells the potential he or she brings to demarcating the stream of auditory stimulation. As Demany et al. (1977) point out, "skills of temporal analysis and synthesis [are] prerequisites for operating with the sequential dimension of language [but] are present well before the stage of speech [p. 719]." In a similar vein, Stern (1977) has revealed some of the intricately developed temporal organization and segmentation that describe even the earliest exchanges between mother and infant; Snow (1972) and Ferguson (1978) have likewise elucidated the functional role of speech segmentation and pause patterning indigenous to "Motherese."

The role of perceptual organization in language extends beyond the texture of comprehension; equivalence classification and prototypicality also contribute to cognitive aspects of language acquisition.[5] One argument is, succinctly, that names tag cognitive concepts that harbor at base perceptual truth. George Miller (1978) tapped our essential reliance on perceptual prerequisites in everyday linguistic knowledge in the following truism: "If the necessary perceptual predicates are satisfied, the sentence, *This is a table*, is accepted as true; if not, the sentence is rejected as indeterminate or false [p. 307]." For language acquisition, some of that perceptual truth lies in the types of organization that I have shown to exist and function near the beginning of life.

Two further strands of evidence show the role of perceptual categorization in language acquisition. Some time ago, Roger Brown (1958) observed that language learning involves "the coordination of speech categories with categories of the nonlinguistic world [p. 247]." Prerequisite to this statement is the assumption that "categories of the nonlinguistic world" already exist in the head. Concept formation research in adults dating back to Hull (1920) had indicated that nonverbal (i.e., perceptual) classification can well precede concept articulation, but only in the last two decades have Brown's developmental assumptions been validated (Anglin, 1977; Clark, 1973, 1974; Macnamara, 1972; Nelson, 1974a). Thus, infants have now been found to engage in sorting and grouping in consistent ways before they acquire language (e.g., Nelson, 1973, 1974a; Riccuiti, 1965). Even very young infants, as I have previously suggested, can form "concepts" (e.g., of color, faces, etc.) that apparently flower from perceptual roots. The results of these developmental studies of early concept formation have been summarized in the following way by Flavell (1970): "there appears to be an ontogenetic shift... from equivalences based on more concrete and immediately given *perceptual*... attributes to equivalences of a more abstract, *verbal*–conceptual sort [p. 996] (author's italics)."

A second strand of evidence supporting the role of perceptual organization in language learning derives from psycholinguistic arguments (e.g., Clark, 1973, 1974) that "over-extensions" that are typical of early semantic development have roots in perceptual behavior such as equivalence classification. Thus, *perceptual similarity* between noninstances and instances of a

---

[5]The two examples cited in the text are selected from language learning, and both are positive. A third, more detrimental example from reading may also be cited. It is that the child's confusion of lateral mirror images may contribute at least in a small way to retarding discrimination of traditionally "confusable" letters, e.g., *b* and *d* (e.g., Davidson, 1935; Gross & Bornstein, 1978; Oyama & Sato, 1975).

category emerges as a most powerful determinant of the child's decision to include a noninstance in a category.

Prototypes, too, facilitate language learning. Thus, young children may learn about semantic categories in ways that parallel the ways that adults verify category membership using prototypes.[6] For example, Heider (1971) showed that 3- and 4-year-old children not only attend to prototypical (focal) colors more often and match them more accurately, but they more frequently choose them (over nonfocal colors) to represent specific color names. Also, Clark and Clark (1977) have given evidence of a perceptual basis for the universal linguistic primacy of vertical and horizontal. On a broader scale, Rosch (1973) and Anglin (1977) both found that children learn about prototypes much earlier than about other members of semantic categories.[7] These same children will grow up to classify items that are prototypical of a semantic category (as *robin* is of *bird*) more reliably, more quickly, and more efficiently than atypical items (e.g., *hawk* and *penguin*, in that order) (Rips, Shoben, & Smith, 1973; Rosch, 1973, 1975b). I have already compared analogous infant–adult data for color (vide supra) (Bornstein & Monroe, 1981).

Finally, we can find in the linguistic coding of equivalence classes structural and developmental principles that have parallels in later semantic categorization. As Anglin (1977) has summarized, the inclusiveness of semantic noun categories expands and their boundaries sharpen as a function of experience with language. For example, Nelson (1974b) found that children between 5 and 8 years of age not only learn more names of flowers, but also learn to omit trees, etc., from their list of flowers. Hue categorization shows exactly similar developmental improvements, only 2 or 3 years earlier. Raskin, Maital, and Bornstein (1979) asked groups of children and adults (including elderly) to categorize in a binary way wavelengths from the short to middle and middle to long parts of the visible spectrum. The results showed that significant boundary sharpening (and its complementary process, category broadening) takes place between 3 and 4 years of age. Fig. 2.24 shows representative color-naming data from individuals 3, 4, 21, and 74 years of age. Three-year-olds showed the least consistent and widest classification among these age groups. Previously, Wolf (1973) and Zlatin and Koenigsknecht (1975) determined that exactly the same processes occur in the early categorization of "phonemes."

The study of perceptual organization near the beginning of life thus contributes to our understanding of the development of language that is to

---

[6]It is appropriate to point out that only a very few semantic categories are natural in the way of equivalence classes of "hues", "mirror images", or "phonemes", and only a few categories may form around prototypical instances (Medin & Schaffer, 1978). Rather, the majority of linguistic categories are learned (Hunt, 1962) and vary among cultures (Kluckhohn, 1954; Triandis 1964).

[7]Typicality *ought* to be related to semantic development because parents typically teach prototypes first and hold them out to children as exemplary (Anglin, 1977).

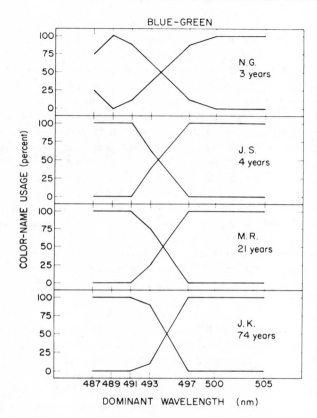

FIG. 2.24.   Three-year-old children show less regular color-name usage (blue or green) than children of 4 years, adults, and elderly, whose usages are quite similar to one another. Each plot represents one individual's data, but the width of the boundary (at 75%) between color-naming functions for that individual is representative of the age group mean.

follow soon. It tells us that several processes characteristic of language development are manifest earlier in perceptual development, and it tells us that even the youngest child possesses rules for understanding and intercourse that themselves begin to guarantee an orderliness and predictability to incipient linguistic interaction.

In brief, perception also "teaches" language.

CONCLUSIONS

For some time we have counted in the infant's repertoire a variety of congenitally organized behaviors thought (now or earlier) to have recognizable "survival value." Grasping and rooting are two. More recently, psychologists like Kessen and Papoušek have shown that the infant possesses other less obvious, but no less important, organized behaviors. Stimulus seeking and the ability to learn soon after birth were duly added to the list of organized infant behaviors. The evidence I have marshaled in the foregoing pages suggests that yet a third class of organized behaviors, perceptual equivalence classification and prototypicality, could be added to the infant's repertoire. Human beings precociously perceive the world into which they are born in organized ways; in particular, they see, hear, taste, and perhaps feel qualities of sensation, and they select particular stimuli from these different perceptual domains as special. Both kinds of perceptual organization afford a startling reduction of Jamesian confusion in the first half of the first year of life. In light of this conclusion, it may be important to add that the studies reviewed in this chapter have not addressed what infants can do in terms of discrimination, but what they do naturally in terms of classification and selection.

Categorization and selection may be innate or quickly learned—it does not matter. Independent of the relative role of genetics and experience, perceptual organization is an important psychological phenomenon in its own right. The phylogenetic ubiquity, early ontogenetic availability, remarkable developmental continuity, and certain cross-sensory prevalence of equivalence classes and prototypes together suggest that these behavior mechanisms are meaningful and significant, and that they are not psychological constructs but objective features of perception that may be critical to early development.[8] Elucidation of these two kinds of perceptual organization in infancy, as elucidation of other organized infant behaviors previously, forces us to begin to revise our conceptions of this period of life so often (and so often justly) conceived as volatile, variable, and essentially mysterious.

EPILOGUE: A PSYCHOLOGICAL REPLY

William Molyneux's epistemological speculation to Locke, though phrased specifically in the hypothetical, translates easily into a real, practical, and essentially developmental question. It is the question of perceptual organization near the beginning of life. Many philosopher–psychologists, including Locke, Hume, Berkeley, Kant, Helmholtz, Hering, and Mach, have seen this developmental interpretation clearly.

---

[8]This essay focuses on invariance, not change. Both obviously take place in human development; neither is primary. Further, I have been speaking of species averages, and I have underemphasized individual or group differences as well as the role of language and culture in inducing or modifying various types of organization. Finally, I have emphasized the potential benefits of infant perceptual organization and omitted any discussion of its cognitive costs.

The foregoing chapter reviews the results of a contemporaneous psychological inquiry into the question of perceptual organization and endeavors to catalog some of the ways in which two kinds of perceptual organization lend structure to otherwise little organized and persistently novel experiences near the beginning of life. This line of investigation suggests that organisms are naturally biased to generalize over physical variation of particular sorts and to attend selectively to certain kinds of information. Classification is a central theme of long-standing appeal in philosophy and the psychology of sense perception; and, attention has long been recognized to be a gateway to perception, thought, and action. These twin characteristics of perceptual organization help the child go beyond elementary units of sensing to perceiving with understanding; further, they provide one solution for the developmental "problem of structure" as Bruner (1978, p. 1354) has termed it: "If we must already know something in order to learn anything, how do we get started learning at all?"

In memory of Mollie Pepper, who effected her own transitions.

ACKNOWLEDGMENTS

Research reported in this chapter was partially supported by the Spencer Foundation and the National Institutes of Health. I wish to express much gratitude to Helen Bornstein, Nancy Cantor, Charles Gross, William Kessen, and Diane Ruble for constructive criticism of earlier versions of this chapter, and to Kay Ferdinandsen, Arlene Kronewitter, and Mary Ann Opperman for invaluable aid in preparing the manuscript.

REFERENCES

Anglin, J. M. *Word, object, and conceptual development.* New York: Norton, 1977.

Appelle, S. Perception and discrimination as a function of stimulus orientation: The "oblique effect" in man and animals. *Psychological Bulletin,* 1972, *78,* 266–278.

Aristotle. *Metaphysica.* In J. A. Smith & W. D. Ross (Eds.), *The works of Aristotle* (Vol. 8). Oxford: Clarendon Press, 1908.

Arnheim, R. *Art and visual perception.* Berkeley: University of California Press, 1974.

Aslin, R. N., & Pisoni, D. B. Some developmental processes in speech perception. In G. Yeni-Komshian, J. F. Kavanaugh, & C. A. Ferguson (Eds.), *Child phonology: Perception and production.* New York: Academic Press, 1980.

Attneave, F. Physical determinants of the judged complexity of shapes. *Journal of Experimental Psychology,* 1957, *53,* 221–227. (a)

Attneave, F. Transfer of experience with a class-schema to identification–learning of patterns and shapes. *Journal of Experimental Psychology,* 1957, *54,* 81–88. (b)

Attneave, F. Triangles as ambiguous figures. *American Journal of Psychology,* 1968, *81,* 447–453.

Bartleson, C. J. Memory colors of familiar objects. *Journal of the Optical Society of America,* 1960, *50,* 73–77.

Bauer, J. A., Jr., Owens, D. A., Thomas, J., MacDonald, G., & Held, R. *A behavioral assessment of the oblique effect in monkeys.* Paper presented at the meeting of the Eastern Psychological Association, Washington, D.C., March 1978.

Beare, A. C. Color-name as a function of wave-length. *American Journal of Psychology,* 1963, *76,* 248–256.

Berlin, B., & Kay, P. *Basic color terms: Their universality and evolution.* Berkeley: University of California Press, 1969.

Blakemore, C. Binocular depth discrimination and the nasotemporal division. *Journal of Physiology,* 1969, *205,* 417–497.

Blough, D. S. The shape of some wave-length generalization gradients. *Journal of the Experimental Analysis of Behavior,* 1961, *4,* 31–40.

Boltz, R. L., Harwerth, R. S., & Smith, E. L. Orientation anisotropy of visual stimuli in Rhesus monkey: A behavioral study. *Science,* 1979, *205,* 511–513.

Bornstein, M. H. Color vision and color naming: A psychophysiological hypothesis of cultural difference. *Psychological Bulletin,* 1973, *80,* 257–285.

Bornstein, M. H. Perceptual generalization: A note on the peak shift. *Psychological Bulletin,* 1974, *81,* 804–808.

Bornstein, M. H. The influence of visual perception on culture. *American Anthropologist,* 1975, *77,* 774–798. (a)

Bornstein, M. H. On light and the aesthetics of color: Lumia kinetic art. *Leonardo,* 1975, *8,* 203–212. (b)

Bornstein, M. H. Qualities of color vision in infancy. *Journal of Experimental Child Psychology,* 1975, *19,* 401–419. (c)

Bornstein, M. H. Infants are trichromats. *Journal of Experimental Child Psychology,* 1976, *21,* 425–445. (a)

Bornstein, M. H. Name codes and color memory. *American Journal of Psychology,* 1976, *89,* 269–279. (b)

Bornstein, M. H. Chromatic vision in infancy. In H. W. Reese & L. P. Lipsitt (Eds.), *Advances in child development and behavior* (Vol. 12). New York: Academic Press, 1978. (a)

Bornstein, M. H. Visual behavior of the young human infant: Relationships between chromatic and spatial perception and the activity of underlying brain mechanisms. *Journal of Experimental Child Psychology,* 1978, *26,* 174–192. (b)

Bornstein, M. H. Perceptual development: Stability and change in feature perception. In M. H. Bornstein & W. Kessen (Eds.), *Psychological development from infancy.* Hillsdale, N.J.: Lawrence Erlbaum Associates, 1979.

Bornstein, M. H., Ferdinandsen, K., & Gross, C. G. Perception of symmetry in infancy. *Developmental Psychology,* 1981.

Bornstein, M. H., Gross, C. G., & Wolf, J. Z. Perceptual similarity of mirror images in infancy. *Cognition,* 1978, *6,* 89–116.

Bornstein, M. H., Kessen, W., & Weiskopf, S. Color vision and hue categorization in young human infants. *Journal of Experimental Psychology: Human Perception and Performance,* 1976, *2,* 115–129.

Bornstein, M. H., & Monroe, M. D. Time to categorize chromatic information: Effects of psychological complexity. *Psychological Research,* 1981.

Boswell, S. L. Young children's processing of asymmetrical and symmetrical patterns. *Journal of Experimental Child Psychology,* 1976, *22,* 309–318.

Bouma, H., & Andriessen, J. J. Perceived orientation of isolated line segments. *Vision Research,* 1968, *8,* 493–507.

Bourne, L. E. *Human conceptual behavior.* Boston: Allyn & Bacon, 1966.

Bower, T. G. R. The visual world of infants. *Scientific American,* 1966, *215,* 80–92.

Boynton, R. M. Color, hue, and wavelength. In E. C. Carterette & M. P. Friedman (Eds.), *Handbook of perception* (Vol. 5). New York: Academic Press, 1975.

Boynton, R. M., & Gordon, J. Bezold-Brücke hue shift measured by color-naming technique. *Journal of the Optical Society of America,* 1965, *55,* 78–86.

Bradshaw, J., Bradley, D., & Patterson, K. The perception and identification of mirror-reversed patterns. *Quarterly Journal of Experimental Psychology,* 1976, *28,* 221–246.

Braine, L. G. A new slant on orientation perception. *American Psychologist,* 1978, *33,* 10–22.

Brown, R. W. *Words and things.* New York: Free Press, 1958.

Brown, R. W. *A first language: The early stages.* Cambridge, Mass. Harvard University Press, 1973.

Brown, R. W., & Lenneberg, E. H. A study in language and cognition. *Journal of Abnormal and Social Psychology,* 1954, *49,* 454–462.

Bruce, V. G., & Morgan, M. J. Violations of symmetry and repetition in visual patterns. *Perception,* 1975, *4,* 239–249.

Bruner, J. S. On perceptual readiness. *Psychological Review,* 1957, *64,* 123–152.

Bruner, J. S. The course of cognitive growth. *American Psychologist,* 1964, *19,* 1–15.

Bruner, J. S. Evidence of intent (Review of *Experience and the growth of understanding* by D. W. Hamlyn). *Times Literary Supplement,* 1978, No. *3999,* 1354–1355.

Bruner, J. S., Goodnow, J. J., & Austin, G. A. *A study of thinking.* New York: Wiley, 1956.

Bruner, J. S., Olver, R., & Greenfield, P. *Studies in cognitive growth.* New York: Wiley, 1966.

Cantor, N., & Mischel, W. Prototypes in person perception. In L. Berkowitz (Ed.), *Advances in experimental social psychology* (Vol. 12). New York: Academic Press, 1979.

Carroll, J. B. (Ed.). *Language, thought, and reality: Selected writings of Benjamin Lee Whorf.* Cambridge, Mass.: M. I. T. Press, 1966.

Clark, E. V. What's in a word? On the child's acquisition of semantics in his first language. In T. E. Moore (Ed.), *Cognitive development and the acquisition of language.* New York: Academic Press, 1973.

Clark, E. V. Some aspects of the conceptual basis for first language acquisition. In R. L. Schiefelbusch & L. L. Lloyd (Eds.), *Language perspectives: Acquisition, retardation, and intervention.* Baltimore, Md.: University Park Press, 1974.

Clark, H. H., & Clark, E. V. *Psychology and language.* New York: Harcourt, Brace, Jovanovich, 1977.

Cohen, L. B., DeLoache, J. S., & Strauss, M. S. Infant visual perception. In J. Osofsky (Ed.), *Handbook of infancy.* New York: Wiley, 1979.

Cohen, L. B., & Gelber, E. R. Infant visual memory. In L. Cohen & P. Salapatek (Eds.), *Infant perception: From sensation to cognition* (Vol. 1). New York: Academic Press, 1975.

Cohen, L. B., & Salapatek, P. *Infant perception: From sensation to cognition.* New York: Academic Press, 1975.

Cohen, L. B., & Strauss, M. S. Concept acquisition in the human infant. *Child Development,* 1979, *50,* 419–424.

Corballis, M. C., & Beale, I. L. *The psychology of left and right.* Hillsdale, N.J.: Lawrence Erlbaum Associates, 1976.

Corballis, M. C., & Roldan, C. E. On the perception of symmetrical and repeated patterns. *Perception & Psychophysics,* 1974, *16,* 136–142.

Cornsweet, T. N. The Bezold-Brücke effect and its complement, hue constancy. In J. C. Armington, J. Krauskopf, & B. R. Wooten (Eds.), *Visual psychophysics and physiology.* New York: Academic Press, 1978.

Crudden, C. H. Reactions of new-born infants to thermal stimuli under constant tactual conditions. *Journal of Experimental Psychology,* 1937, *20,* 350–370.

Cutting, J. E., & Rosner, B. S. Categories and boundaries in speech and music. *Perception & Psychophysics* 1974, *16,* 564–570.

Darwin, C. R. *The descent of man, and selection in relation to sex.* London: John Murray, 1913. (Originally published, 1871.)

Darwin, C. R. *The expression of the emotions in man and animals.* New York: D. Appleton, 1915. (Originally published, 1872.)

Davidson, H. P. A study of the confusing letters, b, d, p, and q. *Pedagogical Seminary and Journal of Genetic Psychology,* 1935, *47,* 458–468.

Demany, L., McKenzie, B., & Vurpillot, E. Rhythm perception in early infancy. *Nature,* 1977, *266,* 718–719.

Desor, J. A., Maller, O., & Greene, L. S. Preference for sweet in humans: Infants, children, and adults. In J. W. Weiffenbach (Ed.), *Taste and development.* Bethesda, Md.: DHEW, 1977.

Desor, J. A., Maller, O., & Turner, R. E. Taste in acceptance of sugars by human infants. *Journal of Comparative and Physiological Psychology,* 1973, *84,* 496–501.

Dethier, V. G. Other tastes, other worlds. *Science,* 1978, *201,* 224–228.

DeValois, R. L. Central mechanisms of color vision. In R. Jung (Ed.), *Central processing of visual information* (Vol. 7/3A of *Handbook of sensory physiology*). New York: Springer-Verlag, 1973.

DeValois, R. L., & DeValois, K. K. Neural coding of color. In E. C. Carterette & M. P. Friedman (Eds.), *Handbook of perception* (Vol. 5). New York: Academic Press, 1975.

Eimas, P. D. Speech perception in early infancy. In L. B. Cohen & P. Salapatek (Eds.), *Infant perception: From sensation to cognition* (Vol. 2). New York: Academic Press, 1975.

Eimas, P. D. Developmental aspects of speech perception. In R. Held, H. Leibowitz, & H.-L. Teuber (Eds.), *Handbook of sensory physiology: Perception.* New York: Springer-Verlag, 1978.

Eisenberg, R. B. *Auditory competence in early life.* Baltimore, Md.: University Park Press, 1976.

Engen, T., Lipsitt, L. P., & Peck, M. B. Ability of newborn infants to discriminate sapid substances. *Developmental Psychology,* 1974, *10,* 741–744.

Fagan, J. F. Infant color perception. *Science,* 1974, *183,* 973–975.

Fagan, J. F. The origins of facial pattern recognition. In M. H. Bornstein & W. Kessen (Eds.), *Psychological development from infancy.* Hillsdale, N.J.: Lawrence Erlbaum Associates, 1979.

Fantz, R. L. Visual experience in infants: Decreased attention to familiar patterns relative to novel ones. *Science,* 1964, *146,* 668–670.

Faulkender, P. J., Wright, J. C., & Waldron, A. Generalized habituation of concept stimuli in toddlers. *Child Development,* 1974, *45,* 1002–1010.

Ferguson, C. A. Talking to children: A search for universals. In J. H. Greenberg (Ed.), *Universals of human language* (Vol. 1). Stanford, Calif.: Stanford University Press, 1978.

Fisher, C. B., Ferdinandsen, K., & Bornstein, M. H. *The role of symmetry in infant form discrimination.* Manuscript submitted for publication, 1980.

Flavell, J. H. Concept development. In P. H. Mussen (Ed.), *Carmichael's manual of child psychology* (Vol. 1). New York: Wiley, 1970.

Frank, M. The distinctiveness of responses to sweet in the chorda tympani nerve. In J. M. Weiffenbach (Ed.), *Taste and development.* Bethesda, Md.: DHEW, 1977.

Freeman, R. D., & Thibos, L. W. Electrophysiological evidence that abnormal early visual experiences can modify the human brain. *Science,* 1973, *180,* 876–878.

Ganz, L. Hue generalization and hue discriminability in *Macaca mulatta. Journal of Experimental Psychology,* 1962, *64,* 142–150.

Garner, W. R. To perceive is to know. *American Psychologist,* 1966, *21,* 11–19.

Garner, W. R. Good patterns have few alternatives. *American Scientist,* 1970, *58,* 34–42.

Garner, W. R. Aspects of a stimulus: Features, dimensions, and configurations. In E. Rosch & B. B. Lloyd (Eds.), *Cognition and categorization.* Hillsdale, N.J.: Lawrence Erlbaum Associates, 1978.

Gibson, J. J. Vertical and horizontal orientation in visual perception. *Psychological Bulletin,* 1934, *31,* 739–740.

Gibson, J. J. Adaptation, after-effect, and contrast in the perception of tilted lines. *Journal of Experimental Psychology,* 1937, *20,* 553–569.

Gibson, J. J. *The senses considered as perceptual systems.* Boston: Houghton-Mifflin, 1966.

Gilbert, J. A. Researches in the mental and physical development of school children. *Studies of the Yale Psychological Laboratory,* 1894, *2,* 40–150.

Graham, C. H. Discriminations that depend on wave-length. In C. H. Graham (Ed.), *Vision and visual perception.* New York: Wiley, 1965.

Gregory, R. L., & Wallace, J. G. Recovery from early blindness: A case study. *Experimental Psychology Society Monograph,* 1963, No. 2.

Gross, C. G., & Bornstein, M. H. Left and right in science and art. *Leonardo,* 1978, *11,* 29–38.

Harkness, S. Universal aspects of learning color codes: A study in two cultures. *Ethos,* 1973, *1,* 175–200.

Heider, E. R. "Focal" color areas and the development of color names. *Developmental Psychology,* 1971, *4,* 447–455.

Heider, E. R. Universals in color naming and memory. *Journal of Experimental Psychology,* 1972, *93,* 10–20.

Hendrickson, L. N., & Muehl, S. The effect of attention and motor response pretraining on learning to discriminate b and d in kindergarten children. *Journal of Educational Psychology,* 1962, *53,* 236–241.

Hochberg, J. Perceptual constancy (Review of *Stability and constancy in visual perception: Mechanisms and processes* by W. Epstein, Ed.). *Science,* 1978, *201,* 1218–1219.

Howard, I., & Templeton, W. *Human spatial orientation.* New York: Wiley, 1966.

Hubel, D. H., & Wiesel, T. N. Receptive fields and functional architecture of monkey striate cortex. *Journal of Physiology,* 1968, *195,* 215–243.

Hull, C. L. Quantitative aspects of the evolution of concepts: An experimental study. *Psychological Monographs,* 1920, *28,* (1, Whole No. 123).

Hume, D. *An inquiry concerning human understanding* (C. W. Hendel, Ed.). New York: Bobbs-Merrill, 1955. (Originally published, 1748.)

Hunt, E. B. *Concept learning: An information processing problem.* New York: Wiley, 1962.

Inhelder, B., & Piaget, J. *The early growth of logic in the child.* New York: Norton, 1964.

Jacobs, H. L., Smutz, E. R., & DuBose, C. N. Comparative observations on the ontogeny of taste preference. In J. M. Weiffenbach (Ed.), *Taste and development.* Bethesda, Md.: DHEW, 1977.

James, W. *The principles of psychology.* New York: Henry Holt, 1890.

Jeffrey, W. E. Variables in early discrimination learning: I. Motor responses in the training of a left–right discrimination. *Child Development,* 1958, *29,* 269–275.

Jeffrey, W. E. The orienting reflex and attention in cognitive development. *Psychological Review,* 1968, *75,* 323–334.

Julesz, B. *Foundations of cyclopean perception.* Chicago: University of Chicago Press, 1971.

Jusczyk, P. W., Rosner, B. S., Cutting, J. E., Foard, C. F., & Smith, L. B. Categorical perception of nonspeech sounds by 2-month-old infants. *Perception & Psychophysics,* 1977, *21,* 50–54.

Kaas, J. H. The organization of visual cortex in primates. In C. R. Noback (Ed.), *Sensory systems of primates.* New York: Plenum Press, 1978.

Kessen, W., Haith, M. M., & Salapatek, P. H. Human infancy: A bibliography and guide. In P. H. Mussen (Ed.), *Carmichael's manual of child psychology.* New York: Wiley, 1970.

Kessen, W., & Nelson, K. What the child brings to language. In B. Z. Presseisen, D. Goldstein, & M. H. Appel (Eds.), *Topics in cognitive development* (Vol. 2). New York: Plenum Press, 1978.

Kessen, W., Salapatek, P., & Haith, M. The visual response of the human newborn to linear contour. *Journal of Experimental Child Psychology,* 1972, *13,* 9–20.

Kluckhohn, C. Culture and behavior. In G. Lindzey (Ed.), *Handbook of social psychology* (Vol. 2). Cambridge, Mass.: Addison-Wesley, 1954.

Koffka, K. *Principles of Gestalt psychology.* New York: Harcourt, Brace, 1935.

Kopp, J., & Lane, H. Hue discrimination related to linguistic habits. *Psychonomic Science,* 1968, *11,* 61–62.

Kuhl, P. K., & Miller, J. D. Speech perception by the chinchilla: Voiced–voiceless distinction in alveolar plosive consonants. *Science,* 1975, *190,* 69–72.

Lashley, K. S. The mechanisms of vision: XV. Preliminary studies of the rat's capacity for detailed vision. *Journal of General Psychology,* 1938, *18,* 123–193.

Lasky, R. E. Serial habituation or regression to the mean? *Child Development,* 1979, *50,* 568–570.

LeBarbera, J. D., Izard, C. E., Vietze, P., & Parisi, S. A. Four- and six-month-old infants' visual responses to joy, anger, and neutral expressions. *Child Development,* 1976, *47,* 535–538.

Leehey, S. C., Moskowitz-Cook, A., Brill, S., & Held, R. Orientational anisotropy in infant vision. *Science,* 1975, *190,* 900–902.

Leventhal, A. G., & Hirsch, H. V. B. Effects of early experience upon orientation sensitivity and binocularity of neurons in visual cortex of cats. *Proceedings of the National Academy of Science,* 1977, *74,* 1272–1276.

Liberman, A. M., Cooper, F. S., Schankweiler, D. P., & Studdert-Kennedy, M. Perception of the speech code. *Psychological Review,* 1967, *74,* 431–461.

Lipsitt, L. P. Taste in human neonates: Its effects on sucking and heart rate. In J. M. Weiffenbach (Ed.), *Taste and development.* Bethesda, Md.: DHEW, 1977.

Locke, J. *An essay concerning human understanding.* London: Dent, 1961. (Originally published, 1690.)

Luria, A. R. [*The mind of a mnemonist*] (L. Solotaroff, trans.). New York: Avon, 1968. (Originally published, 1965.)

Maccoby, E. E. The development of stimulus selection. In J. P. Hill (Ed.), *Minnesota symposia on child psychology* (Vol. 3). Minneapolis: University of Minnesota Press, 1969.

Mach, E. [*The analysis of sensations*] (C. M. Williams, trans.). New York: Dover, 1959. (Originally published, 1885.)

Mackintosh, N. J. *The psychology of animal learning.* New York: Academic Press, 1974.

Mackintosh, N. J., & Sutherland, N. S. Visual discrimination by the goldfish: The orientation of rectangles. *Animal Behaviour,* 1963, *11,* 135–141.

Macnamara, J. Cognitive basis of language learning in infants. *Psychological Review,* 1972, *79,* 1–13.

Maffei, L., & Campbell, F. W. Neurophysiological localization of the vertical and horizontal visual coordinates in man. *Science,* 1970, *167,* 386–387.

Mansfield, R. J. W. Neural basis of orientation perception in primate vision. *Science,* 1974, *186,* 1133–1135.

Marg, E., Adams, J. E., & Rutkin, B. Receptive fields of cells in the human visual cortex. *Experientia,* 1968, *24,* 348–350.

Marler, P. Sensory templates in species-specific behavior. In J. Fentress (Ed.), *Simpler networks and behavior.* Sunderland, Mass.: Sinauer, 1976.

McBurney, D. H., & Gent, J. F. On the nature of taste qualities. *Psychological Bulletin,* 1979, *86,* 151–167.

McCall, R. B., & Kagan, J. Stimulus–schema discrepancy and attention in the infant. *Journal of Experimental Child Psychology,* 1967, *5,* 381–390.

McGurk, H. Visual perception in young infants. In B. Foss (Ed.), *New perspectives in child development.* Baltimore: Penguin, 1974.

McKenzie, B., & Day, R. H. Orientation discrimination in infants: A comparison of visual fixation and operant training methods. *Journal of Experimental Child Psychology,* 1971, *11,* 366–375.

Medin, D. L., & Schaffer, M. M. Context theory of classification learning. *Psychological Review,* 1978, *85,* 207–238.

Miller, D. J. Visual habituation in the human infant. *Child Development,* 1972, *43,* 481–493.

Miller, G. A. The magical number seven plus or minus two: Some limits on our capacity for processing information. *Psychological Review,* 1956, *63,* 81–97.

Miller, G. A. Practical and lexical knowledge. In E. Rosch & B. B. Lloyd (Eds.), *Cognition and categorization.* Hillsdale, N.J.: Lawrence Erlbaum Associates, 1978.

Moffett, A. Stimulus complexity as a determinant of visual attention in infants. *Journal of Experimental Child Psychology,* 1969, *8,* 173–179.

Morse, P. A., & Snowdon, C. T. An investigation of categorical speech discrimination by rhesus monkeys. *Perception & Psychophysics,* 1975, *17,* 9–16.

Moskowitz, H. R. The sweetness and pleasantness of sugars. *American Journal of Psychology,* 1971, *84,* 387–405.

Mowatt, M. H. Configuration properties considered 'good' by naive subjects. *American Journal of Psychology,* 1940, *53,* 46–49.

Nelson, K. Some evidence for the cognitive primacy of categorization and its functional basis. *Merrill–Palmer Quarterly of Behavior and Development,* 1973, *19,* 21–39.

Nelson, K. Concept, word, and sentence: Interrelations in acquisition and development. *Psychological Review,* 1974, *81,* 267–285. (a)

Nelson, K. Variations in children's concepts of age and category. *Child Development,* 1974, *45,* 577–584. (b)

Newton, I. New theory about light and colors. *Philosophical Transactions of the Royal Society,* 1671–1672, *80,* 3075–3087.

Nickerson, D., & Newhall, S. M. A psychological color solid. *Journal of the Optical Society of America,* 1943, *33,* 419–422.

Nissen, H. W., & McCulloch, T. L. Equated and non-equated stimulus situations in discrimination learning by chimpanzees. *Journal of Comparative Psychology,* 1937, *23,* 165–189.

Nowlis, G. H. *Quality coding in the rodent gustatory system: A labeled line system?* Paper presented at the Rockefeller University, New York, February 1978.

Nowlis, G. H., & Kessen, W. Human newborns differentiate differing concentrations of sucrose and glucose. *Science,* 1976, *191,* 865–866.

Odom, R. D. Effects of perceptual salience on the recall of relevant and incidental dimensional values: A developmental study. *Journal of Experimental Psychology,* 1972, *92,* 285–291.

Odom, R. D., & Guzman, R. D. Development of hierarchies of dimensional salience. *Developmental Psychology,* 1972, *6,* 271–287.

Olson, D. R. *Cognitive development: The child's acquisition of diagonality.* New York: Academic Press, 1970.

Olson, R. K., & Attneave, F. What variables produce similarity grouping. *American Journal of Psychology,* 1970, *83,* 1–21.

Orton, S. *Reading, writing and speech problems in children.* London: Chapman and Hall, 1937.

Oyama, T., & Sato, K. Relative similarity of rotated and reversed figures to the original figures as a function of children's age. *Journal of Comparative and Physiological Psychology,* 1975, *88,* 110–117.

Paraskevopoulos, I. Symmetry, recall, and preference in relation to chronological age. *Journal of Experimental Child Psychology,* 1968, *6,* 254–264.

Parriss, J. R. A technique for testing cat's discrimination of differently oriented rectangles. *Nature,* 1964, *202,* 771–773.

Pettigrew, J. D., Nikara, T., & Bishop, P. O. Responses to moving slits by single units in cat striate cortex. *Experimental Brain Research,* 1968, *6,* 373–390.

Pfaffmann, C. Biological and behavioral substrates of the sweet tooth. In J. M. Weiffenbach (Ed.), *Taste and development.* Bethesda, Md.: DHEW, 1977.

Piaget, J. [*The mechanisms of perception*] (G. N. Seagrim, trans.). London: Routledge & Kegan Paul, 1969. (Originally published, 1961).

Pick, H. L., Yonas, A., & Rieser, J. Spatial reference systems in perceptual development. In M. H. Bornstein & W. Kessen (Eds.), *Psychological development from infancy.* Hillsdale, N.J.: Lawrence Erlbaum Associates, 1979.

Pomerantz, J. R., Sager, L. C., & Stoever, R. J. Perception of wholes and of their component parts: Some configural superiority effects. *Journal of Experimental Psychology: Human Perception and Performance,* 1977, *3,* 422–435.

Posner, M. I. *Cognition: An introduction.* Glenview, Ill.: Scott, Foresman, 1973.

Quine, W. V. Natural kinds. In W. V. Quine, *Ontological relativity and other essays.* New York: Columbia University Press, 1969.

Raskin, L. A., Maital, S., & Bornstein, M. H. *Perceptual classification: A life-span study.* Manuscript in preparation, 1979.

Ray, V. F. Techniques and problems in the study of human color perception. *Southwestern Journal of Anthropology,* 1952, *8,* 251–259.

Ray, V. F. Human color perception and behavioral response. *Transactions of the New York Academy of Sciences,* 1953, *16,* 98–104.

Ricciuti, H. Object grouping and selective ordering in infants 12–24 months old. *Merrill-Palmer Quarterly of Behavior and Development,* 1965, *11,* 129–148.

Riopelle, A. J., Rahm, U., Itoigawa, N., & Draper, W. A. Discrimination of mirror-image patterns by Rhesus monkeys. *Perceptual and Motor Skills,* 1964, *19,* 383–389.

Rips, L. J., Shoben, E. J., & Smith, E. E. Semantic distance and the verification of semantic relations. *Journal of Verbal Learning and Verbal Behavior,* 1973, *12,* 1–20.

Rosch, E. Natural categories. *Cognitive Psychology,* 1973, *4,* 328–350.

Rosch, E. Cognitive reference points. *Cognitive Psychology,* 1975, *7,* 532–547. (a)

Rosch, E. The nature of mental codes for color categories. *Journal of Experimental Psychology: Human Perception and Performance,* 1975, *1,* 303–322. (b)

Rosch, E. Human categorization. In N. Warren (Ed.), *Studies in cross-cultural psychology* (Vol. 1). London: Academic Press, 1978.

Rubin, E. [Figure and ground.] In D. C. Beardslee & M. Wertheimer (Eds.), *Readings in perception.* Princeton, N.J.: Van Nostrand, 1958. (Originally published, 1915.)

Rudel, R. G., & Teuber, H.-L. Discrimination of direction of line in children. *Journal of Comparative and Physiological Psychology,* 1963, *56,* 892–898.

Sandell, J. H., Gross, C. G., & Bornstein, M. H. Color categories in macaques. *Journal of Comparative and Physiological Psychology,* 1979, *93,* 626–635.

Schiller, P. H., Finlay, B. L., & Volman, S. F. Quantitative studies of single-cell properties in monkey striate cortex. II. Orientation specificity and ocular dominance. *Journal of Neurophysiology,* 1976, *39,* 1320–1333.

Sinnott, J. M., Beecher, M. D., Moody, D. B., & Stebbins, W. C. Speech sound discrimination by monkeys and humans. *Journal of the Acoustical Society of America,* 1976, *60,* 687–695.

Snow, C. E. The development of conversation between mothers and babies. *Journal of Child Language,* 1972, *4,* 1–22.

Sokal, R. R. Classification: Purposes, principles, progress, prospects. *Science,* 1974, *185,* 1115–1123.

Steiner, J. E. Facial expressions of the neonate infant indicating the hedonics of food-related chemical stimuli. In J. W. Weiffenbach (Ed.), *Taste and development.* Bethesda, MD.: DHEW, 1977.

Stellar, E. Sweet preference and hedonic experience. In J. M. Weiffenbach (Ed.), *Taste and development.* Bethesada, Md.: DHEW, 1977.

Stern, D. *The first relationship: Infant and mother.* London: Open Books, 1977.

Stone, J., Leicester, J., & Sherman, S. M. The nasotemporal division of the monkey's retina. *Journal of Comparative Neurology,* 1973, *150,* 333–348.

Street, R. F. *A Gestalt completion test: A study of a cross section of intellect.* New York: Teachers College Press, 1931.

Sutherland, N. S. Visual discrimination of orientation and shape by the octopus. *Nature,* 1957, *179,* 11–13.

Szilagyi, P. G., & Baird, J. C. A quantitative appraoch to the study of visual symmetry. *Perception & Psychophysics,* 1977, *22,* 287–292.

Tomie, A., & Thomas, D. R. Adaptation level as a factor in human wavelength generalization. *Journal of Experimental Psychology,* 1974, *103,* 29–36.

Triandis, H. C. Cultural influences on cognitive processes. In L. Berkowitz (Ed.), *Advances in experimental social psychology* (Vol. 1). New York: Academic Press, 1964.

Tversky, A. Features of similarlity. *Psychological Review,* 1977, *84,* 327–352.

Van Hof, M. W. Discrimination between striated patterns of different orientation in the rabbit. *Vision Research,* 1965, *6,* 89–94.

von Frisch, K. *Bees: Their vision, chemical senses, and language.* Ithaca: Cornell University Press, 1950.

von Uexküll, J. A stroll through the worlds of animals and men. In C. H. Schiller & K. S. Lashley (Eds.), *Instinctive behavior.* New York: International Universities Press, 1934.

Warren, J. M. Discrimination of mirror-images by cats. *Journal of Comparative and Physiological Psychology,* 1969, *69,* 9–11.

Waters, R. S., & Wilson, W. A., Jr. Speech perception by rhesus monkeys: The voicing distinction in synthesized labial and velar stop consonants. *Perception & Psychophysics,* 1976, *19,* 285–289.

Wertheimer, M. [Principles of perceptual organization.] In D. C. Beardslee & M. Wertheimer (Eds.), *Readings in perception.* Princeton, N.J.: Van Nostrand, 1958. (Originally published, 1923.)

Whorf, B. L. *Collected papers on metalinguistics.* Washington D.C.: Foreign Service Institute, 1952.

Wiseman, S., & Neisser, U. Perceptual organization as a determinant of visual recognition memory. *American Journal of Psychology,* 1974, *87,* 675–681.

Wohlwill, J. F. Responses to class-inclusion questions for verbally and pictorially presented items. *Child Development,* 1968, *39,* 449–465.

Wolf, C. G. The perception of stop consonants by children. *Journal of Experimental Child Psychology,* 1973, *16,* 318–331.

Wolff, P. Mirror-image confusability in adults. *Journal of Experimental Psychology,* 1971, *91,* 268–272.

Wright, A. A. Psychometric and psychophysical hue discrimination functions for the pigeon. *Vision Research,* 1972, *12,* 1447–1464.

Wright, A. A., & Cumming, W. W. Color-naming functions for the pigeon. *Journal of the Experimental Analysis of Behavior,* 1971, *15,* 7–17.

Wright, J. C., & Vlietstra, A. G. The development of selective attention: From perceptual exploration to logical search. In H. W. Reese (Ed.), *Advances in child development and behavior* (Vol. 10). New York: Academic Press, 1975.

Wright, W. D. *Researches on normal and defective colour vision.* St. Louis: C. V. Mosby, 1947.

Yoshida, S., Iwahara, S., & Nagamura, N. The effect of stimulus orientation on the visual evoked potential in human subjects. *Electroencephalography and Clinical Neurophysiology,* 1975, *39,* 53–57.

Young-Browne, G., Rosenfeld, H. M., & Horowitz, F. D. Infant discrimination of facial expressions. *Child Development,* 1977, *48,* 555–562.

Zlatin, M. A., & Koenigsknecht, R. A. Development of the voicing contrast: Perception of stop consonants. *Journal of Speech and Hearing Research,* 1975, *18,* 541–553.

Zusne, L. *Visual perception of form.* New York: Academic Press, 1970.

3 Constraints on Structure: Evidence from American Sign Language and Language Learning

Elissa L. Newport
University of Illinois at Urbana-Champaign

The general question I will consider in this chapter is this: Why are languages structured the way they are? What is it about human language users that leads to certain universal aspects of langauge design? The fact that there are universal patterns of language organization has been pointed out in recent times by linguists like Joseph Greenberg (1963, 1966) and, most notably, Noam Chomsky (1965, 1975). Chomsky has suggested that there are innate constraints on the forms human languages can take, constraints that arise from a special language faculty.

More recently, a number of investigators have attempted to address these questions by studying the structure and acquisition of American Sign Language, a natural language that has arisen independently of English or any other spoken language, for use among the deaf of North America. The study of American Sign Language (ASL) permits a kind of natural analysis of variance, since it differs from spoken language in at least two ways:

1. In modality: In ASL, the eyes and hands are used as communication channels rather than the ears and mouth. In fact, as I will argue, these modalities do offer rather different potential resources and options for language structure (cf. Friedman, 1977; Klima, Bellugi, et al., 1979; Siple, 1978).

2. In circumstances of acquisition: Because of the place of the deaf community within a dominant hearing, English-speaking world, ASL may be acquired either early or late in life, either from native speakers of the language or from speakers who themselves acquired the language very late in life (cf. Fischer, 1978; Woodward, 1973).

The study of ASL therefore offers us the opportunity to consider which, if any, of these factors contributes to the shape and structure of a natural language.

The traditional view of language structure has been that modality is all-important. Chomsky (1965, 1975), Wasow (1973), Osherson & Wasow (1976), Liberman (1970), and others have argued that there is a privileged ear–language connection, a specially evolved spoken language faculty that gives spoken languages their formal character. Part of the evidence for this claim has been the view that communication systems outside the spoken medium look very different from spoken languages in organizational structure (Cohen, Namir, & Schlesinger, 1977; Friedman, 1977; Osherson & Wasow, 1976; Schlesinger, 1970; Wasow, 1973).

In the present chapter, I will argue a rather different view. Although the visual modality in fact offers rather different *potential* resources and options for language structure, ASL looks in many detailed ways strikingly the same as spoken languages. Our findings thus suggest that the modality, for both spoken language and signed language, is not the crucial constraining factor. In contrast, communication systems, whether spoken or signed, look quite systematically different as a function of the number of preceding generations of native speakers of the language, and therefore the number of learners through which the system has been passed. Thus what I will suggest is that there is something about the character of the learning process itself that gives structure to languages.

ANALOG REPRESENTATION
AND MORPHOLOGICAL ORGANIZATION

To what extent is the formal organization of ASL like that of spoken languages? In previous literature it has often been argued that the grammatical structure of signed languages is very different from that of spoken languages. For example, although spoken languages universally use word order or case marking to express grammatical relations (e.g., subject versus object), there is some question about the existence of such formal devices in sign languages (Fischer, 1974; Schlesinger, 1970). Moreover, it has been suggested that sign languages do not distinguish between nouns and verbs (Cohen, et al., 1977; Stokoe, Casterline, & Croneberg, 1965), while in spoken languages such a form-class distinction is universal (Hockett, 1963; Slobin, 1977). Wasow (1973) and Osherson and Wasow (1976) have used such evidence to argue for the task specificity of at least some linguistic universals. On the other hand, more recent studies of sign language have often uncovered formal devices, initially overlooked in early investigations, that have turned out to be quite analogous to those of spoken language. For example, in ASL, word order and spatial arrangement, along with grammatically functioning facial expressions, operate quite systematically to mark subject versus object (Fischer & Gough, 1978; Liddell, 1977). Similarly, Supalla and Newport (1978) have found a consistent distinction in ASL between related nouns and verbs in manner and frequency of movement.

This question is not merely a point of interest for those who study sign languages. As noted earlier, if in fact sign languages are quite different in organization from spoken languages, the notion of a special spoken language faculty would receive strong support; at minimum, such a finding would suggest important contributions of the auditory–vocal modalities to language structure. If, however, sign languages are very similar to spoken languages, there is little reason to hypothesize a special faculty restricted to spoken language, and little reason to suggest that modality is a significant contributor to language structure.

Morphology in Spoken Language

Spoken languages tend to be what I will call *analytic* in character. I use this term not as it is used in linguistics (as equivalent to "isolating"); rather, I use it to mean that sentences, and words within sentences, are made up of (i.e., are analyzable into) a number of discrete morphological parts, components of form that have a consistent meaning.[1] Across languages, there is a relatively small number of morphological parameters, and on each of these parameters, a small number of discrete morphological distinctions. For example, in English one morphologically distinguishes number into singular versus plural (e.g., "boy" versus "boys"); there is no continuum on which a short -s means just a few boys and a longer and longer -s means more and more of them. Note that there are not always just two distinctions; my point is that there are always discrete alternatives.

Moreover, there are consistent ways in which these morphemes are organized within the word (Aronoff, 1976; Nida, 1949): Derivational morphemes must be encompassed within inflectional morphemes.[2] The

---

[1]A few spoken languages (e.g., Vietnamese, Chinese) are isolating; that is, they uniformly consist of words that are unanalyzable single morphemes. However, most spoken languages have fairly complex morphologies, i.e., words that are analyzable into a number of regular parts.

[2]As has been pointed out by many investigators (Aronoff, 1976): "the distinction [between derivational and inflectional morphemes] is delicate, and sometimes elusive, but nonetheless important [p. 2]." Nida (1949) and Matthews (1974) suggest the following: If a simple form can be substituted for a complex form in a sentence, then the complex form is derivational (that is, a property of the lexical item but not the construction). If a simple form cannot be substituted for a complex form in a sentence, but instead every lexical item that can go in the slot must be likewise complex, the complex form is inflectional (that is, a property of the grammatical construction). This criterion must be supplemented by other facts, e.g., the paradigmatic nature of inflections, to deal with special problems like suppletion. See Matthews (1974) and Aronoff (1976) for more extensive discussion.

central morpheme of a word is known as the root; this root is immediately preceded (in prefixing languages) or followed (in suffixing languages) by derivational morphemes, which add components of meaning to the root or change its grammatical category (e.g., from a verb to a noun); and the derivational morphemes are then preceded or followed by inflectional morphemes, which apply paradigmatically to the word to signal such things as number, tense, or aspect. For example, in English the root "estimate" may take derivational morphemes immediately surrounding it, like "over-" or "-ion" (→"overestimation"). Inflectional morphemes, like the plural "-s," must then appear outside of these derivational morphemes (→"overestima-tions," but not *"overestimates-ion"). Inflectional morphemes cannot appear inside of derivational morphemes (e.g., one cannot say "drover" to indicate a person who was a driver in the past; "-er" is a derivational morpheme, while the past tense morpheme is inflectional).[3] In short, the characteristic pattern is: [INFL + [DERIV + [ROOT] + DERIV] + INFL], a shell-like or layered arrangement of discrete units.

In fact, in spoken languages, these constraints are strong enough that, as elements change from being separate words to being morphemes within the same word, the placement of inflections shifts. For example, "teaspoons full" → "teaspoonsful" → "teaspoonfuls"; the loss of a word boundary between "teaspoons" and "full" is currently resulting in a rearrangement of morphemes to observe the patterning constraint.[4]

Morphology in American Sign Language

I have argued (Newport, in press) that the visual modality seems to make accessible a great deal more richness than the auditory mode (at least in that portion of the auditory mode that spoken language uses). In theory, then, signed languages could be quite different in organization from spoken languages. What is, in fact, the morphological character of American Sign Language?

To answer this question, one must consider two domains in ASL. First, there is what I will call *the frozen lexicon*. These are the single-morpheme signs that are well standardized among signers, typically listed in standard dictionaries of ASL, learned early by adults and children acquiring ASL, and borrowed for use in Signed English. Most of the current literature on ASL has concentrated on these signs. (For further discussion, see Supalla, in press.) Second, there is another portion of the language that has been called

---

[3]Technically, the correct generalization concerns rule ordering: Derivational changes must apply before inflectional changes. For most languages, these two ways of stating the generalization are equivalent. However, for languages in which inflections are infixed to the root, only the latter statement is accurate. I am grateful to Mark Aronoff (1976 and personal communication) for a discussion of this issue.

[4]I would like to thank Lila Gleitman for suggesting this example to me.

"mimetic," "nonstandardized," "analogue," or "nonlinguistic"; by deaf people, it is called "sign mime." These signs seem to reflect aspects of the real world in form: Handshapes often refer to shapes of objects, and movement of these handshapes through space in front of the signer is used to represent the motion of objects through real-world space. Fig. 3.1 presents an example of a sign sequence of this type of "mimetic depiction." Table 3.1 presents an English translation.

In the ASL literature, there have been two rather different points of view on the character of mimetic depiction. On one view, only the frozen lexicon is the lexicon of the language; "mimetic depiction" is considered a nonlinguistic extension of the mode, analogous to "vroom-vroom" for the sound of a motorcycle in the auditory mode (Klima, Bellugi, et al., 1979, p. 13–15). On this view, ASL becomes like spoken languages by excluding from the bounds

a. VEHICLE-WANDER-
UPWARD-ACROSS-
HORIZONTAL-WIDE-
STRAIGHT-SHAPE

b. VEHICLE-ROTATE-ON-
HORIZONTAL-WIDE-
STRAIGHT-SHAPE

c. VEHICLE-MOVE-ACROSS-
HORIZONTAL-WIDE-
STRAIGHT-SHAPE

d. VEHICLE-MOVE-THRU-
FOUR-HORIZONTAL-THIN-
STRAIGHT-SHAPES

e. VEHICLE-TURN-PAST-TREE

f. VEHICLE-MOVE-TO-
VERTICAL-THIN-STRAIGHT-
SHAPE

g. PERSON-FALL-FROM-
VEHICLE

h. LONG-VERTICAL-THIN-
STRAIGHT-SHAPE-SWING-TO-
HORIZONTAL

FIG. 3.1.   A sequence of ASL "mimetic depiction."

TABLE 3.1
English Translations of ASL "Mimetic Depiction" in Fig. 3.1

(a) A car wanders uphill.	(e) The car turns to avoid hitting a tree.
(b) The car skids on the road.	(f) The car hits a telephone pole.
(c) The car goes across the road.	(g) A person falls out of the car.
(d) The car crashes through a fence.	(h) The telephone pole falls down.

of the language proper much of the communicative use of the modality. However, several investigators have recently suggested a second, radically different position: that "mimetic depiction" is part of ASL proper, that it is built on an analogue use of movement and space, and therefore that ASL is dramatically different in organizational character from spoken languages. For example, DeMatteo (1977) has proposed that these signs vary continuously in form and meaning, in an analogue way, to match the visual images they represent. This is in sharp contrast to the discrete distinctions of spoken language. Moreover, DeMatteo has suggested that the grammar of ASL, in contrast to that of spoken languages, must include mechanisms for mapping continuously varying forms onto visual images. Similarly, Cohen et al. (1977) have claimed that many signs in Israeli Sign Language covary continuously and indefinitely with their meanings, a property that they attribute to the iconic potential of the visual–gestural mode. This view, then, argues that the organizational character of a language is highly determined by the modality in which that language is transmitted.

It is quite true that the modalities used by a signed language have the *potential* for an analogue, rather than a discrete, system. In an earlier paper (Newport, in press) I presented evidence that perception and immediate memory for sign-like items are continuous rather than categorical. Moreover, with a system of gestures that uses handshape to represent shape, and hand movement to represent movement, there is clearly the possibility for analogue flexibility. In fact, Carol Schwartz, Ted Supalla, and I (Schwartz, Newport, & Supalla, in preparation) have demonstrated experimentally that hearing subjects, using sign-like gestures nonlinguistically, vary their mimetic gestures continuously in correspondance with continuous variations in real-world stimuli. However, what I will argue is that the language does not take advantage of this potential: Despite the additional and somewhat different resources offered by the visual–gestural modality, the language looks in many ways the same as spoken languages. In particular, our analyses suggest that "mimetic depiction" in ASL is strikingly like morphology in spoken languages: "Mimetic" forms within American Sign Language are not at all analogue in nature; rather, like morphologically complex forms in spoken language, they are constructed from a relatively small number of discrete components, which mark familiar distinctions of meaning and are combined in familiar ways. Unlike spoken language, these morphemes are largely simultaneous rather than sequential; moreover, the form of each morpheme has some clear relation to its meaning (i.e., the morphemes are iconic). However, the ways in which these components are organized is like that of other languages of the world.

The evidence for these claims comes from a linguistic analysis of "mimetic depiction" in American Sign Language conducted by Ted Supalla and me (Newport & Supalla, in preparation; Supalla, in press), as well as from suggestions in prior work of Coulter (1975, in press) and Newport and Bellugi (1978). Supalla and I have initially focused our attention on ASL depictions of motion and location, using standard linguistic methodologies to elicit from native speakers judgments of what forms are possible in the language, what forms are contrastive in meaning, and then determining the internal structure of these forms from the range of possibilities and contrasts within the set. The results of this analysis are presented, in overview, below; for further detail, see Newport & Supalla (in preparation).

Handshape as a Classifier. There is a limited number of discretely different handshapes that can be used in "mimetic depiction," each with its own consistent meaning. The handshape of a sign within "mimetic depiction," then, is itself a morpheme. (This is not generally the case within the frozen lexicon; for frozen signs, handshape is a phonological parameter with no associated meaning.) In the mimetic depiction sequence rendered in Table 3.1, handshapes are roughly translated into English nouns (e.g., the horizontally extended index and second finger and the vertically extended thumb, a handshape known within the ASL literature as a 3–hand, is translated as "car"). However, a more precise translation is given in Fig. 3.1 (i.e., "vehicle" for the example just described; for other signs in Fig. 3.1, "person," "long–vertical–thin–straight shape," etc.). The handshapes of these signs mark the semantic category or the size and shape of the associated noun. In actual discourse, these forms are preceded by full nouns from the frozen lexicon: for example, CAR*frozen* VEHICLE–WANDER–UPWARD.[5]

As noted by Frishberg (1975), Kegl and Wilbur (1976), and Supalla (1978), these handshapes function similarly to morphemes known in spoken languages as *classifiers,* which commonly appear in verbs of motion and location. For example, in Navajo the final morpheme of the verb of motion or location varies according to the shape of the object involved in the action (from Allan, 1977):

béésò sì-ʔá	= money lie–of round entity	"A coin is lying (there)."
béésò sì-ltsòòz	= money lie–of flat flexibile entity	"A bill is lying (there)."
béésò sì-nìl	= money lie–of collection	"A pile of change is lying (there)."

---

[5]Following the notational conventions of the ASL literature, I use an English gloss in capitals to represent a sign, and an English gloss or translation in lower case, enclosed in quotation marks, to represent the meaning. Wherever possible, multimorphemic signs are represented by multiple words, in capitals, with one word glossing each morpheme and hyphens between the words.

The corresponding sentences of ASL are formally analogous, with the classifier morpheme occurring simultaneous with the movement or location morpheme:

MONEY ⌈FLAT–ROUND–SHAPE (F–handshape)⌉   "A coin is lying
      ⌊BE–LOCATED (contact movement) ⌋   there."
MONEY ⌈FLAT–WIDE–SHAPE (B–handshape)⌉   "A bill is lying
      ⌊BE–LOCATED (contact movement) ⌋   there."
MONEY ⌈DOME–SHAPE (5̆–handshape)   ⌉ "A pile of change
      ⌊BE–LOCATED (contact movement)⌋ is lying there."

The ASL verbs from these three sentences are illustrated in Fig. 3.2

ASL has several different handshapes that function as classifiers in "mimetic depiction;" on the basis of characteristics of form as well as meaning, these fall into two main groups.[6] One group includes size-and-shape specifiers (SASSes), which classify objects on the basis of their size and shape. The other group is abstract classifiers, which classify objects on the basis of semantic characteristics. All of these classifiers fall within the types Allan (1977) has found in spoken classifier languages of the world.

The SASS handshapes actually consist not of a single handshape morpheme, but of a group of simultaneous hand-part morphemes: Each finger, as well as the thumb and forearm, is a possible morpheme that can combine in specifiable ways to form a handshape (Supalla, 1978). Fig. 3.3 presents examples of two morphologically related groups of SASSes. The SASSes on the left all share the morpheme STRAIGHT; those on the right all share the morpheme ROUND. The rows differ formationally in whether the index finger (and, for the round shapes, the thumb) occurs alone (row 1), or whether the middle finger (row 2)[7] or the full hand (row 3) is involved as well; the meanings of these forms differ correspondingly, as indicated in the Figure. In addition, there are discrete morphological values of size that must be marked on the SASSes as well; for further details, see Newport and Supalla, in preparation, and Supalla, 1978, in press. In sum, for the SASSes there is a limited number of discrete values along several dimensions of handshape; hand parts form a morphophonological system that relates the phonology of the hand with the visual–geometric features of the referent object.

---

[6]The discussion here focuses on intransitive verbs of motion. There are also transition verbs of motion (e.g., bring, carry) that have other sets of classifiers. The latter classify the instrument (e.g., "by hand" versus "by forklift") as well as the object or patient of the action.

[7]The SASS for shallow cylindrical shape (i.e., both the index finger and middle finger bending along with the thumb into a circle) does not occur in many signers' dialects. In this case, the handshape with only the index finger and thumb is used for both the flat round shape and the shallow cylindrical shape.

a. FLAT-ROUND-SHAPE-BE-
LOCATED

b. FLAT-WIDE-SHAPE-BE-
LOCATED

c. DOME-SHAPE-BE-LOCATED

FIG. 3.2.   Three ASL verbs of location.

The second group of classifier handshapes, although they may have originated as SASSes (see Supalla, in press), are currently composed of a single morpheme (rather than a group of morphemes), and represent the semantic category of the associated object (rather than its visual–geometric properties). Fig. 3.4 presents several examples of these semantic classifiers. The first, a V–handshape oriented downward (in its unmarked orientation[8]), is used with animate human nouns, as illustrated in Fig. 3.1g for a person. The second example, a bent-V oriented downward (in its unmarked orientation), is used with animate nonhuman nouns—for example, a dog, a bird, or a bug.

 THIN & STRAIGHT   FLAT & ROUND (circle)

 NARROW & STRAIGHT   SHALLOW & ROUND (shallow cylindrical)

 WIDE & STRAIGHT   DEEP & ROUND (cylindrical)

FIG. 3.3.   Morphologically related size-and-shape specifiers.

---

[8]Each semantic classifier has an unmarked orientation; changes of orientation are additional morphological parameters. For further discussion, see the section *Other Internal Morphemes*.

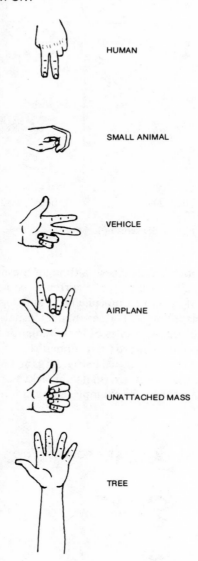

HUMAN

SMALL ANIMAL

VEHICLE

AIRPLANE

UNATTACHED MASS

TREE

FIG. 3.4. Some examples of semantic classifiers.

The 3–handshape, used for vehicles (e.g., a car, a boat, or a motorcycle), was illustrated in Fig. 3.1 a–g. In contrast, the airplane classifier is used only for airplanes (but not helicopters). The fifth example, a fist with the thumb extended upward, is used for three-dimensional objects that are separable from their ground: a flowerpot, a house, a bottle, a potted tree. In contrast, a rooted tree must be classified by the last example, a classifier for trees that is used for palm trees or evergreens as well as for more prototypically shaped trees. In short, although there is some clear iconic relationship between the form of the classifier and its meaning, these forms within contemporary ASL are used in semantic and grammatical ways extended systematically beyond their iconic properties.

As one may notice from the descriptions of the domains of these classifiers, for any given noun more than one classifier might be appropriate. In ASL, as in spoken classifier languages (cf. Allan, 1977), different classifiers may be used with the same noun to focus on different characteristics of the referent. For example, to talk about a person moving, one could use the index finger oriented upward (VERTICAL–THIN–STRAIGHT–SHAPE) or the V–handshape; the former classifies the noun in terms of its visual–geometric properties (classifier languages commonly include people in the category of long, thin things), while the latter classifies the noun as two-legged human and requires further morphemes to specify manner of movement (e.g., walk versus slide).

These classifier handshapes, then, are a set of discrete morphemes that occur within "mimetic depiction." These handshape morphemes occur in combination with movements that are described in the next section.

Movement as a Root Morpheme.   Movement within "mimetic depiction" appears on first inspection to vary continuously with movement in the real world; prior linguistic investigations, as well as more superficial observation, have suggested that classifier handshapes can be manipulated through the signing space to mirror the paths and manners of movement taken by the referent object. However, our own analyses (Newport & Supalla, in preparation; Supalla, in press) have suggested that movement, like handshape, does not vary continuously or indefinitely in either form or meaning. Rather, as in spoken classifier languages, the classifier is combined with a limited number of discretely different morphemes representing categories of movement to form a verb of motion or location.

Not all conceivable paths of movement are acceptable or contrastive in ASL "mimetic depiction." Those paths of movement that are acceptable in the language are constructed from only seven basic movement patterns, or *movement roots;* each root is a morpheme within verbs of motion or location. (As with handshape, the same movements may occur within the frozen lexicon, but within the frozen lexicon these movements are phonological entities with no associated meaning of their own.) These roots may each occur alone (in combination with morphemes from the other morphological parameters) to represent simple events, or may combine with each other (and morphemes from the other morphological parameters) to represent complex events. The seven roots are listed in Fig. 3.5

The first is the *hold root,* in which there is no movement and the hand remains in one place. This root has the meaning "be stationary." For example,

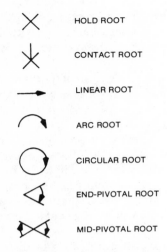

FIG. 3.5.   Movement roots.

a bent–V handshape combined with the hold root (that is, held stationary in neutral space in front of the signer) means "small animal (e.g., a bird) is stationary"; a 3–handshape with the same movement means "vehicle is stationary"; the airplane–handshape with the same movement means "airplane is stationary."

The next is the *contact root*, in which there is a brief movement before the hand stops at a specified location. This root has the meaning "be located" and is found in all verbs of location. (It is therefore the movement occurring in all three ASL equivalents of the Navajo verbs discussed previously and illustrated in Fig. 3.2.) This root in combination with a bent–V handshape means "small animal (e.g., a bird) is located (there)" and forms a minimal morphological pair with the first example in the previous paragraph; the same movement in combination with a 3–handshape means "vehicle is located (there)" and forms a minimal pair with the second example of the previous paragraph; the same movement in combination with the airplane–handshape means "airplane is located (there)" and forms a minimal pair with the third example in the previous paragraph.

The contact root can also be extended for more abstract grammatical purposes. In this case, classifiers are combined with the contact root to establish arguments whose spatial locations will later be used in marking case relations. For example, to sign "the dog bites the cat," one can sign the following sequence: the frozen noun DOG, followed by the animal classifier with the contact root performed on one side of signing space; then the frozen noun CAT, followed by the animal classifier with the contact root performed on the other side of signing space; and finally the sign BITE, performed directionally from the location of the dog classifier to the location of the cat classifier.[9] In contrast, to sign "the cat bites the dog," the sequence may be identical[10] except that BITE is performed from the location of the cat classifier to the location of the dog classifier. In this type of usage, the contact root does not necessarily indicate an actual physical location for the referent objects, but rather a grammatical location to be used in a later verb.

The remaining five roots in Fig. 3.5 are used in verbs of motion. In all these roots the hand starts at an initial point in the signing space and moves to an end point; they differ from one another in the form of the movement path. In the *linear root*, the hand moves in a straight path from the initial point to the end point. For example, this root in combination with the bent–V handshape means "small animal (e.g., bird) moves from one place to another"; the root in combination with a 3-handshape means "vehicle moves from one place to another"; and the root in combination with the airplane–handshape means "airplane moves from one place to another." Again, these examples form minimal pairs with the examples given for the hold root and the contact root.

In the *arc root*, the hand moves in an arc from the initial point to the end point. This root has a concrete meaning, "to move through an arc"; but it also has a more abstract meaning, "to move from one point to another (with the path unspecified)." For example, in combination with the bent-V handshape, the more likely reading would be "small animal jumps from one point to another." In contrast, for the same root in combination with the 3-handshape, the more likely reading (given the abilities of vehicles) is "vehicle moves (in an unspecified path) from one location to another"; the vehicle could have moved in a straight line, in a zigzag, it could have been lifted from one place to another, or it could have vanished at the point of origin and reappeared at the final point. For the same root in combination with the airplane–classifier, either reading is likely.

In the *circular root*, the hand moves through a circular movement path, with the meaning "move in a circle." In combination with the bent–V handshape, it means "small animal (e.g., bird) moves in a circle"; in combination with the 3-handshape, it means "vehicle moves in a circle"; in combination with the airplane–handshape, it means "airplane moves in a circle."

In the three previous roots, the whole hand moves across space. In contrast, for the last two movement roots, one part of the hand is fixed in space while other parts of the hand move across space; both of these roots signal changes of orientation. In the *end-pivotal root*, one end of the hand is fixed while the other end moves, with the meaning "swing." For example, Fig. 3.1h shows

---

[9]It is not yet clear whether this ASL sequence is one sentence with three clauses, or three separate sentences. This question awaits further analyses of ASL syntax.

[10]When directional verbs are used, word order is relatively free (Fischer, 1974).

this root in combination with the LONG–VERTICAL–THIN–STRAIGHT–SHAPE SASS, with the meaning "long vertical thin straight shape swings to the ground." The same movement performed horizontally[11] in combination with the WIDE–STRAIGHT–SHAPE SASS means "wide straight shape (e.g., gate) swings." In the *mid-pivotal root,* the hand changes orientation with the middle of the hand fixed. For example, this root in combination with the bent–V handshape means "small animal (e.g., bird) turns upsidedown"; in combination with the 3–handshape, it means "vehicle turns upsidedown" (pivoting vertically) or "vehicle rotates (e.g., slips on the ground)" (pivoting horizontally). The latter example is illustrated in Fig. 3.1b.

All of the preceding examples involve one movement root per sign. However, certain movement roots may also combine within a verb of motion to represent more complex events. Fig. 3.6 shows several permissible combinations.

Certain movement roots may combine simultaneously, as in the first example in Fig. 3.6. In this case, the arc root is combined simultaneously with the mid-pivotal root with the meaning "fall" (= "move" + "change of orientation"). This complex movement contrasts in meaning and in form with the simple arc movement meaning "jump"; the latter involves the arc root alone and signifies only movement to a new location (without a change of orientation).

In other combinations, the roots are combined in sequence, as in the second example in Fig. 3.6. In this case, a linear root is combined with a mid-pivotal root and another linear root, with the three sequential roots well-merged and performed with smooth transitions. This movement combination has the meaning "turn," as in the example VEHICLE–TURN in Fig. 3.1e. Like the other movement forms previously described, this form is not limited to an analogue usage: The referent movement need not be precisely 90° and the form is unchanged for a wide range of referent movements. Rather, like the English word "turn," the form refers to a category of real-world events.

The last example in Fig. 3.6 is a movement pattern in which sideways linear movement is combined simultaneously with forward linear movement, with the meaning "move randomly" or "wander." Again, this form is used not for one particular path, but for a variety of random paths. For example, this complex movement in combination with the 3–handshape (VEHICLE–WANDER) is shown in Fig. 3.1a.

In sum, movement in "mimetic depiction" does not vary continuously as an analogue to real-world movement. Rather, there is a small number of movement categories that are marked in ASL; complex paths of movement are marked by combinations of these forms. The analyses described thus far,

----

[11]For all movement roots, the plane in which the movement is performed is an additional morphological parameter; see the section *Other Internal Morphemes.*

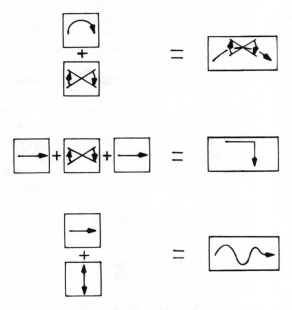

FIG. 3.6.   Some combinations of movement roots.

then, suggest that these signs are *not* mimetic depictions, but multimorphemic verbs of motion and location.[12] Additional sets of morphemes within these verbs are described below.

Base Point as a Morpheme.   Thus far I have described the handshape and movement of the active, or dominant, hand (for right-handed signers, this is typically the right hand). In verbs of motion and location, this hand marks the action of the central or moving object and is, of course, an obligatory part of the sign. The nondominant hand, known as the base hand, is optionally part of the verb as well, remaining in one place while the active hand moves. We have found that this base hand and its placement in verbs of motion and location involve several independent morphemes; all of these morphemes

---

[12]On very rare occasions, signers may attempt to outline the precise path of a moving object or the precise shape of an object. However, this continuous type of movement differs in a number of ways from the discrete movement forms previously described. First, it is produced very slowly, with the eyes oriented toward the hands rather than toward the listener's face. Second, its use is restricted to the special purpose of specifying precise outlines; it is considered unacceptable for ordinary conversation. This type of signing is thus like the "drawing in air" that a hearing person might produce for similar functions, and it is marked by speed and eye gaze as being outside the normal use of the language. This is not what previous investigators have called "mimetic depiction," "sign mime," or "analogue signing." For a further discussion of these distinctions, see Coulter (in press).

mark aspects of a secondary object (for example, the source or goal) related to the action of the central object. (As with handshape and movement, the base hand within the frozen lexicon is a phonological entity with no associated meaning of its own.)

First, the handshape of the base hand is a classifier for the secondary object, just as the handshape of the active hand is a classifier for the central object. For example, the base hand with the index finger oriented upward (VERTICAL–THIN–STRAIGHT–SHAPE) can be combined with an active hand with a 3–handshape (VEHICLE) and a linear movement to mean "vehicle moves to a vertical thin straight shape" (e.g., "the car hits the telephone pole"). This verb is shown in Fig. 3.1f. In contrast, the base hand with a bent–V handshape (ANIMAL) can be combined with the same active handshape and movement to mean "vehicle moves to a small animal" (e.g., "the car hits the bird"). Since the base hand classifiers are identical to those of the active hand,[13] I will not dicuss them further; see the section *Handshape as a Classifier*.

Second, the placement of the base hand with respect to the path of the active hand is another morpheme, marking the semantic relationship of the secondary object to the central object. There is a limited number of possible locations around the movement path that can be marked with a base hand. We have called these locations *base points*. The set of all base points for a given movement root is called the *base grid system*.

Fig. 3.7 illustrates the base point morpheme possibilities by showing the possible locations of a base hand along or adjacent to the linear movement root. As shown in this figure, there are only three possible locations for a base hand on the movement path of the linear root: the initial point, the midpoint, and the endpoint. For example, a base hand with the index finger oriented upward (VERTICAL–THIN–STRAIGHT–SHAPE) is placed at the initial point, marking the source of the movement, with a 3–handshape of the active hand, to mean "vehicle moves from a vertical thin straight shape" (e.g., "the car leaves the telephone pole"). The same handshapes and movements with the base hand placed at the midpoint means "vehicle moves through a vertical thin straight shape" (e.g., "the car goes through the telephone pole"). The same handshapes and movements with the base hand placed at the end point, marking the goal, means "vehicle moves to a thin straight shape" (e.g., "the car hits the telephone pole"). The last example is illustrated in Fig. 3.1f. Figs. 3.1a, c, d, and g illustrate other base handshapes at the mid- and end points of the movement path.

---

[13]Within the frozen lexicon, the phonological possibilities for the base hand are more restricted than those of the active hand; see Battison, 1974, for a description of these phonological constraints. However, in complex verbs of motion and location, where the base handshape is itself a morpheme, these constraints do not apply.

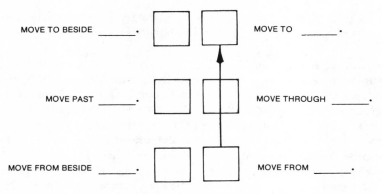

FIG. 3.7.   Base points of the linear movement root.

Fig. 3.7 also shows three locations adjacent to the linear movement path at which a base hand may be placed: adjacent to the initial point, mid point, and end point. For example, the handshapes and movements just described with the base hand placed beside the initial point would mean "vehicle moves from next to a vertical thin straight shape"; with the base hand placed beside the mid point, the meaning is "vehicle moves past a vertical thin straight shape"; and with the base hand placed beside the end point, the meaning is "vehicle moves (to) next to a vertical thin straight shape."

Finally, there are several more base points not illustrated in Fig. 3.7: ahead of or behind the movement path, or along the movement path. (In the last, the entire movement path is marked with a base hand, with the meaning "moves along on." An example with the mid-pivotal movement root is shown in Fig. 3.1b.)

Other Internal Morphemes.   By this time it should be clear that there is a large number of morphological dimensions in ASL verbs of motion and location. Although this degree of morphological complexity is unlike English, it is not uncommon in languages of the world: some languages, known as *polysynthetic* languages, may have as many as 10 or 15 possible morphemes within a single word.

Thus far I have described only some of the ASL morphological dimensions. There are several others—for example, a set of morphemes that mark the orientation of the central and secondary objects with respect to the movement path and to the external world; a set of morphemes that mark the orientation and spatial plane (e.g., above the ground versus below the ground) of the movement path and the base grid; and a set of morphemes that mark the manner of movement of the central object (e.g., rolling versus sliding). For further details, see Supalla (in press) and Newport & Supalla (in preparation). Like the morphological dimensions previously described, each of these consists of a discrete set of alternatives; although each of the morphemes is iconic (i.e., there is a clear relationship between the form of the morpheme and its meaning), none varies continuously or indefinitely.

Noun Derivation and Inflectional Processes.   The movement root along with handshape, orientation, (optionally) manner, and (depending on the syntactic context) base hand morphemes together form the *stem* of the verb of motion or location. There are in addition several *process morphemes*[14] that can be added to this stem, to form a noun rather than a verb, and to inflect either the noun or verb for number or temporal aspect. Formal rules for these processes are presented in Supalla & Newport (1978).[15]

When semantically appropriate, certain verb stems can undergo a change in the manner of movement to become *noun stems.* While the movement of verb stems is either a continuous or a hold movement, that of noun stems is *restrained* in manner: The movement is quick and stiff (rather than smooth), and the hand bounces back to its initial position. In addition, when the noun is not inflected, repetition is also added to the stem to form the surface noun. This morphological process is a highly regular and systematic way of forming concrete nouns in ASL (Supalla & Newport, 1978). Figs. 3.8a and 3.9a illustrate this distinction for the verb FLY (airplane–classifier + linear movement) and the noun AIRPLANE: The hand moves steadily forward for the verb, while it moves in a restrained fashion for the noun.

Inflectional processes can then be applied to the verb stem to form an inflected verb, or to the noun stem (including restrained manner of movement) to form an inflected noun. For example, a slow reduplication process can be applied to either stem, as illustrated in Fig. 3.8b for the verb and in Fig. 3.9b for the noun. Notice that, although the inflection itself has the same form for the two stems (a reduplication with a slow, arc-shaped transition back to the initial point between reduplicated units), the resulting inflected stems are distinct: The inflected verb is continuous in manner of movement, while the inflected noun is restrained in manner of movement. In short, the inflection operates on the stem, reduplicating its constituent morphemes. In a related way, the inflection has a somewhat different interpretation for the two types of stems: When applied to the verb, it has the interpretation of *continuous aspect,* marking the verb for iteration or elongation of the action (e.g., "flying and flying and flying") (Fischer, 1973;

---

[14]In spoken languages, some morphemes are *segmental* (that is, have as their surface form an isolable component of the stem), while others are *process* morphemes (that is, have as their form processes applied to the stem). For example, in many languages the marking for a derived noun or for continuous aspect is a reduplication of the unmarked verb stem. Similarly, in ASL derived nouns, number, and aspect are marked by various types of reduplication processes.

[15]Our earlier description treated noun derivation and inflections as applying to a single-morpheme underlying form, or root. Our current analysis, as presented in this chapter, differs in one significant respect: What was previously treated as the underlying form, or root, of the sign, we are now claiming is, at least for verbs of motion and location, a complex stem composed of several independent morphemes.

a. FLY   b. SLOW REDUPLICATION FORM   c. DUAL FORM

FIG. 3.8.   FLY: base form and two inflected forms.

a. AIRPLANE   b. SLOW REDUPLICATION FORM   c. DUAL FORM

FIG. 3.9.   AIRPLANE: base form and two inflected forms.

Fischer & Gough, 1978). When applied to the noun, it has the interpretation of *serial pluralization* (e.g., "airplane after airplane after airplane") (Supalla & Newport, 1978). Both are common inflections in spoken languages of the world.

There are many other inflections that can be applied to verbs or nouns in ASL; see Fischer & Gough, 1978, and Klima, Bellugi, et al., 1979, for a more exhaustive description of inflectional processes. I will describe only one more example: Like many spoken languages, ASL inflects verbs and nouns for *dual,* as well as multiple, plural. In the dual inflection, the stem is performed once in each of two locations in space. This inflection applied to the verb stem FLY is shown in Fig. 3.8c, and applied to the noun stem AIRPLANE is shown in Fig. 3.9c. Again the inflection has the same form in both cases, but the resulting inflected verb is continuous in manner, while the inflected noun is restrained in manner. When applied to the verb stem, the inflection has the meaning of performing the action twice (e.g., "fly to two places or at two times"); when applied to the noun stem, it means two objects (e.g., "two airplanes").

These inflectional processes can also both be applied to the same stem, with the order of application corresponding to the semantic scope of the inflections. For example, the verb stem FLY can be inflected for continuous aspect, and then that stem inflected for dual: [[FLY $_{cont}$]$_{dual}$]. This complex inflected form has the meaning "flying and flying on two different occasions." The noun AIRPLANE with the same sequence of inflections, [[AIR-PLANE$_{serial}$]$_{dual}$], has the meaning "two rows of airplane after airplane." In

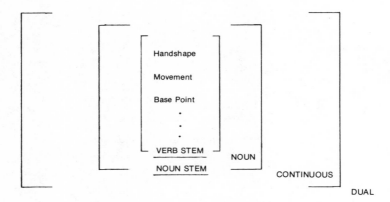

FIG. 3.10.   Structure of the "word" in American Sign Language.

contrast, the same inflections can be applied in the reverse order, with the dual inflection applying before, or inside of, the inflection for continuous aspect. The verb form, $[[FLY_{dual}]_{cont}]$, has the meaning "flying twice over and over again"; the noun form, $[[AIRPLANE_{dual}]_{cont}]$, has the meaning "pairs of airplanes, pair after pair." Finally, the same inflection may be applied recursively to the stem, for example, $[[FLY_{cont}]_{cont}]$, "flying continuously over and over again." In short, like certain inflectional processes in spoken languages (Chapin, 1967, 1970), the inflections of ASL operate hierarchically and recursively (Supalla & Newport, 1978; Klima, Bellugi et al., 1979).

Summary: Structure of the "Word" in American Sign Language

As we have seen, what appeared to be continuously varying "mimetic depiction" in ASL turns out to be complex morphology much like that in spoken languages. In ASL, the morphemes are often high iconic, and they are most often combined simultaneously rather than sequentially. However, as in spoken languages, complex forms are made up of a limited number of discrete components. Moreover, these discrete units are combined with a *shell-like structure* like that in spoken languages. Fig. 3.10 summarizes the internal structure of the "word" in American Sign Language. Significantly, the inner layer of this shell consists of the root and derivational morphology, those components that add basic meanings to the root; operating outside of these is the derivational morphology that changes the grammatical category of the stem from verb to noun; and outside of these is inflectional morphology.[16] In

---

[16]The evidence for the distinction between derivational and inflectional morphology in ASL comes not only from the meanings of the morphemes in question, but also from the substitutability criterion presented in Footnote 2.

short, American Sign Language has the same kind of analytic character, with discrete units inside of discrete units, that is displayed by spoken languages. It therefore appears that language demands this type of organization, even when the modality would permit other quite different organizational possibilities.

THE INFLUENCE OF LEARNING ON LANGUAGE

Why are languages organized in this way? Apparently the reason is not that the modality requires a particular type of linguistic organization. As I have argued here and elsewhere (Newport, in press; Schwartz, Newport, & Supalla, in preparation), there is richness available in the visual, if not the auditory, mode that would permit a rather different type of organizational system. I would like to suggest that the property of having highly analytic forms, with units inside of units organized in constrained ways, arises from the learning processes through which such systems are passed. Let us begin by examining the acquisition of "mimetic depiction" in young deaf children of deaf parents.

Acquisition of Morphology
in American Sign Language

Our linguistic work demonstrates that the final product of the ASL acquisition process is a formal morphological system much like that of spoken languages; but one might well still wonder about the early stages of acquisition. To what extent do the early stages show the influence of the analogue potential of the modality, and to what extent do they look like a formal morphological analysis despite this potential? Given exposure to "mimetic depiction" signs, the child could in principle make either of two kinds of inductive generalizations: First, s/he could attend to the iconic, analogue aspects of the input and predict new forms on the basis of an analogue organization. On this route, one should expect the child to make a kind of flying leap into the language by producing mimetic forms very early relative to frozen forms. Alternatively, s/he could attend to the formal morphological organization, analyzing new signs as part of a combinatorial system. In the latter case, the "mimetic" forms, morphologically the more complex, would be acquired relatively late. Characteristic errors in the early stages would likewise be expected to differ for these two alternatives.

I have examined the signing of three young deaf children, videotaped in their homes once a month, to answer this question (Newport, 1979). The videotapes are part of a much larger study of ASL acquisition being conducted by Supalla (in progress), and were loaned to me for this purpose. The subjects are deaf children from deaf families, where ASL has been used in the home for several generations. The children are thus acquiring ASL in infancy, as their native language, as did their parents. The videotapes include both spontaneous signing and elicited productions of verbs of motion and location. I have analyzed only the elicited productions of verbs of motion. For this portion of a session each month, the child is shown a set of 20 animated films constructed to test the morphemic contrasts of interest. For example, the child watches a dog jumping over a bed, a car driving uphill, or a boy jumping into a toilet, and is then asked to say what happened. There are three such sets, so the child receives a different set of films each month. In the videotapes I have analyzed, the three children together cover the age range from 2½–5 years of age.[17]

Table 3.2 presents the results of this analysis of terms of the percentage of correct productions versus errors of various kinds, for simple movements (that is, those productions requiring only one movement morpheme) and complex movements (those productions requiring more than one movement morpheme). Complex movements are further subdivided into those that the child produced as a frozen sign versus those that the child produced as a nonfrozen "mimetic depiction." I have concentrated on the movement parameter alone since this parameter seemed a priori the most likely to involve analogue forms, if they were to occur. Since the children (particularly the youngest child) often did not respond to every film within a set, the data are collapsed over three sets,[18] and nonresponses are excluded from analysis.

As can be seen from Table 3.2, simple movements (i.e., those we analyze as single morphemes) are produced correctly virtually 100% of the time throughout the period from 2½–5 years. This in and of itself suggests that the child is not beginning with an analogue strategy, since many of the filmed events involve paths of movement that are not perfectly analogous to the single-morpheme movement that represents them in ASL. However, the strongest evidence that children are acquiring the discrete components of the adult system, morpheme by morpheme, comes from the responses to complex movements.

Complex movements (i.e., those we analyze as consisting of more than one movement morpheme in their target adult forms) are often avoided, particularly by the youngest child, and are replaced with frozen signs that are performed the same over a number of contrasting films. (See also Ellenberger & Steyaert, 1978, for related findings.) For example, the children at the youngest ages produced the sign FALL in its citation form, regardless of whether the referent object was a person or an inanimate object, and regardless of whether the path of the fall was a downward arc or merely a

---

[17]During the sessions I have analyzed, the children were shown pilot films. Supalla (in progress) and our adult study in progress described in the section *Language Evolution* involve similar, but more well controlled, films.

[18]Anne I and Randy I were shown all three sets in one session. Otherwise, the three sets were shown over a period of 3 months, one set per month.

TABLE 3.2

Elicited Productions: % of Simple Movements, Complex Frozen Movements, and Complex Nonfrozen Movements that are Correct versus in Error over Age

| | Simple Movement | | Complex Movement | | | | | | |
| | | | Frozen Sign | | Nonfrozen Sign | | | | |
	Correct	Error	Correct	Error	Correct	Missing Morpheme(s)	Separated Morphemes	Analogue	Other
Anne I (2;4)	100% (3)		100% (3)		50% (2)	50% (2)			22% (2)
Anne II (2;6–2;9)	100% (4)		100% (3)		0% (0)	78% (7)			
Anne III (2;11–3;1)	100% (7)		100% (6)		11% (1)	89% (8)			
Janie I (3;4–3;6)	85% (16)	15% (3)	67% (2)	33% (1)	19% (3)	56% (9)	6% (1)	19% (3)	
Randy I (4;5)	100% (23)		100% (5)		29% (7)	58% (14)	8% (2)	4% (1)	
Randy II (4;7–4;10)	100% (22)		100% (6)		35% (6)	35% (6)	18% (3)	12% (2)	
Randy III (4;11–5;1)	100% (21)		75% (3)	25% (1)	43% (10)	35% (8)	13% (3)	9% (2)	

change of orientation (e.g., from standing to face down). The proportion of complex movements that are signed by the young child as frozen signs is 43% for the youngest child (Anne I) and declines with age to 15% for the oldest child (Randy III). Moreover, as shown in Table 3.2, when a frozen sign is performed, it is virtually always correct.

In contrast, when complex movements are represented by nonfrozen "mimetic depictions," they are almost always produced incorrectly. Table 3.2 shows that accuracy on nonfrozen signs increases steadily from 0% correct in Anne II[19] to 43% correct in Randy III. More importantly, the predominant error pattern throughout this period from 2½–5 involves producing one or two of the movement morphemes correctly, but omitting the one or two other morphemes required for a fully correct movement. The frequency of errors of this type (that is, errors that omit whole morphemes but have no other inaccuracy) is 78% at Anne II, age 2½, and 89% at Anne III, age 3; it then declines with age to 35% at Randy II, age 5, as correct productions increase.

For example, the children are shown a film of a hen jumping from the ground to the roof of a barn. The correct adult form is an upward arc movement ($\nearrow$), which we analyze within the linguistic system as a simultaneous combination of an arc root ($\frown$) and an upward linear root ($\nearrow$). The child of 2;6 produced only an arc, omitting any upward component. The child of 4;5 produced a new kind of error: a simple arc omitting any upward component, followed by an upward linear movement. (Such productions are classified in Table 3.2 as "separated morphemes," where the child produces sequentially morphemes that are produced simultaneously by the adult.) At 5;0 the fully correct form was produced. Similarly, the children were shown a truck turning a fence corner; the correct adult form is one that we analyze as consisting of a sequential linear root, followed by a pivot, and then a linear root. The youngest child produced only a linear movement; the child of 4;5 produced all three roots but in a clearly sequential fashion, with distinct pauses between each root; and only the child of 5;0 produced the smooth, well-merged adult form. When shown a yellow dot moving randomly, a movement correctly represented by a simultaneous combination of a linear back and forth root and a linear forward root, the children produced only a back and forth linear movement; the correct form was not produced within the age range we examined. Finally, when shown a cow hopping uphill, a movement correctly represented by a series of arcs simultaneous with a linear upward root, the youngest child produced only a series of arcs, with no upward component; the middle child produced an up-and-down movement in one place, which she followed by taking a step with her own body; the oldest child produced the correct adult form.

---

[19]Although Anne I produces 50% correct, this is only two signs. Given the clear pattern for the other six scores, this appears to be an unreliable figure.

Although the criterion I adopted for analogue productions (any movement that went in an analogue fashion beyond producing the adult morphemes, even when the child appeared to be playing, e.g., by adding a crash to the flight of an airplane) was purposely generous, the number of analogue productions is small and comparatively unpatterned over age. Moreover, analogue productions do not appear at all in the youngest child and do not begin to show up until the children are producing a relatively larger proportion of complex movements correctly.

In short, the developmental pattern is as follows: Only simple movements and frozen signs are produced correctly in the early stages. The former consist of only one movement morpheme. The latter also consist of only one morpheme, in that they are phonologically complex forms whose internal parts are not analyzed by the child. These are like what MacWhinney (1978) has called *amalgams* in the early stages of acquiring spoken languages with complex morphology. With increasing age, the child apparently begins to analyze internal morphemes, producing some individual morphemes correctly while omitting others. On occasion, this stage is followed by the production of multiple morphemes produced sequentially. Only later does the child produce correct complex forms, with multiple morphemes combined appropriately. This process, like that in the acquisition of spoken languages with complex morphology, is apparently not completed until after the age of 5. In fact, the overall pattern and the ages at which these types of productions occur are in general quite similar to those of the acquisition of spoken language morphology (MacWhinney, 1978; Slobin, 1968).

The young child, then, begins the acquisition process with unanalyzed forms and proceeds to analyze the system into discrete components; s/he apparently makes precious little use of the analogue possibilities, but rather treats the input as part of a formal morphological system. Thus even when the modality appears to offer a kind of inductive generalization that seems intuitively obvious and that would give the child a leap into the system at the start, s/he doggedly continues doing what the linguist does, analyzing discrete morphemes in a formal way and acquiring them one at a time. This similarity of pattern with spoken languages, despite the additional alternatives the visual medium appears to offer, suggests how strongly biased the learning mechanism is to approach the problem analytically and to find an internal analysis that relates forms across the language. For related findings in the acquisition of spoken languages, see Karmiloff-Smith (1979).

Language Evolution

I began the description of ASL acquisition by suggesting that the tendency for languages to have highly analytic forms, with units inside of units organized in constrained ways, may arise from the learning process through which such systems are passed. Our acquisition work demonstrates that learners, at least in infancy, are biased to interpret their input as part of such a system, even in the face of reasonable alternatives. In accompaniment with the findings of others on language evolution and acquisition, our work further suggests that this bias for learners to find an internal analysis of previously unanalyzed forms may itself be responsible for the tendency of languages to have highly analytic forms.

What is the evidence for this claim? In fact, not all communication systems are organized in this fashion; early, newly evolved communication systems display this analytic character to a lesser degree than older, more successively learned communication systems. One example of this contrast can be found in the history of writing systems (Gelb, 1952; Gleitman & Rozin, 1977). The earliest writing systems were first pictographic, representing a complex idea through a global picture, and then logographic, representing the spoken language at the level of the whole word. As these writing systems were picked up by new cultures, they apparently were reanalyzed in more and more analytic ways, resulting in a systematic progression from logography to syllabary, with representation of the internal syllables of the spoken word, to alphabet, with representation of the morphemic and phonemic structure of the word (Gelb, 1952; Gleitman & Rozin, 1977). Significantly, these evolutionary changes generally occur not within a single culture, where the use of the system tends to become frozen, but rather when the system is adopted and reanalyzed by a new culture for use with its language.[20]

A similar phenomenon occurs within the invention and evolution of new spoken languages. *Pidgins* are communication systems invented by adults for communication with other adults with whom they do not share a language (typically in trade situations). Pidgin languages are universally isolating, with little or no morphology internal to the word and with grammatical functions performed through separate words and word order; this is true even when the creators of the pidgin are all native speakers of languages with rich morphologies (Broch, 1927; Kay & Sankoff, 1974; Slobin, 1977). When children are born to pidgin speakers and acquire the pidgin in infancy, as a native language, the communication system is known as a *creole*. In contrast to pidgins, creole languages universally include morphology internal to the word; this internal morphological structure is apparently added to the system through reanalysis of the input language by the second generation learner (Sankoff & Laberge, 1973; and see Slobin, 1977, for an important discussion of the significance of these facts to language acquisition).

Finally, the deaf community presents an exceptionally striking example of the same phenomenon. The linguistic and acquisition work on ASL previously described has concentrated on second- and third-generation deaf, those for whom ASL is a native language acquired in infancy. However, 90%

---

[20]I am indebted to Jay McClelland for reminding me of this fact.

of the deaf population in America are first-generation deaf, deaf children born to hearing parents. The earliest communication system for the latter children is often a "home sign" system invented for use within the family in the absence of any exposure to other gestural communication systems. Recent studies of "home sign" (Feldman, Goldin-Meadow, & Gleitman, 1978; Goldin-Meadow, 1978) have revealed that it is composed of sign-like gestures without internal morphology and with fairly consistent gesture ordering. Our own work in progress suggests that these first-generation deaf individuals go on later in life to acquire predominantly the frozen lexicon of American Sign Language, those signs lacking much of the internal morphology discussed in this chapter. The highly analyzed morphology I have described is largely a property of the sign competence of only second-generation deaf (and subsequent generations), those who learn ASL as a native language in infancy.[21]

This suggestion is in line with the findings of Woodward (1973), who has shown that the use of certain rules of ASL inflectional morphology is related to having deaf parents and to acquiring ASL before the age of 6, and of Fischer (1978), who has presented evidence that ASL has arisen under creolizing circumstances. Moreover, it is supported by our own observational work on "mimetic depiction," as well as by an experimental study of compounding rules conducted by Ursula Bellugi and me. In the latter study (Newport & Bellugi, in preparation), we presented to both first- and second-generation adult signers a set of sentential contexts, each containing a blank that the subject was to fill in. Some of these contexts grammatically required two signs in a phrase (e.g., "Yesterday all day long I *was painting the house.*"[22]); others required the same two signs in a noun–verb compound (e.g., "My occupation is *house-painting.*"). While second-generation signers were uniformly correct on this test, first-generation signers made a number of inconsistent errors. These findings suggest that first-generation signers, unlike second-generation, often did not have productive compounding rules (an aspect of derivational morphology not described in the present chapter) that they could apply to the task.

More relevant to the present discussion, Ted Supalla, Carol Schwartz, and I are currently conducting a systematic study of first- versus second-

---

[21]Some first-generation deaf have older deaf siblings from whom they learn ASL in infancy or early childhood; others enter residential schools for the deaf early in life and learn ASL from other children through the signing "underground." These individuals show some significant mastery of complex ASL morphology; a more precise statement must await further analysis of our generational data. However, because, until recently, most schools for the deaf prohibited signing whenever possible, a large number of first-generation deaf individuals are not exposed to ASL until later in life. My statements about first-generation signers are most true of these signers.

[22]For the reader's convenience, these examples are presented in English translation; in the actual experiment, all presentations were in ASL. In this example, although in English the blank is filled by more than two words, the ASL response is two signs (PAINT[++]HOUSE).

generation adult signers' control of the internal morphology of "mimetic depiction" in ASL. In this study we are presenting to signers a series of animated film scenes like those described in our acquisition study, carefully constructed to elicit minimally contrasting verbs of motion and location. In each trial, the subject is asked to sign what happened. The films are presented in random order. Since the set of films is constructed to elicit minimally contrasting verbs, by examining the whole set of responses we can determine which individual morphemes of verbs of motion and location are correctly controlled by the signer. Data collection and analysis in this study are still in progress. However, initial results generally appear to support the claim that there are very striking differences between first- and second-generation signers in the extent of morphological analysis and control: While second-generation signers generally produce all of the contrasting morphemes described in our linguistic analysis, first-generation signers lack many or all of the contrasts and often produce frozen signs for a group of films that second-generation signers distinguish with contrasting internal morphemes.

Since first-generation deaf are of course the parents of second-generation deaf, these findings suggest that complex internal morphological analysis is performed by second-generation deaf on an input that does not itself contain this morphology. This is not to say that such analysis occurs entirely in the absence of environmental support; in fact, Newport, Gleitman, & Gleitman (1977), Feldman, Goldin-Meadow, & Gleitman (1978), and Goldin-Meadow (in press) have presented evidence that grammatical morphemes are acquired with dependence on a linguistic environment. The frozen lexicon of ASL, which is the predominant linguistic input for most second-generation signers, includes the handshapes, movements, etc., of complex verbs of motion and location as phonological entities inconsistently associated with particular components of meaning. The second-generation learner, then, regularizes these associations, ending up with productive form–meaning components that were not characteristic of the language of his or her parents.

All of these examples, taken together, suggest that the learning process itself may contribute certain types of organizational characteristics to languages. This is not an entirely new claim: It has been argued by Chomsky (1965), McNeill (1966), and others that there must be strong constraints on the learning process for any language to be learned from only a sample of input strings. I am suggesting even more strongly that learning may go well beyond what is justified by the input, that the output of such a process may be more highly structured than the input (see also Kiparsky, 1971). Moreover, our current work on the acquisition of artificial languages in the laboratory (Morgan & Newport, in press) suggests that these contributions to structure may be made by a general learning process, which is not necessarily specific to language.

We are just beginning studies of the acquisition process in second-generation deaf children, and our studies of first- and second-generation deaf adults, as previously described, are still in progress. These studies will eventually provide us with information not only about the precise competences of the various groups of signers and their acquisition, but also about the relation of these competences to age at first exposure to the language and to details of input as well. At present, I can offer little insight into *why* the learning process leads in consistent directions. Nevertheless, the evidence suggests that it does, and that it may, under certain circumstances, change the language.

SUMMARY

According to our linguistic analyses, signed languages (at least American Sign Language) have the same kind of analytic character as spoken languages. First, ASL marks the same kinds of semantic distinctions marked by many spoken languages. More importantly, ASL has the same kind of formal apparatus for marking these distinctions: a limited number of parameters along which a limited number of discrete values are signaled, and a shell-like, hierarchically organized combinatorial system governing the permissible ways in which these discrete units may co-occur. Moreover, this analytic kind of organization appears in ASL despite the very clear iconic base for these forms, and despite the resulting potentially different options the visual–gestural modality makes available.

Our linguistic analyses are supported by our studies of the acquisition of ASL: Young deaf children appear to enter the system making precious little use of the iconic or analogue possibilities; rather, they doggedly perform their own formal analyses, morpheme by morpheme, over a period of several years.

Finally, and more speculatively, it appears that certain of these learners perform this analysis on an input that is not itself fully analyzed, creating morphological structure where their parents had mastered predominantly frozen, unanalyzed forms. This finding, along with others in the literature on language evolution and acquisition, suggests that the explanation of such structural regularities may lie in an understanding of the learning process itself.

ACKNOWLEDGMENTS

This research was supported in part by a grant from the Research Board, University of Illinois, by NSF grant #BNS–76–12866 to the Salk Institute for Biological Studies, and by PHS grant #MH–15828 to the Center for Human Information Processing, University of California, San Diego. All figures were drafted by Ted Supalla; Figs. 1, 2, 5, 6, 7, 8, 9, and 10 are reproduced, with permission, from Supalla (in press). I would like to thank Ted Supalla, my collaborator, for his crucial participation in every aspect of this work; Geoff Coulter, who, along with Ted, made important suggestions that started me thinking about "mimetic depiction;" Jean Mandler and Len Talmy for stimulating discussion; and Carolyn Mervis, Michael Maratsos, and Lila Gleitman for extremely helpful comments on an earlier draft of this chapter.

REFERENCES

Allan, K. Classifiers. *Language*, 1977, *53*, 285–311.

Aronoff, M. *Word formation in generative grammar.* Cambridge, Mass.: M. I. T. Press, 1976.

Battison, R. Phonological deletion in American Sign Language. *Sign Language Studies*, 1974, *5*, 1–19.

Broch, O. Russenorsk. *Archiv für slavische Philologie*, 1927, *41*, 209–262.

Chapin, P. *On the syntax of word derivation in English.* Information Systems Language Studies #16, MITRE Corp., Bedford, Mass., 1967.

Chapin, P. On affixation in English. In M. Bierwisch & K. Heidolph (Eds.), *Progress in linguistics.* The Hague: Mouton, 1970.

Chomsky, N. *Aspects of the theory of syntax.* Cambridge, Mass.,: M. I. T. Press, 1965.

Chomsky, N. *Reflections on language.* New York: Random House, 1975.

Cohen, E., Namir, L., & Schlesinger, I. M. *A new dictionary of sign language.* The Hague: Mouton, 1977.

Coulter, G. *American Sign Language pantomime.* Salk Institute Working Paper, La Jolla, Calif., 1975.

Coulter, G. Continuous representations in American Sign Language. In W. Stokoe (Ed.), *1977 National symposium on sign language research and teaching.* Washington, D.C.: National Association of the Deaf, in press.

DeMatteo, A. Visual imagery and visual analogues in American Sign Language. In L. Friedman (Ed.), *On the other hand.* New York: Academic Press, 1977.

Ellenberger, R. & Steyaert, M. A child's representation of action in American Sign Language. In P. Siple (Ed.), *Understanding language through sign language research.* New York: Academic Press, 1978.

Feldman, H., Goldin-Meadow, S., & Gleitman, L. R. Beyond Herodotus: The creation of language by linguistically deprived deaf children. In A. Lock (Ed.), *Action, symbol & gesture: The emergence of language.* New York: Academic Press, 1978.

Fischer, S. Two processes of reduplication in the American Sign Language. *Foundations of Language*, 1973, *9*, 469–480.

Fischer, S. Sign language and linguistic universals. In C. Rohrer & N. Ruwet (Eds.), *Actes du colloque Franco–Allemand de grammaire transformationelle, Band II: Etudes de semantique et autres.* Tubingen: Max Niemeyer Verlag, 1974.

Fischer, S. Sign language and creoles. In P. Siple (Ed.), *Understanding language through sign language research.* New York: Academic Press, 1978.

Fischer, S., & Gough, B. Verbs in American Sign Language. *Sign Language Studies*, 1978, *18*, 17–48.

Friedman, L. (Ed.) *On the other hand.* New York: Academic Press, 1977.

Frishberg, N. Arbitrariness and iconicity in American Sign Language. *Language*, 1975, *51*, 696–719.

Gelb, I. *A study of writing: The foundations of grammatology.* Chicago: University of Chicago Press, 1952.

Gleitman, L., & Rozin, P. The structure and acquisition of reading I: Relations between orthographies and the structure of language. In A. S. Reber & D. Scarborough (Eds.), *Toward a psychology of reading.* Hillsdale, N.J.: Lawrence Erlbaum Associates, 1977.

Goldin-Meadow, S. Structure in a manual communication system developed without a language model: Language without a helping hand. In H. Whitaker & W. A. Whitaker (Eds.), *Studies in neurolinguistics* (Vol. 4). New York: Academic Press, 1978.

Goldin-Meadow, S. Recursion in a communication system developed without a conventional language model. In L. R. Gleitman & E. Wanner (Eds.), *Language acquisition: The state of the art.* New York: Cambridge University Press, in press.

Greenberg, J. H. (Ed.) *Universals of language.* Cambridge, Mass.: M. I. T. Press, 1963.

Greenberg, J. H. *Language universals.* The Hague: Mouton, 1966.

Hockett, C. F. The problem of universals in language. In J. H. Greenberg (Ed.), *Universals of language.* Cambridge, Mass.: M. I. T. Press, 1963.

Karmiloff-Smith, A. *Language as a formal problem space for children.* Paper presented at the Conference "Beyond description in child language," Max Planck Gesellschaft, Nijmegen, The Netherlands, June 1979.

Kay, P., & Sankoff, G. A language–universals approach to pidgins and creoles. In D. DeCamp & I. Hancock (Eds.), *Pidgins and creoles: Current trends and prospects.* Washington, D.C.: Georgetown University Press, 1974.

Kegl, J., & Wilbur, R. Where does structure stop and style begin? Syntax, morphology and phonology vs. stylistic variation in American Sign Language. *Chicago Linguistic Society,* 1976, *12,* 376–396.

Kiparsky, P. Historical linguistics. In W. O. Dingwall (Ed.), *A survey of linguistic science.* College Park, Md., University of Maryland Press, 1971.

Klima, E., Bellugi, U., Battison, R., Boyes-Braem, P., Fischer, S., Frishberg, N., Lane, H., Lentz, E., Newkirk, D., Newport, E., Pederson, C., & Siple, P. *The signs of language.* Cambridge, Mass.: Harvard University Press, 1979.

Liberman, A. M. The grammars of speech and language. *Cognitive Psychology,* 1970, *1,* 301–323.

Liddell, S. *An investigation into the syntactic structure of American Sign Language.* Unpublished doctoral dissertation, University of California, San Diego, 1977.

MacWhinney, B. The acquisition of morphophonology. *Monographs of the Society for Research in Child Development,* 1978, *43*(1–2), Serial No. 174.

Matthews, P. H. *Morphology: An introduction to the theory of word structure.* Cambridge, England: Cambridge University Press, 1974.

McNeill, D. The creation of language by children. In J. Lyons & R. Wales (Eds). *Psycholinguistics papers.* Edinburgh: Edinburgh University Press, 1966.

Morgan, J., & Newport, E. The role of constituent structure in the induction of an artificial language. *Journal of Verbal Learning and Verbal Behavior,* in press.

Newport, E. *The acquisition of morphology in American Sign Language.* Paper presented in "The child's formation of grammatical categories and rules," Society for Research in Child Development, 1979.

Newport, E. Task specificity in language learning? Evidence from speech perception and American Sign Language. In L. R. Gleitman & E. Wanner (Eds.), *Language acquisition: The state of the art.* New York: Cambridge University Press, in press.

Newport, E., & Bellugi, U. Linguistic expression of category levels in a visual–gestural language: A flower is a flower is a flower. In E. Rosch & B. B. Lloyd (Eds.), *Cognition and categorization.* Hillsdale, N.J.: Lawrence Erlbaum Associates, 1978.

Newport, E., & Bellugi, U. Productivity of compounding rules in American Sign Language. Manuscript in preparation, 1980.

Newport, E., Gleitman, H., & Gleitman, L. R. Mother, I'd rather do it myself: Some effects and non-effects of maternal speech style. In C. Snow & C. Ferguson (Eds.), *Talking to children: Language input and acquisition.* Cambridge, England: Cambridge University Press, 1977.

Newport, E., & Supalla, T. Morphological structure of American Sign Language. Manuscript in preparation, 1980.

Nida, E. *Morphology: The descriptive analysis of words* (2nd Ed.). Ann Arbor, Mich.: University of Michigan Publication in Linguistics II, 1949.

Osherson, D. N., & Wasow, T. Task-specificity and species-specificity in the study of language: A methodological note. *Cognition,* 1976, *4,* 203–214.

Sankoff, G., & Laberge, S. On the acquisition of native speakers by a language. *Kivung,* 1973, *6,* 32–47.

Schlesinger, I. M. The grammar of sign language and the problems of language universals. In J. Morton (Ed.), *Biological and social factors in psycholinguistics.* Urbana, Ill.: University of Illinois Press, 1970.

Schwartz, C., Newport, E., & Supalla, T. Discrete vs. continuous encoding in American Sign Language and non-linguistic gestures. Manuscript in preparation, 1980.

Siple, P. (Ed.) *Understanding language through sign language research.* New York: Academic Press, 1978.

Slobin, D. *Early grammatical development in several languages with special attention to Soviet research.* Working paper no. 11, Language–Behavior Research Laboratory, University of California, Berkeley, 1968.

Slobin, D. Language change in childhood and history. In J. Macnamara (Ed.), *Language learning and thought.* New York: Academic Press, 1977.

Stokoe, W. C., Jr., Casterline, D., & Croneberg, C. G. *A dictionary of American Sign Language on linguistic principles.* Washington, D.C.: Gallaudet College Press, 1965.

Supalla, T. *Morphophonology of hand classifiers in American Sign Language.* Working paper, University of California, San Diego, 1978.

Supalla, T. Morphology of verbs of motion and location in American Sign Language. In F. Caccamise (Ed.), *1978 National symposium on sign language research and teaching.* Washington, D.C.: National Association of the Deaf, in press.

Supalla, T. *Acquisition of morphology of American Sign Language verbs of motion and location.* Unpublished doctoral dissertation, University of California, San Diego, in progress.

Supalla, T., and Newport, E. L. How many seats in a chair? The derivation of nouns and verbs in American Sign Language. In P. Siple (Ed.), *Understanding language through sign language research.* New York: Academic Press, 1978.

Wasow, T. The innateness hypothesis and grammatical relations. *Synthese,* 1973, *26,* 38–56.

Woodward, J. C. Inter-rule implication in American Sign Language. *Sign Language Studies,* 1973, *3,* 47–56.

4

Comparative Cognitive Research: Learning from a Learning Disabled Child

Michael Cole
Kenneth Traupmann
University of California
San Diego

The work that we describe in this chapter is part of a general effort by members of the Laboratory of Comparative Human Cognition at the University of California, San Diego to characterize the ways in which culturally organized activities influence intellectual behavior. Almost all of our work has been comparative in some respect: comparisons of children of different ages, children from different home backgrounds, schooled and unschooled children, literate and nonliterate adults, and normal and psychotic adults. In this chapter we will describe the beginnings of a different line of comparative research that is directly motivated by problems arising in the course of our earlier studies.

As long ago as 1971, Cole and his colleagues asserted that cultural differences in learning and problem solving reside more in the situations to which people of different cultures apply their cognitive skills than in the existence of such cognitive processes in one cultural group and their absence in another (Cole, Gay, Glick & Sharp, 1971). That conclusion made sense in the context of their research. However, it was an unsatisfying conclusion in several respects. First, there was little more than a casual description of the various everyday tasks in which people seemed to exhibit skills that they appeared to lack in more tightly controlled laboratory tasks. This led us to question whether it was reasonable to assume that laboratory and naturally occurring tasks were measuring the same skills. For example, when somebody learns and remembers riddles, the names of leaves, or one's ancestors, and does so in a fashion that appears remarkable to us, are the essential skills the same as those required in free recall, paired associates, or any other well-analyzed cognitive task?

A second cause of dissatisfaction with the conclusion from our early cross-cultural work was its vagueness; it was unsatisfying because the immediate source of differences in cognitive task performance *within* the controlled laboratory settings was by no means clear. This point was brought home to us in the course of our reseasrch on the cognitive consequences of education conducted in the early 1970s in Mexico (Sharp, Cole, & Lave, 1979).

On the face of it, the results of this latter research strongly supported the notion that attendance at school is responsible for many of the intellectual achievements that are associated with the term "cognitive development" in the United States. Vis-a-vis their uneducated brethren, schooled Yucatecans could remember longer lists of words, they more often organized words according to taxonomic principles, and they performed better on tests of logical reasoning. So long as we confine our inferences to those traditionally made in view of this evidence there can be little doubt that schooling produces a very significant transformation in the ways people think about problems.

But, we think it possible that the traditional line of reasoning is in error. As Sharp et al. (1979) pointed out, the tasks of virtually all cross-cultural cognitive research are extremely similar in their structure to the tasks constructed by Alfred Binet for the purpose of predicting children's success in school. Binet designed tasks to sample problems set for children in educational settings, not all the possible settings that confront children and adults. It is possible that, because of this bias in sampling tasks, the implication that education is central to the development of cognitive skills might be no more than a tautology built upon unquestioning belief in the validity of these tasks as the metric of intellectual competence. After all, why should it be surprising that people who are given extensive training on school-like tasks are more skilled at doing them than people who have rarely, if ever, encountered them, at least within the context of the typical testing format?

Our cross-cultural problem can be stated concretely as follows: In order to decide whether unschooled people perform poorly on currently popular cognitive tasks because they have had less exposure to such tasks than their educated peers, it is necessary to determine how frequently schooled and unschooled individuals confront such tasks inside and outside of the classroom. In order to determine frequency, we must be able to identify the tasks. But identifying intellectual tasks outside of the carefully constructed and constrained confines of the laboratory or formal psychometric test is a nontrivial problem. There exists no set of rules, no guidelines, no accepted procedures in the social sciences for evaluating the similarity of cognitive tasks unless the analyst has constructed the task in the first place (in which the task-as-constructed provides the basis for claims about task similarity). It follows, then, that there is no accepted method of specifying whether an individual's behavior is, except for topography, the same or different when it occurs in different contexts.

Because none of the prerequisites for intercontext comparison exist currently in the social sciences, we are in a precarious position when making professional statements about the effects of education on human thinking. Statements about the impact of different cultures are even more problematic because we are even less able to specify the relevant aspects of general cultural experience than the relevant aspects of formal educational experience.

These problems took us in several directions. First, we examined the literature in psychology that had led us to believe that it would be possible to discover the "same task occurring in different settings." This work produced an examination of the scattered writings on generalizing from experiments, the concept of ecological validity, and the conditions necessary for asserting that a task had occurred in the absence of standard experimental-psychological methods (Cole, Hood, & McDermott, 1978). This literature review led us to conclude that psychological experiments typically rest on procedures that render them systematically unrepresenative of intellectual tasks encountered outside of schools and tests.

We also designed a research program in which we deliberately set out to provide structure for children's activities in a number of settings in an attempt to determine the kinds of activities psychologists would have to engage in if they wanted to *make* the same task happen in different settings (Griffin, Cole, & Newman, in press).

One of these was the study of children for whom some claim had been made that their behavior *was* the same in different settings. We challenged ourselves to discover the grounds for such claims. Included among our concerns were the following: How often are the cognitive tasks that have been studied in the laboratory actually encountered in various classroom and club settings? Could we show similarity (or differences) in the behavior of individual children for tasks encountered in the different setttings? Granting that the exact form of a given task would vary according to the context in which it occurred, could we specify how the context influenced the particular form of the task and the child's response to it?

CONTEXTS OF OBSERVATION

In the fall of 1976, we undertook a study with 17 children, 8–10 years of age, who attended a small, private school in mid-Manhattan, New York City. We made both video and audio tapes of the children's activities in a variety of school settings and in an after-school club modeled loosely on those one would encounter at a community center. During one of the club sessions' we conducted an Information Bee in which club members were divided into two teams and competed for prizes by attempting to answer questions from the Wechsler Intelligence Scale for Children (WISC).

We also recorded hour-long individual testing sessions during which each child was presented a variety of laboratory-derived intellectual tasks. The series of tests we selected were meant to be representative of tests used to evaluate scholastic aptitude or cognitive development. Our battery included: (1) the similarities subtest of the WISC, which was modified so that, in cases in which the child experienced difficulty, a third item was added to the original pair (e.g., we added onion to turnip-carrot); (2) a mediated memory test first developed by Leontiev (1932) and Luria (1928) that allowed children to use one set of pictures to help them recall another set; (3) a figure-matching task of the sort used to assess impulsiveness; (4) a syllogistic reasoning task; and (5) a classification task involving common cooking and eating utensils. These tasks were administered by a professional tester who did not know the purpose of the study.

The Initial Paradox

As the project got under way, some members of the group began spending time in the classroom observing the children and looking for examples of laboratory-styled intellectual tasks. Others began to conduct club sessions. The teacher and other school personnel were naturally curious about the children and they wanted to check impressions with us. There was little surprise about the difficulty we experienced with Ricky, a child who was often disruptive in the classroom. But, we were asked, had Archie been a problem?

This question was puzzling to us because Archie had most certainly *not* been a problem. He had worked cheerfully and industriously with his partner during the cooking sessions we had conducted thus far. Except for his unwillingness to let Ricky join with him in baking, there was nothing remarkable about Archie, as far as we could tell. The teacher's reason for suspecting that Archie might experience difficulties in the club was even more surprising, conditioned as we were to think of "problems" as problems of deportment. Archie, we were told, is a child with a rather severe learning disability.

By this time, those of us who conducted club sessions had spent several hours with the children. We had observed the children in conversation and while implementing recipes that require reading, measuring, and coordination with other people. Only once had we noticed anything special about Archie that was consistent with his teacher's report. Like many younger children, he mispronounced spaghetti as "pischetti," to the howling laughter of several club members. In general, Archie appeared to us one of the more competent members of the group.

This simple disjunction between the teacher's knowledge of Archie as learning disabled and our naivete was the paradox initiating this work. Once the teacher laid out the list of Archie's problems, we had difficulty understanding how he could simultaneously suffer such general deficits when engaged in scholastic activity and appear to us well within the range of normal behavior in our cooking club.

It required only a little reflection to realize that Archie represented a very interesting special case of the general problem that we were tackling. Here was a child about whom it was asserted that he behaved the same way in a variety of different settings. The challenge was clear: How could it simultaneously be true that Archie was the "same" yet "different" as he moved from one context to another in the course of a single day? In addressing this challenge, we took as our point of departure the strong claims about Archie's specific deficits (e.g., "He has an... auditory language problem."). We reasoned that such characterizations might be used as a template against which to evaluate the similarity of tasks and behaviors across settings.

In the sections that follow, we first examine Archie's behavior in rather standard "learning disability" terms. We claim that these disabilities, as well as a wide range of striking abilities, are identifiable in all the settings we observed. We use our observations as the basis for a discussion intended to clarify claims about similarity of cognitive tasks and behaviors across settings.

The reader is cautioned to treat the entire discussion that ensues as an exploration in comparative research method, and not as a set of strong claims about learning disabilities.

MANIFESTATIONS OF LEARNING DISABILITY: FORMAL TESTS

At no time during our work did we administer tests designed to reveal learning disabilities. However, we were able to interview the psychologist who had made the initial assessment of Archie. She had been following him since he began school, was directing a program of special tutoring for him, and she graciously cooperated in our work.

The psychologist told us that Archie was different from other children even when he started school; he often appeared "disoriented" and "highly distractible." Not long before we first encountered Archie, she administered a WISC that showed his full-scale IQ to be in the normal range. At the same time, his subscale scores fit the pattern reported for children with learning disabilities (e.g., Smith, Coleman, Dokecki, & Davis, 1977; Traupmann & Goldberg, 1979). Both his Coding score and his Digit Span score were below what one would expect on the basis of his overall IQ score. Although learning-disabled children tend to show depressed Arithmetic scores as well, Archie did not.

Consistent with the standardized test performance of learning disabled children, Archie displayed no indication of neurological problems. In response to rather intensive probing from us, the psychologist appeared certain that were Archie to be given an intensive neurological examination, no evidence of brain dysfunction would emerge.

Archie had been seeing a reading tutor for more than two years at the time we met him, yet he continued to have considerable difficulty reading. He was almost two full years below his third-grade level in terms of standardized reading achievement. He was able to read only a few words by sight. For the most part, he read by sounding out the constituent letters or letter clusters of words. He then combined these into an English word. The reading tutor referred to her instructional method as "blending." At the time we met him, Archie read simple words like "cat" as "/k/-at, /k/-at, cat." His reading tutor remarked that, Archie could see the word "cat" 100 times, but, each time, he would say "/k/-at"; he would not recongize it by sight.

Several other characteristic manifestations of learning disability were mentioned in our interviews, including misperception of auditory verbal stimuli (although his hearing acuity was quite normal), misnaming of objects and their representations, difficulty with higher-order concepts, and so on.

These data are, of course, second hand. We present them because they yield such a prototypical picture of a child with a specific learning disability. We now turn to the observations we made ourselves examining first data from the formal test session and the Information Bee.

Misperceiving Auditory Verbal Stimuli

The two examples of misperceptions that follow are especially interesting because both came in the midst of a similarities test; one occurred in the formal testing session and the other in the Information Bee.

Most of the similarities items were taken directly from the WISC. One pair, "wing-fin," was included in the formal test because the class had just been studying vertebrate taxonomies and one of their lessons concerned means of locomotion. We wondered whether the children would incorporate into their answers what they might have learned in the classroom. The following interaction took place between Lisa (the tester) and Archie, after Lisa said, "Wing and fin."

(1) A: Well, wing and thin.   [Thin was whispered and Lisa may very well have been unable to hear it.]

      A wing is thin.   [Archie laughed as this was said as if to indicate that it was not to be taken as an answer.]

(2) L: Not thin, wing and fin.   [Lisa emphasized the articulation of
                                          /f/ in fin.]

(3) A: Oh fin. I thought it
        was thin.

(4) L: No.

(5) A: Um, flying fish   [Said tentatively and
        um, well, what does   with a laugh.]
        a wing have to do
        with a thin?

Consider also the following example excerpted from the Information Bee at the time that Helen, one of Archie's teammates, was asked:

(1) K: Helen, in what way are
        beer and wine alike?

(2) H: They're both drinks.   [Her response was very quick.]

(3) A: A deer isn't a drink!   ["Hot on Helen's heels."]

(4) H and other children
        simultaneously: Beer!   [All responded in a loud and
                                         drawn out manner.]

In both instances, the specific misperceptions are predictable on the basis of phoneme discriminability (he heard /th/ instead of /f/ and /d/ instead of /b/). These two instances are especially interesting because they occurred in the context of a similarities test in which perception of one component of the stimulus pair could be expected to guide perception of the other. Archie's perception (interpretation?) of "fin" and "beer" apparently was not influenced by aspects of the companion items that might be expected to exert some control over his response (something like *appendage* or *part of a body* in the case of "wing" and *drink* in the case of "wine.")

Misnaming Objects, People, and Their Representations

According to his psychologist, "even though (Archie) does perfectly average verbally, it is very difficult for him to express himself in language. He gets very mixed up in terms...(and when) looking (at) a series of pictures, he can't produce the word for a lot of common things." Misnaming occurs, the psychologist told us, despite the fact that often he "know(s), of course, exactly what it is." Consider some of the examples of our corpus that correspond to the psychologist's impressions.

We encountered many examples of misnamed pictures in the course of the Luria mediated memory task in which Archie first had to name each picture, after which he was tested for recall. He called the picture of an igloo an "Eskimo," a pipe was called a "cigar", and a brush was called a "comb."

Notice that just as the sound discrimination errors Archie made were "near misses" based on acoustic similarity, so too the names offered by Archie, although incorrect, are clearly related to the standard labels. No one reading this chapter should have difficulty imagining how Archie might have come to say Eskimo instead of igloo, cigar instead of pipe, or comb instead of brush. Such errors suggest that some aspect of the stimulus common to both responses (e.g., "hair-grooming utensil" in the case of brush and comb) effectively controls Archie's response, but aspects critical to distinguishing between the common label and the one offered by Archie (e.g., having teeth as opposed to having bristles) are ineffective.

We elaborate on the "brush-comb" example; it illustrates that Archie *can* use the word "brush," and also it suggests something of the complexity of variables controlling Archie's lexical choices. It happened that while Archie was naming one set of 12 pictures, he named several quite rapidly, including "comb" instead of "brush." Lisa was instructed to correct him should he misname any of the pictures. Although she did so on all other occasions, this time she failed. After naming all of the pictures, Archie was asked to recall them and one of the six items he recalled was "comb." He was then shown 12 more pictures. The picture paired with the brush in this second set featured the rear view of a woman's head in which her hair was the most salient aspect. Archie said "hair" in response to the picture. He was then asked to "tell . . . how the pairs of pictures are related," and, arriving at the brush–hair pair, he said, "Hair, comb goes to hair because it brushes it."

Archie's use of "brush" here indicates that his previous naming error could not have occurred because he could not say the word. However, although Archie failed to respond appropriately to the picture of a brush, the brush's function appears to have exercised satisfactory control over the name, brush. The same lexical response was involved in both cases, but the pictorial representation of a brush did not produce "brush" whereas its function did. This example suggests that, although Archie displays some difficulty naming things and their representations, he has less difficulty naming the relationship between things. However, even tasks that permit naming relationships in which one object acts with or on others may yield evidence of difficulty.

In one part of the formal testing session, Archie was required to classify various cooking utensils and tableware items that we included because all of the children had experience with them in the cooking club sessions. In fact, Archie acknowledged this connection when, as Lisa was placing the articles on the table before him, he said: "I'm beginning to think this is the cooking club."

He placed the plate, the glass, and the tablespoon in a group in which he had originally included the mug, but he placed the mug aside when he included the glass. When asked why he constructed this grouping, he explained, "Because drink with this (picking up the glass), you eat off of this (pointing to the plate), and you eat with this (picking up the tablespoon), n' you drink out of this (pointing again to the drinking glass—not the mug). "And," he continued, "they're sort of like a lunch." Moments later, as Lisa was recording his response, he said, placing the mug in this group, "And, you could put a mug here too with it."

In a second group, he included the measuring cup, the pot, the wooden spoon, and the measuring spoon, "Because these are all used for cooking."

Archie's groups suggest that he "understands" the relationships between the objects, but the names (or phrases) that he uses to designate those groups were not class-inclusion labels. Either they specified constituents (e.g., "they're all glasses, they're all cups") or they specified a likely action that one would carry out with the objects (e.g., "they're all things to slurp with"). This is supported by the high frequency with which action references emerged in his answers throughout the formal test. For instance, in the mediated memory task, he said that "feet *go into* shoes;" he acted out smoking in response to the similarity between cigarettes and a pipe, he said that a bat and a football go together "because they're both *used* for sports," and so on.

Despite the difficulties Archie displays in naming conceptual relationships, it would be inappropriate to conclude that he shows no "understanding" of such relationships. For instance, when in the mediated memory task, he was asked to tell how cigarettes and a pipe are related, it was clearly the act of smoking that Archie mimicked. And, when pressed by Lisa, he said the word "smoke." Responses like these call to mind his psychologist's remark that he "knows" the answer. We suggest that one reason he gives this appearance is that, even when his response is not acceptable according to the criteria of the test, it reflects knowledge of culturally shared aspects of the situation that typically determine "adequate" responses.

Distractibility

Occasionally, Archie appears to be engaged in one task when his behavior is suddenly inappropriate. The following scene, in which Archie called his teammate by the wrong name, provides an example.

The incident occurred during the Information subtest when a member of the opposing team, Laura, was asked, "From what country did America become independent in 1776?" The videotape shows Archie looking towards the opposing team; he may have been attending specifically to Laura. Archie's friend, Peter, was next to Laura. Peter raised his hand when Laura was slow to respond. (Peter's response was entirely in keeping with the rules governing the Bee, which allowed teammates to answer questions not answerable by the one whose turn it was.) Immediately after Peter raised his hand, Ricky, a member of Archie's team, called out, "Oh, I know, I know, I know."" His third "I know" occurred as Peter's hand reached its full extension. Simultaneously,

Archie turned toward Ricky who was seated to Archie's left. Within a half second of the time Ricky finished saying his third "I know," Archie, now facing Ricky, said, "Well, raise your hand, then, Peter." More than a second elapsed while Ricky stared at Archie. Ricky asked, "Huh?" Archie replied, "Raise it, raise your hand then." Again, more than a second elapsed before Ricky finally reported, "I'm not Peter, I'm Ricky" "I mean Ricky, raise your hand," was Archie's immediate reply.

It appears that Archie's misnomer was, at least in part, a function of his having attended to Peter as Peter raised is hand. Because Archie's utterance was directed at Ricky, as indicated by the ensuing dialogue, Archie appears to have been "distracted" by Peter's action. As in other examples of erroneous behaviors, however, Archie's response can be seen as appropriate to certain aspects of Ricky's behavior as it occurred in the context of the Information Bee. Raising a hand was the surest route to a chance at the question and, except for misnaming his friend, Archie's verbal behavior was appropriate. Here again is an indication that Archie's verbal behavior manifests "understanding" at the same time that he responds erroneously to certain aspects of his environment.

Controlling His Own Subsequent Behavior

It is unusual for a person to emit a misnomer (for example) and not detect it (imagine, for example, a harried mother calling her child first the name of another child, then by the name of the family dog, and eventually by the child's given name). Archie, on the other hand, often appears oblivious to such behavior. The interchange in which he called Ricky by Peter's name illustrates this phenomenon, but it appears in other contexts as well. Consider the "wing-fin" example discussed previously. When Archie asked Lisa, "Well, what does a wing have to do with a thin?" he gave no clue that just seconds earlier he had said both "fin" and the wing–fin associate "flying fish." Another illustration of this phenomenon occurred when he correctly named the pictures of a pot and of a stove, but when asked how it is that the two go together, he said: "The pot goes on the *oven.*"

Two other examples reveal Archie responding twice to the same aspect of a stimulus. Especially significant was that, in neither case, did he indicate that he had responded to that aspect previously. To the similarities problem "fork–spoon," he said, "Ya can eat with a fork and you can eat with a spoon." Later, after having given two other satisfactory similarities, he again returned to their function, saying, "They're both used for eating." Similarly, he both began with and ended with the drinking glass when justifying the grouping that he described as "sort of like a lunch."

The evidence presented in this section leaves us with little doubt, and we hope the reader is similarly inclined, that Archie manifests the kinds of erroneous behaviors that led him to be referred to a psychologist upon entering school and which eventually produced the diagnosis of "learning disabled." However, we did not gather and present this information as a means of proving that Archie is a learning-disabled child. Rather, we have presented these examples because we want to examine the applicability of our description to Archie when he is not in a formal test. The fact that we can plausibly argue that he commits what we have been terming errors is, implicitly, a claim about the context (environment, controlling stimuli) in which the behavior occurs. It is, in short, a claim about tasks and behaviors.

We can now address the question of whether such claims can also be made when we move outside of relatively constrained, test-like scenes into a situation that was not constructed for the detection of errors. In doing so, we will also hope to discover why casual observation does not make any existing difficulties visible.

DESCRIPTION AND ASCRIPTION IN AN INFORMAL SETTING

As we said at the outset, we did not know that Archie was identified as "learning disabled" on the basis of his behavior in the club. To us, he was simply one of the eight children who invaded our senses and sensibilities once each week as we, in our attempts to solve the riddles of human cognition, presented them with cooking tasks of varying (and quite unknown) difficulty. In order to illustrate the kind of data we are dealing with we offer a somewhat lengthy transcript of a segment of one of the club sessions.[1]

The kids are about to make a cranberry bread. The situation differed from our usual club sessions because Ken, the club leader, left the room on the pretense of work he had to perform in an adjoining room. We arranged matters this way in order to evaluate the children's performance when they worked without the aid of adults. Archie worked with Ricky this time, because his usual partner and close friend, Peter, was absent. The previous week Archie and Ricky had great difficulty working together, but on this occasion, Ricky began by explicitly offering to be cooperative.

As we pick up their interaction, Archie was standing at the end of the table where the two boys had elected to work. To Archie's right three girls were working together; at the opposite end of the table stood Ricky recipe in hand. He was kneeling on a chair observing the group of girls.

---

[1]Some readers may find reading transcripts especially difficult. They are advised to skip over this particularly long one and come back to it after reading our discussion of it.

(1)   A: One and one-half of...

[Archie then shook his arms up and down and, while standing in place, he looked about the room.]

(2)   A: Oh, damn where'd our stripeh...(closest English equivalent)

[At this point, Ricky returned and offered the recipe, which Archie was quick to take from him. Ricky kneeled in the chair next to Archie and proceeded once again to watch the girls. Archie began to read the recipe.]

(3)   A: One and one-half of what? Ricky, Ricky check the *Ric-ky*!

(4)   R: What, what, what?

[uttered with disdainful emphasis.]
[Simultaneously, one of the neighboring girls referred to the second step of the recipe.]

(5)   RB: Orange peels, orange peels, where's the orange peels?

[Now that Archie had Ricky's attention, and while he was pointing to the first line on the recipe, he nevertheless spoke in reference to orange peels.]

(6)   A: Orange peels we have to do that, too, but w–

[Ricky began to read where Archie was pointing.]

(7)   R: One, what's this?

(8)   A: One and one-half...

(9)   A: One and one-half chopped raw cranberries.

(10)   A: What are raw cranberries?

[As Archie asked the question, Ricky pointed to the girls across the table who, by this time, were measuring the cranberries for their own bread. Archie looked and then proceeded to the other end of the table where a can of cranberries sat. He picked up the can and a measuring cup and started to pour the cranberries.]

(11)   A: One and one-half...

[Archie poured very carefully, holding both the can and measuring cup at eye level and attending to the graduations on the cup.]

(12) R: I don't know what one and one-half is so Archie you have to do it by yourself.

(13) A: I know, I know.

[The girls were observing them on occasion too, and, at this point, one of them interrupted.]

(14) L: Not that much cranberries.

(15) A: *One cup* it says.

(16) L: One and one-half cups.   [Reading from the recipe]

(17) A: *Right!*
         And that's what I'm doing, you stupid

(18) L: I'm not stupid.

(19) A: We're almost there, almost there.

(20) R: It looks like a big-

(21) A: Yeah! I done it.

[All this while Archie poured the cranberries very deliberately. On reaching the one and one-half cup mark, he was clearly pleased, and before returning to his work station, he placed down on the table the now empty can. He made no reference to the fact that it contained exactly one and one-half cups. After the boys finished pouring the cranberries from the measuring cup to a mixing bowl, they continued.]

(22) A: Okay, what's the next one?

[He then picked up the recipe, simultaneously touching R on his forearm.]

(23) A: Okay next.
         Four table-

(24) R: Four teaspoons of grate, grated orange peels.

[Said as Archie put down the recipe and went for the orange rind, and while Ricky eyed the cranberries.]

(25) A: Uh, what did you guys do...

(26) R: Can I taste a little of this?

(27) A: No, don't, please.

[Said as he located a teaspoon among the measuring spoons.]

How many? Read it again.

(28) R: Four.

(29) A: Four? Okay.

(30) R: One...

[As Archie put in the first teaspoon of orange rind]

Let me put that in.

(31) A: Okay, just a minute.
           I'll do the other,
           third one.

[Archie then left Ricky to the orange peels and went around the table to where the recipe was laying. He sat at the chair in front of it and began to read.]

(32) A: One tablespoon of sugar.

[He read "sugar" as though it was the solution to a tricky problem. He then began to search, presumably for measuring spoons. His search continued for over 20 seconds when he asked one of the girls at his table:]

(33) A: Is that, are you th-through
           with those things?

[He then picked up the spoons and Ricky excused himself from the proceedings.]

(34) R: I have to go to the
           bathroom.

(35) A: Okay did you do four?

(36) R: Yeh.

(37) A: Okay good, of baking
           powder.

This last statement occurred 31 seconds after he read the recipe which called for sugar. It also occurred just 4 seconds after a child at a neighboring table read aloud the instruction: "Three teaspoons of baking powder." No other child uttered the words baking powder during this period. Archie then located a can of baking powder, picked it up, and questioned one of the girls at his table concerning its contents.]

(38) A: Is this baking powder?

(39) H: Read the box, stupid!

(40) A: Ba-king pow-

[Midword, another of the girls swiped the baking powder from him.]

(41) L: C'mon. I'm using it.
          That is 3 tablespoons,
          not 3 teaspoons.
(42) A: Dammit! It says right   [This time, he read "sugar as
          here one tablespoon   though surprised by defeat.]
          of sugar, ah, I was
          wrong.

This episode lasted 2 minutes and 56 seconds of an hour-long session.

Disabilities in Club

We recognize that transcripts such as the foregoing one are difficult to read and incomplete in several important respects. We have not, for example, included all the utterances and other behaviors of the participants who were part of this scene and whose behavior might plausibly be expected to have influenced Archie. Nor have we described every physical move that Archie made. The issue of how to produce a relevantly detailed transcript is a serious one, but we cannot deal with it in detail here. Despite its shortcomings, we believe that the transcript contains numerous examples of the phenomena we encountered in test-like settings. Consider the following, nonexhaustive list:

1. At the very outset of the segment (line 2), Archie mispronounced "recipe" ("stripeh").

2. Later, when he apparently was searching for measuring spoons, he asked the girls whether they were done with "those things" (line 33). Use of such a general term is, we believe, similar to his difficulty in naming things discussed earlier.

3. There were two instances when Archie, seemingly distracted by the activity of others, appeared to lose track of his own verbalizations. At one point, he was "distracted" by the girls whose reference to orange peels occurred just at the moment that he obtained Ricky's attention to the recipe (line 6). At another point, he appears to have been distracted by the girls at the next table who were discussing baking powder. Measuring spoons in hand, he began searching for the sugar, but he ended up obtaining baking powder (line 37).

4. There are three instances when Archie displayed reading difficulties. One occurred at the outset of the scene (line 3). A second occurred in reading the second line of the recipe (line 23), which Archie started as "Four table...," whereupon Ricky began reading, "Four teaspoons..." The third instance occurred when, in response to the command from a neighboring girl to read the label himself, Archie read, "Ba-king pow..." (line 40). He read the label in just the halting manner described earlier by his reading tutor.

5. He quickly forgot the number of spoonfuls of orange rind called for by the recipe (line 27).

We could enlarge this list of examples, but we hope that we have provided enough evidence to show that it is plausible to conclude that the same kind of difficulties Archie manifests in formal test settings *are* detectable in the cooking club.

Archie as an Active Agent in Cooking Club.   In the examples of task and behavior similarity we have described so far, the emphasis has been on specifying the environmental (task, stimulus) conditions in which Archie makes errors. We have, in fact, used these errors in the manner of chemical tracers, to suggest something about the common task conditions. Crudely speaking, we have seen Archie responding to various environmental demands and have identified some of those responses as inadequate (using variable, poorly specified criteria). However, our observations of Archie in the club make available for analysis a different kind of environment-person interaction, one in which *Archie is an active initiator and constructor of the environments to which he responds.*

Ironically, the first piece of evidence that Archie is "learning disabled" provides the first piece of evidence for his skill in organizing his own and other's behavior in order to accomplish better the tasks at hand (here we have in mind getting the cake baked as well as getting a piece of print decoded or keeping track of how many spoonfuls of chopped orange peel are necessary for fulfilling the next step in the recipe).

When Archie said, "Oh, damn, where'd our stripeh (recipe) ... (line 2) he was not responding to a direct instruction to begin baking or to begin looking at the recipe. Rather, speaking loosely, he was responding to the overall task of baking the cake, a plausible first step of which was to get the recipe. His behavior contrasted sharply with that of Ricky at the same moment. Ricky was watching the girls; the recipe was in his hand. Whatever task Ricky was working on, it did not appear to be in the service of getting the cake baked.

Line 3 offers further evidence of "an information processing disability" accompanied by what we might refer to as a "strategic ability." Archie was standing, head bent, over the recipe as he started to "read." (Here, the question of whether or not he *was* reading is posed sharply by the fact that he said "One and one-half of" while *Ricky* had the recipe in hand (line 1). Encountering trouble, he reached for Ricky, both figuratively (through the escalating salutations) and literally (by taking Ricky's arm, pointing to the exact place on the recipe that needed reading, and bending over with Ricky as he read). No sooner was this accomplished than Ricky looked up and started to nibble at some food on the table while observing the girls. Archie, on the other hand, despite a momentary distraction, went to get the cranberries and the necessary measuring cup. Ricky's sole contribution to this part of the exchange was to point to the girls when Archie asked what cranberries are (line 10). To Archie went the problem of "measuring" the cranberries. Having accomplished this, he returned to the recipe, saying, "Okay. What's the next one?"

Ricky was still wandering, but Archie, again confronting his trouble reading, reached out and physically moved Ricky into the task of reading: "Four teaspoons of grate, grated orange peels" (line 24). Archie put down the recipe and went for the orange peels. In contrast Ricky eyed the cranberries, saying, "Can I taste a little of this?" (line 26). Later, when Ricky excused himself to go to the bathroom, Archie checked to see that Ricky had completed the step on which he had been working.

It seems clear that baking a cake requires two kinds of activities. First, it is important to engage in activity such as retaining information about how many spoonfuls of orange peel are required; it is equally important to decode print. But skill at these kinds of activity are not sufficient to get the cake baked; one must also engage in reading and remembering relevant material at the right time. In short, the various component tasks involved in baking a cake must be assembled in the right sequence. Furthermore, each must be completed successfully. If this is not accomplishable by one's own skills (reading knowledge, for example), it must be accomplished indirectly by arranging for someone close to perform that component task. We believe that, just as Archie is manifestly weak in dealing directly with the former kinds of task, he is outstanding in the latter. Unable to read, he nevertheless knows that reading is important and he engaged in it to the extent possible; he moves from step to step in the recipe on completing the prior step; he garners materials as he needs them, and so on. He is particularly skilled at recruiting human resources to circumvent the particular difficulties that were our initial focus of concern.

Ricky is adept at executing just those tasks that bedevil Archie. He reads far above grade level and displays no evidence of any kind of "learning disability." Yet, he seems hopelessly "disabled" when it comes to assembling bits of activity to make up the cake. In common parlance, he is inattentive, his mind wanders. Nowhere in this session did we see Ricky engage in the kind of planful, controlled behavior vis-a-vis baking the cake that Archie displayed. If Ricky "recruits" someone else, it is likely to signal interpersonal trouble. *Together*, in strikingly complimentary fashion, they get the job done.

Archie as an Active Agent in Tests.   These kinds of observation, which occurred consistently in the cooking club, led us to analyze more carefully Archie's performance in the settings from which we had initially drawn our hypotheses about cognitive tasks, the formal test and the Information Bee. Our analysis led us to reason that Archie's behavior in the club setting both reveals examples of the organism-environment interactions that we label disabilities and a class of other interactions that we refer to as active modification of the problem environment. The logic of our approach urged on us the possibility that these same two classes of interaction would be observable in test-like settings as well. It is, then, to Archie as an active organizer of his formal test environment that we now turn.

That Archie was effective in organizing formal testing situations had been hinted by his psychologist who told us that he needed to have the Arithmetic subtest problems of the WISC repeated over and over. She justified her deviation from standard procedure by suggesting that, if she "had presented them (Arithmetic problems) in a different way, he might have gotten more right." What concerns us is how Archie behaved to generate an impression of competence that was otherwise beyond the immediate display of his ability.

The formal testing-situation reveals a number of examples of Archie soliciting help directly. He usually, but not always, failed, reflecting the constraints that constitute psychological testing when compared, for example, with baking in the cooking club. The tester is constrained heavily by the procedures specified because deviation from these procedures will ultimately reduce the validity of the tester's statements. Our tester, Lisa, was very experienced and clearly followed the dictates of formal testing. In fact, the constraints may even have been somewhat magnified by the presence of our video camera. All the same, there were instances when Lisa responded to Archie in a way that was not dictated by test procedures, ways that we think reflected her response to Archie as he, in turn, was responding to difficult problems. Consider the following example drawn from the similarities test:

(1) L: How about anger and joy?
(2) A: Um...um Anger I can't...too good. Anger and joy would be, Anger and joy is um um (clears throat) Anger and joy are sometimes. Anger is mad...Hmm...But those don't match. Anger is different from joy.
(3) L: Well, can you think of some way that they are the same?
(4) L: Well they're both different ways, they're both expressions.
(5) L: Okay, there, that's very good.

Archie's initial response lasted a full 51 seconds, before he said that "Anger is different from joy." According to our instructions, which she followed on earlier items, Lisa was to have given Archie a third member of the "expressions" category, in this case "sorrow," but she did not. Despite the difficulty of the problem, Archie continued to generate false attempts at a solution, each one aborted in turn. At the same time, he displayed considerable distress; his head was lowered and he pulled his sleeves until he eventually had covered his hands. Lisa also revealed evidence of her distress. When he made eye contact with her, saying, "But, those don't match...," she responded, giving him all of the help that the constraints of her situation allowed; she gave him more time and possibly an "instruction" to respond to the pair in a different way.

Consider another example that occurred during the Information Bee: Archie had several attempts to answer during the first series of questions, which were taken from the Information subtest of the WISC, and he missed all of them. He was the only child who, on switching to the next test, had failed to garner any points for his team. The next was Digit Span, and it was clear to Archie that, by the time it was his turn again, the string of digits would be far too long for him to succeed. He can be heard to say, "Why are they always so hard when they get to me?" At this point, still several turns before his, he bowed his head to the table. Later, but still two turns before his, one of his teammates asked, "Archie, why are you crying?" We pick up the dialogue as Ken said, "Okay, Archie, is it your turn now?"

(1) *Teammate 1*:	Will you pass it to me, please Archie?
(2) *A*:	I'm not passing it to anybody.
(3) *Ken*:	It's your turn now Archie, right? All right.
(4) *Teammate 1*:	Why are you crying Archie?
(5) *Opposing Player 1*:	'Cause it's hard. It's hard for him.
(6) *Mike*: (other clubleader):	Well, just pass it by, that's all. It's no big deal.
(7) *Teammate 1*:	I'll do it for your Archie, please?
(8) *Teammate 2*:	You want...
(9) *A*:	No, I don't want to pass it by.
(10) *Opposing player 2*:	No, let him do it by himself.
(11) *Peter*:	He wants to answer questions but they're hard.
(12) *Ken*:	He can try it.
(13) *Mike*:	Everybody misses some of them.
(14) *Opposing player 1*:	Um-hm...
(15) *Ken*:	Okay, Archie, you ready? Six, one, five, eight.
(16) *A*:	Six, one, five, eight?
(17) *All*:	Yeah!
(18) *Teammate 2*:	Give me five, Archie. Please?

But, Archie did not reply. Instead, he resumed his head-in-hands posture, indicative of the Pyrrhic victory he had achieved. It turned out that the pain he displayed, no doubt exacerbated because of the competition, led to a change in the task he was about to receive. His turn called for Ken, the tester, to administer a seven-digit string, one that Archie was very unlikely to reproduce correctly. Ken administered a four-digit (!) string instead. Archie was able to reproduce this string, but not without informing everyone that he was accorded special status because of his difficulty in such tasks. That, however, did not prevent all present from cheering on as if they had been released from an extremely painful situation.

Of course, in a formal test, Ken would not have been able to restructure the task in this way (although, that some restructuring typically occurs is evident in Lisa's actions and in those of Archie's psychologist). Nor is it likely that he would have had to because the procedures for administering the WISC, for example, call for termination of the task when the child demonstrates consistent failure. That is, formal tests are arranged so as to preclude the extreme situation that the competition of the Information Bee provided, competition that rendered highly aversive the impending failure on Archie's part. It is also significant that the Information Bee allowed Ken the freedom to alter the problem confronting Archie so as to permit his turn to end with a success and alleviate social disaster.

GENERAL DISCUSSION

Across all situations in which we have observed him, Archie has shown us that he experiences difficulties when confronted with certain kinds of tasks and that he actively organizes his environment to avoid or mitigate the consequences of his difficulties. Dozens of instances, gleaned from the club, classroom, and both formal and informal testing sessions suggest that such behaviors can be identified in whatever context they occur. Now, we turn to the more general questions motivating this work. What has Archie taught us about describing cognitive tasks that can be of use not only to the study of learning diabilities, but to comparative cognitive research more generally? Recall that the discussion began with the issue of how to specify the cognitive consequences of education. We knew that in many cognitive tasks, years of education predicts performance when other variables, such as age, do not. Why be surprised we asked? After all, experimental contexts require some quite specific skills in addition to the general abilities they may entail. Schooled individuals, by definition, benefit from a lot of practice in such tasks, so of course they should have mastered the tricks of that particular trade (to use Goodnow's, 1972, expression).

In order to move beyond speculation on this topic to hard evidence, we set out to discover what it would take to specify cognitive tasks outside of school so that we could make the relevant population comparisons on tasks of equal familiarity to schooled and nonschooled populations. That search led us to a classroom of 9- and 10-year-olds and our cooking club.

The cooking club perplexed us because intellectual tasks were so difficult to identify. Like Charlesworth (1978), we would have had to conclude that problem solving is a very rare event if we used the evidence provided by task environments borrowed from experimental psychology.

The problem of task specification that we encountered in the cooking club rendered even more acute the issue that embarked us on this journey in the first place. If we could not do the necessary descriptive work in the confines of specially designed clubs with microphones and TV cameras present to help us capture details of people's behavior, what chance did we have for implementing such ideas in cross-cultural settings?

Despite the obvious remaining uncertainties and difficulties, we believe that our work has advanced our general goals, in addition to providing some information of more immediate use in the area of learning disabilities. We *have* learned something useful about task specification in different contexts, including more about what we mean by "task." Because the difficulties of talking about cognitive tasks are related to the settings for behavior we have been studying, features of those settings must be considered.

Testing sessions and laboratory experiments show the following features of concern here:

1. The physical environment is highly constrained and the person being evaluated is instructed to respond to certain, specific features of the environment; the fact that the tester constructs these stimulus constraints allows that person to specify (correctly or incorrectly) the relevant stimuli.

2. The person evaluated is told the domain of behaviors that will be observed, making it highly probable that such behaviors will be emitted.

3. The domain of behaviors is chosen to produce hypothetical relations with the stimuli presented.

All these design features of experiments and tests facilitate, among the other things, the identification of errors.

When Archie pointed to the picture of an igloo and said, "Eskimo," we were able to identify his response as a misnomer because: (1) the picture was a line drawing representing an igloo, and it was called an igloo by all the other children in Archie's class; (2) he had named correctly several pictures just previously, indicating that he was responding in accordance with Lisa's instructions to name the pictures; (3) we can identify a reasonable relationship between his response and the acceptable name, so we are led to regard his response as a "misnomer" rather than say, a "misperception"; (4) the tester corrected him in accordance with our instructions, indicating that she, as a participant in the session, also regarded the response as an error; and (5) Archie accepted the correction, saying, "Oh, yeh, Eskimo." Each kind of evidence is made available to us by virtue of the special organizational properties of testing sessions.

Environments such as cooking club differ from tests in several significant respects. Importantly, they are not designed to provide for displays of intellectual behavior that are intentionally graded and controlled so that somewhere in the proceedings the individual has to fail. Intellectual activity is rarely the goal in such settings. Instead, people have come together to construct some thing(s); although individual participants may be interested in creating situations in which someone else commits errors, a great deal more behavior is best interpreted as helping get the agreed-upon task accomplished (in our case, baking a cake). In the course of getting the task done, individuals provide a good deal of assistance to each other precisely because such assistance directly facilitates what they are doing.

The fact that many individuals are involved in such scenes is important, too. Their histories of interaction together provide the potential for many different problems to arise, problems that co-occur with cake baking. Although we believe that tests also embody many different tasks, as a rule, such tasks are ignored in analysis; they contribute to error variance. They are, however, amenable to the same kinds of analysis as any other cognitive task (see, for example, Cicourel, Jennings, Jennings, Leiter, MacKay, Mehan, & Roth, 1974). (We often alluded to this aspect of tests: Lisa was distressed by Archie's difficulties, displaying her task of testing Archie without making him so miserable that negative social sanctions were likely to occur.)

The club was not organized for the purpose of evaluating performance against intellectual criteria; yet, we were able to cull several instances of Archie's appearing "disabled" in just over two minutes. Our identification of his response, "stripeh," as a mispronunciation of "recipe" is a particularly useful case to discuss precisely because of the ways in which the context of its occurrence deviated from the constraints of formal tests. There was no task definable in the sense in which the formal test had called for him to name things. He was not pointing to anything, and there was nothing that we are able to detect in his field of vision resembling a recipe. Nor had he been naming things when he said "stripeh." Moreover, he gave no indication that his question was addressed to anyone in particular.

There are, nevertheless, aspects of Archie's behavior in this context that lead us to identify his response as a mispronunciation:

1. The formal properties of his response, "stripeh," are not recognizable as an English word or words. We have never heard Archie emit such an utterance on any other occasion, so it is at least reasonable to suppose that he mispronounced something. "Recipe" is a likely candidate if only because it resembles Archie's response phonetically.

2. The response occurred in an identifiable linguistic context, his question, "Oh, damn, where'd our stripeh? . . . " The term in question occurred in the place in his utterance appropriate for the name of an object. In addition, "where'd" indicates the absence of some thing that was present previously, and "our" indicates that there are more than one such thing in the vicinity, only one of which belongs to him.

3. Ricky returned from girl watching immediately on orienting to Archie's searching and laid the recipe on the table in front of Archie.

4. Archie's search terminated at the moment he said "stripeh," *and* picked up the recipe. His quickness in retrieving the recipe suggests that the recipe was the object in question.

5. We have often observed Archie referrring to the recipe. For instance, he referred to it for instructions to steps two and three after he completed steps one and two, respectively.

It should be clear to most readers that, however incomplete this list, it is possible to build a rather strong case for claiming that Archie's response, "stripeh," was a mispronunciation. It is possible to do so, moreover, even though the club was not arranged for the purpose of making such errors salient.

There is a second difference between clubs and tests that is relevant to the issues we are addressing. In clubs, the behavior of Archie or of any of the other children is likely to modify their environments in ways that facilitate whatever actions are in progress. But in tests, the environment has been prearranged. The prearrangements determine the response of the environment within constraints over which the subject has minimal control. This frequently gives the interactional dynamics of tests a very peculiar caste. For example, when Lisa gave Archie the similarity pair "turnip-carrot," Archie's response was the "unacceptable" question, "What's a turnip?" Lisa's reply, "Well, suppose I said, turnip, carrot, and onion?" was clearly governed by the testing format, the rules under which she was operating for purposes of making the test work. It is important to note, too, that there is an excellent example of Archie's soliciting help to deal with a difficult problem. In this setting, however, with rules operating to restrict the kinds of help that Lisa can legitimately give, his effort failed.

Learning Disabilities

What emerges with special clarity from the comparative analysis of Archie in different settings is that we cannot understand either his behavior or comparative terms like "similarity" or "difference" that may be attributed to that behavior if we fail to appreciate that we are always describing an organism-environment interaction: Archie acts on his environment, which acts on him.

When we characterize Archie's behavior interactively, we lose faith in the notion that he can be characterized as an organism with fixed attributes. To say that he suffers a particular "memory deficit" or that he is "distractible" turns out to be a statement about the structure of certain interactions he has with only some of the multiple environments he encounters. The use of psychological trait names itself is made possible and plausible because of shared (if poorly analyzed) ideas about the interactions that are possible in those special contexts (tests, for example) that are the criterion settings in which we substantiate labels such as "learning disabled." Without the kind of careful context description that we have struggled with in our work, such terms are static snapshots of a presumably fixed, universally representative environment. It is a mistake to treat the variable factors that organize the contexts producing judgments like "learning disabled" as universal. Because contexts are not universal, descriptions predicated on universality lead inexorably to contradiction.

These remarks frame the implications of our work for the field of learning disabilities. We have tried to make clear that the study of learning disabilities is not our focus, but rather serves as an occasion for solving general problems in cognitive psychology. The implications we can legitimately draw about learning disabilities are understandably limited on this account. However, certain of our observations seem to speak directly to current controversies in that field of research.

First, assuming that there is some generality to our analysis of Archie and his friends, there should be no mystery about the inconsistencies in the application of the diagnostic categories used to describe specific learning disabilities, nor in the supposedly school-based nature of learning disabilities. Both the diagnostic inconsistencies and context dependencies arise from a single source: the fact that different contexts place different constraints on people in terms of which they are permitted (or encouraged) to behave.

By virtue of their socially designated purposes, psychometric tests (and, to a great extent, the school settings in which they predict behavior) seriously restrict the possibilities of organizing conditions for achieving the solutions of the problems posed. Those constraints are part of the task-as-constructed. It is "cheating" to engage in activities that reduce the difficulty of the task. Even so, we can see rudimentary forms of such behaviors in experimental contexts where they appear as "deviations from standard procedure."

It is of interest that our classification of the behavior we see Archie engaging in has a rough parallel in the psychometric literature on learning disabilities. Several investigators (Smith et al., 1977; Traupman & Goldberg, 1979) have pointed out a special patterning in the psychometric test performance of learning-disabled children: a profile of very low scores on tasks involving the holding of information in short-term store (digit substitution, backward memory span), but better-than-average scores on "spatial" subtests. This finding is the essential byproduct of the definition of specific learning disabilities which emphasizes that such children have "normal IQ's." Low scores on part of the test must be balanced by high scores elsewhere.

We know from his diagnostician as well as our own observation of his behavior in our test-like settings that Archie demonstrates this typical learning disability profile. What our cooking club observations yield is a new understanding of the implications of this profile in terms of everyday problem-solving environments. The club setting provides a richer and more detailed notion of what is specific to a specific learning disability. Observations in all the settings from which we have data indicate that Archie frequently misperceives, misnames, and so on. Yet, he steadfastly, almost doggedly, sticks to the task. In doing so, he makes dramatically visible the distinction between general and specific disabilities.

We believe that these observations merit systematic study. For example, some training programs for the learning disabled place them in small, soundproof cubicles to help them learn, free of the distractions of irrelevant stimuli. Even when such isolation proves effective in speeding the acquisition of certain information-processing skills, without supplementary arrangements, such prosthetic environments are not likely to deal comprehensively with the problems facing a child like Archie. Instead, we recommend a program that simultaneously teaches children to make the relevant kinds of discriminations when faced with important tasks such as word recognition and retention while allowing them to exploit existing skills in a flexible manner to deal with the multiple goals that such information-processing activities typically service outside of the sound proof cubicle.

It also seems sensible to arrange environments that overtly reinforce Archie for his successful intellectual behavior. Finally, although Archie's failures are often given attention, his success in organizing his own and others' behavior to deal with the tasks confronting him frequently goes unnoticed. As a result, Archie often has to work to conceal his difficulties and to deal with other people's attempts to make an issue of them. In part, the emphasis on errors can be attributed to the possibility that they are more easily detectable than his successes, but it also seems that Archie's difficulties are an occasional source of reinforcement for his peers (points discussed at greater length in Hood, McDermott, & Cole, Note 1). It is often suggested (e.g., Estes, 1970) that educational programs should build on students' strengths, not their weaknesses. Our investigation of Archie has suggested some specific ways in which this therapeutic goal might be accomplished.

Comparative Cognitive Research

In closing we want to consider briefly the problems in comparative cognitive research that made studying the behavior of a learning-disabled child in different settings seem a promising analytic vehicle.

It should be clear to the reader, as it is to us, that we have failed to produce a general set of rules for identifying the environment-person relations of the sort that we have labeled cognitive tasks. We cannot even offer an abstract set of tasks that we believe relevant to an understanding of Archie. Some of our claims seem very compelling—claims about mispronunciations, for example. Others seem less compelling—the claim that "those things" resembles the misnomers that we encountered in various tests, or the claims to the effect that many of Archie's behaviors recruited help in anticipation of difficulties with a next step of the recipe. The underlying logic in all of these cases is, we believe, the same, but the implementation of this logic varies greatly from one case to another. In all cases, we come to our analysis with some notion of relevant environmental events and potentially appropriate behaviors. The sources of these notions are quite varied. They may come from shared knowledge (often implicit) of the rules of English phonology; they may come from some notion of appropriate levels of specificity in naming objects so that a listener will be able to identify the referent from all other objects; they may come from hypotheses about recipes and the steps in making a cake. Whatever their source, these ideas about the environments for behaving and how responses are related to the environment become our claims about "cognitive tasks."

We have pointed out that, in all settings, behavior is multiply determined; that is, the environment consists of several tasks co-occuring with *the* task in which a person (subject) is engaged. This statement is as true when our data come from specially constructed experimental tasks as it is when we observe behavior in clubs. As experimental psychologists, we tend to forget this fact. For us, the experiment specifies what behaviors are relevant to our analysis. It gives us our dependent variables, as we like to say. In this sense, the experiment is a ready-made coding scheme.

We know, of course, that we omit a great deal of behavior from our descriptions. We also know that our specification of the task can be incorrect. One way of handling this untidiness is to interpret it as part of the error term in an analysis of variance. Another is to run a new experiment that more accurately creates the model system that we assume characterizes the subject-stimulus interaction. Of course, some scientists, even some psychologists think that these procedures simply sweep trouble under the rug. Our oversights as experimenters usually begins to bother us most when someone comes along and claims that our error terms are masking important phenomena; but, because these inadequacies are difficult to deal with and because they are often seen as irrelevant to our concerns with identifying a cognitive process, they receive little systematic attention (we have in mind here work such as that of Cicourel et al., 1974).

We cannot provide a complete specification of all the tasks that Archie engaged in when we observed him (although, as a tour de force, such ethnographers as McDermott, Gospodinoff, & Aron (1978) can take that enterprise surprisingly far). But, because complete specification is not a likely outcome of cognitive research based on experimental manipulations either, this shortcoming of observational studies should not bring enterprises like the current one to a halt. Instead, we must content ourselves with specifying one or more of the tasks that a person is engaged in at any point in our analysis. This specification will always be incomplete. But, the incompleteness of our analysis need not stop the enterprise. If our procedures provide us with interpretable regularities, we can leave to our critics the job of demonstrating how a fuller specification of the tasks at hand will change the conclusions we draw on the basis of our analyses.

This viewpoint has some clear-cut implications for the problems in cross-cultural research that were our starting point. First, it should be evident that it is hopeless to go looking in everyday life for cognitive tasks in general. Nor does the standard tool kit of the cognitive psychologist with its well-defined problems, puzzles, categorized lists, and word associations represent "cognitive tasks in general." The primary environment that we use as the source for cognitive tasks, the school, did not arise by accident; it is an historically conditioned system of interaction with a variety of purposes. Those purposes include the preservation and propagation of cultural knowledge, the supply of labor to modern industrial society, and the sorting of people into varied social roles (this list is intended as illustrative, not exhaustive, cf. Tyack, 1974). If we want to see how exposure to the tasks that arise in an institutionalized setting such as the school affects behavior in other settings (the home, the supermarket, the office) *we must go to those other settings* to determine: (1) if the social organization of behavior there allows for the occurrence of the tasks that we have hypothesized are occuring at our source point; and (2) how people behave in the everyday contexts of occurrence of those tasks.

We should not embark on such an enterprise convinced that we will encounter behavior organized to fit our template-like notion of a cognitive task. For example, we may find that air-traffic controllers have to deal with an environment that involves something like a keeping-track memory task; but, we may not. Rarely could we identify tasks in the clubs using standard cognitive-psychological notions of what a task might be. Should we decide to undertake such an enterprise, two comments seem in order. First, it would be foolish to go looking for cognitive tasks at random. Instead, looking should be constrained to places where our knowledge of the culture tells us that such tasks might occur and where we have a theory of the relevance of experience in one setting for experience in another. When we constructed the cooking club, we had hypothesized, albeit incorrectly, that school tasks would frequently arise in cooking club. We followed this latter strategy more successfully (in terms of finding what we went in looking for) in our recent work on the consequences of learning to read and write (Scribner & Cole, 1978). In that work, we found no "general intellectual consequences" of literate practice. But, when we observed behavior in settings involving literacy, and created detailed model tasks that embodied our notions of what such literate practice might entail, discernible transfer of performance from one socially organized setting for a task to another was detected.

Second, as the previous remarks suggest, when we got into a new setting to study behavior and we are interested in its relation to a previously analyzed setting, we cannot take for granted that the system of activity we call a cognitive task will occur. By virtue of the enduring functions of different domains of activity, they are unlikely to result in the organizations that we are terming cognitive tasks in the same way. Even if something like the same task seems discernible, many of its details may be changed because the constraints on participants that organize the task will vary. This variability will not defeat us unless we demand *a priori identity* of tasks across settings (as we did at the outset of this project). Instead, if our interest is in some real-life domain of activity that we hypothesize to be relevant to, say, the experience of schooling, then we must be willing to study it with the same care that we have put into analyzing cake baking. If we proceed in this way, we can indeed carry out research on such matters as the cognitive consequences of education, but, the objects of our analysis will be tasks-as-organized-in-the-scenes-of-their-everyday-occurrence, not tasks-as-organized-in-tests. That latter strategy will work only in the rare occurrence of identity of larger contexts that are a part of both settings. Not accidently, we hope, this conclusion brings us around to the point of view expressed by Brown and French (1979) in their comments on our cross-cultural work. In response to the difficulties we have belabored here, Brown and French suggest that

> what is needed to clarify the ambiguity (of research based on school-like tasks) is an examination of situations which require schooled and unschooled partici-pants to learn new tasks unrelated to the activities fostered by either schooling or the occupational skills of the unschooled adult [p. 106].

They suggest, further, that metacognitive skills (checking and self-monitoring activity as in "What is the first step?") should be the object of study, because such skills are likely to be relevant to many settings. This suggestion would fit neatly with our observations of Archie, because the activities we have described in terms of active control map so well onto Brown and French's conception of metacognitive skills. However, Brown and French assume that if we pick the right levels of analysis (in their case, analysis of metacognitive activity), we can proceed on the basis of already accepted methods. We believe that whatever the level of analysis, be it mispronunciations or plans, a careful description of the contexts of occurrence is necessary. If such analysis is not carried out, we are not likely to be able to make well-grounded claims about cognition, plain or "meta." This process of describing the tasks that people construct for themselves and each other as part of their lives in society is the enterprise that we (Laboratory of Comparative Human Cognition, 1979) have called elsewhere an "ethnographic psychology of cognition".

Finally, our analysis of thinking in test, club, and classroom has, somewhat unexpectedly, highlighted one hallmark of modern cognitive psychology, the active organism. It has done so in an unusual manner: by contrasting behavior across settings and positing the within-setting factors that control between-setting variation. In attempting to understand Archie's behavior in the club setting we were forced to consider the many ways in which he actively modifies his problem environment. Once alerted to the pervasiveness of such behaviors in the club environment, we were encouraged to reexamine the experimental and classroom contexts. They were there to be seen, but only upon rather close observation.

This asymmetrical situation, in which the experiment highlights one form of interaction and the club another, has far reaching consequences for cognitive psychology in its attempt to characterize the active nature of human cognitive functioning. Experiments, the contexts constructed to make behavior analyzable, are also contexts that discourage the expression of active, adaptive behaviors. This point was made many years ago by one of the few genuine interactive cognitive theorists, L. S. Vygotsky (1978) who pointed out that:

> All stimulus-response methods [which in this context refer to all standard experiments in the tradition following Wundt] share the inadequacy that Engels ascribes to naturalistic approaches in history. Both see the relation between human behavior and nature as unidirectionally reactive. My collaborators and I, however, believe that human behavior comes to have that "transforming reaction on nature" which Engels attributed to tools. We must, then, seek methods adequate to our conception [p. 61].

If our analysis in this chapter has a future, that future will have to include the invention of new experimental and analytic techniques that permit a principled study of *interaction* in addition to *reaction*.

ACKNOWLEDGMENTS

Early phases of this research were conducted collaboratively with L. Hood, R. P. McDermott and Carla Seal to whom we are indebted for their invaluable insights. Conduct of the research and preparation of the manuscript were made possible by a Grant from the Carnegie Corporation.

REFERENCES

Brown, A. L., & French, L. A. Commentary on education and cognitive develoment. *Monographs of the Society for Research in Child Development,* 1979, Serial No. 178, Vol. 44, Nos. 1–2, p. 101–109.

Charlesworth, W. R. Ethology: Its relevance for observational studies of human adapatation. In G. P. Sackett (Ed.) *Observing behavior* (Vol. I). Baltimore: University Park Press, 1978.

Cicourel, A. V., Jennings, K. H., Jennings, S. H. M., Leiter, K. C. W., MacKay, R., Mehan, H., & Roth, D. R. *Language use and school performance.* New York: Academic Press, 1974.

Cole, M., Gay, J. A., Glick, J., & Sharp, D. W. *The cultural context of learning and thinking.* New York: Basic Books, 1971.

Cole, M., Hood, L., & McDermott, R. P. *Ecological niche picking: Ecological invalidity as an axiom of cognitive psychology.* Technical Report. Laboratory of Comparative Human Cognition. 1978.

Estes, W. K. *Learning theory and mental development.* New York: Academic Press, 1970.

Goodnow, J. J. Rules and repertoires, rituals and tricks of the trade: Social and informational aspects to cognitive and representational development. In .S. Farnham-Diggory (Ed.), *Information processing in children.* New York: Academic Press, 1972.

Griffin, P., Cole, M. & Newman, D. Locating tasks in psychology and education. *Discourse Processes,* (in press).

Laboratory of Comparative Human Cognition. What's cultural about cross-cultural cognitive psychology? *Annual Review of Psychology,* 1979, *30,* 145–172.

Leontiev, A. N. Studies in the cultural development of the child. *Journal of Genetic Psychology,* 1932, *40,* 52–83.

Luria, A. R. The problem of the cultural behavior of the child. *Journal of Genetic Psychology,* 1928, *35,* 493–506.

McDermott, R. P., Gospodinoff, K. & Aron, J. Criteria for an ethnographically adequate description of concerted activities and their contexts. *Semiotica,* 1978, *24.*

Scribner, S. & Cole, M. Literacy without schooling: Testing for intellectual effects. *Harvard Educational Review,* 1978, *48* (4), 448–461.

Sharp, D. W., Cole, M. & Lave, C. Education and cognitive development. *Monographs of the Society for Research in Child Development,* 1979, Serial No. 178, Vol. 44, Nos. 1–2.

Smith, M. D., Coleman, J. M., Dokecki, P. R., & Davis, E. F. Recategorized WISC-R scores of learning disabled children. *Journal of Learning Disabilities,* 1977, *10,* 437–443.

Traupmann, K. & Goldberg, N. *The relationship between WISC subscale patterns and tests of underlying memory processes in learning disabled children.* Unpublished manuscript, University of California, San Diego, 1979.

Tyack, D. *The one best system: A history of American urban education.* Cambridge: Harvard University Press, 1974.

Vygotsky, L. S. *Mind in Society: The Development of Higher Psychological Process,* M. Cole, V. John-Steiner, S. Scribner, & E. Souberman (Eds.). Cambridge, Mass.: Harvard University Press 1978.

5 Intrinsic and Extrinsic Motivation in Children: Detrimental Effects of Superfluous Social Controls

Mark R. Lepper
Stanford University

My goal in this chapter is to present an overview of a research program concerned with the effectiveness of different techniques of social control in influencing a person's behavior in subsequent situations in which salient extrinsic controls are minimal. In particular, I wish to examine some of the conditions under which initially successful, but functionally unnecessary, social-control techniques—involving the use of rewards, threats of punishment, and other forms of extrinsic constraint—may sometimes have detrimental effects on subsequent behavior in settings in which such external constraints are no longer salient.

My more specific aims are several: First, I wish to describe briefly a set of studies concerned with the effects of threats of punishmnent on children's "internalization" of adult prohibitions and their behavior in subsequent situations in the absence of further prohibitions. Second, I wish to consider in greater detail more recent research concerned with the effects of extrinsic rewards on children's subsequent intrinsic interest in the activities for which rewards had been previously offered. Both lines of investigation, I wish to suggest, provide evidence that the use of unnecessarily powerful techniques of social control to achieve initial compliance with an adult request may lead to lessened later internalization or subsequent intrinsic interest.

After sketching out these two lines of research, I wish to place this research in a broader context—to make clear that the phenomena examined in these studies are only a small (though, I think, an interesting) part of the larger picture of the ways in which social-influence attempts may affect subsequent behavior and the factors that determine the effects of extrinsic incentives on subsequent behavior. Finally, I wish to conclude with some speculations on potential differences in the dynamics of the effects of rewards and punishments and possible implications of this work for traditional issues in the study of the socialization process.

INTERNALIZATION VERSUS COMPLIANCE: THE EFFECTS OF THREATS OF PUNISHMENT ON CHILDREN'S INTERNALIZATION OF ADULT PROHIBITIONS

There is, of course, a long history in social and developmental psychology to the distinction between compliance and internalization, and to the underlying premise that techniques that are most effective in eliciting immediate "compliance" with some request or command will not always be those most likely to produce "internalized" changes in attitudes or values that would affect behavior in subsequent situations where one's actions are no longer under the immediate control of the stimuli that produced initial compliance. In social psychology, this distinction appears first in experimental work in Lewin's group-dymanics laboratory—in demonstrations, for example, that children's groups run by dictatorial and authoritarian leaders will be more productive and less overtly aggressive, as long as the leader is present, but less productive and more aggressive than other sorts of groups as soon as the leader exercising this power is absent (Lewin, Lippitt, & White, 1939). Over the years, comparable distinctions have also appeared in the study of conformity and attitude change (Hovland, Janis, & Kelley, 1953; Kelman, 1958, 1961), dissonance theory (Aronson, 1969; Festinger, 1957), and attribution and self-perception processes (Bem, 1967, 1972; Kelley, 1967, 1973). In developmental psychology, similar issues have been a persistent focus of investigations concerned with children's internalization of adult values—standards that permit children to inhibit antisocial behavior (Sears, Whiting, Nowlis, & Sears, 1953) and promote their acquisition of moral standards (Hoffman, 1970, 1975) or prosocial behavior patterns (Rosenhan, 1969; Staub, 1978, 1979). Yet, despite its central theoretical significance, this problem has received surprisingly little empirical investigation.

The "Insufficient-Justification" Paradigm

My own concern with generalized effects of social controls derived initially from an interest in a now-classic series of studies in social psychology that examined the effects of more and less severe threats of punishment used to induce children to comply with an initial adult prohibition of a particular activity on children's later evaluation of that previously prohibited activity and their later behavior in similar settings in which further prohibitions were lacking. Let us begin with a consideration of this work.

The paradigmatic study in this area, by Aronson and Carlsmith (1963), can be summarized simply. Preschool children were first asked to rank a number of desirable toys in terms of their relative attractiveness. Then, under a suitable pretext, the experimenter indicated that he would need to leave the child alone briefly. During that period, the experimenter continued, the child would be free to play with all of the toys, except one particularly attractive toy that he or she was not to touch. For half of the children, this initial prohibition was accompanied by a relatively "mild" threat of punishment for disobedience—the experimenter indicated that he would be annoyed if the child were to play with the forbidden toy in his absence. For other children, this prohibition was accompanied by a much more severe threat—the experimenter indicated that he would be very angry and might tell the child's teacher, or leave the school, if the child transgressed. Importantly, by means of careful pretesting, the mild-threat procedure was selected to be sufficient, though barely so, to induce all children to comply with the prohibition. Hence, the severe-threat procedure added yet further, but functionally superfluous, justification for not playing with the forbidden toy. At the end of the temptation period, during which all children did, indeed, comply with the prohibition, children's personal preferences for the different toys were then reassessed. The study showed that children who had resisted the temptation to play with the forbidden toy under mild threat of punishment were significantly more likely to devalue or derogate that toy than children in the severe-threat condition.

Within a dissonance framework, these preferences were conceptualized as a function of the amount of justification provided by the two threat manipulations for the child to refrain from engaging in an activity he or she would normally have enjoyed—a response that was otherwise inconsistent with the child's prior attitudes. When the child is provided with compelling external justification for not playing with this attractive toy, as in the severe-threat conditions, he or she should experience little dissonance about the decision to comply with the adult's request; when the external justification is minimal and psychologically "insufficient" (Aronson, 1969), dissonance will be produced. One way of reducing this dissonance, the theory suggested, would be to decide that the activity is itself not worth undertaking—to bring one's private attitudes into line with one's overt behavior. These findings were of particular interest, of course, because they appeared to contradict a simplistic associationistic view that the pairing of an activity with a more powerful threat of punishment would increase subsequent compliance with the prohibition of that activity. The results presupposed an active and cognitive, rather than a passive and automatic, response to temptation.

At the time I became interested in this work, considerable further research had already been conducted using this basic "forbidden-toy" paradigm. These studies both attested to the strength and persistence of these effects over time (e.g., Freedman, 1965; Pepitone, McCauley, & Hammond, 1967; Turner &

Wright, 1965) and demonstrated that children's subsequent behavior, as well as their reported attitudes, towards the previously forbidden activity was influenced by the strength of the prior prohibition. In the most impressive of these follow-up studies, Freedman (1965) showed significant increases in avoidance of the prohibited toy among mild-threat subjects some 6 weeks later, when these children were tested by another adult in a very different setting in which they were only inadvertently confronted with an opportunity to play with any or all of the toys they had previously encountered. Increased avoidance of the toy was not apparent, however, under either mild- or severe-threat conditions when the children had been kept under close surveillance by the experimenter during the initial "temptation period." These data suggested that it was the experience of resisting temptation under conditions of minimal justificiation, and not the specific content of the two threats of punishment, that led to later devaluation and continued avoidance of the activity in the absence of further constraints.

These impressive behavioral consequences, obtained in a different setting weeks after the initial experimental sessions, suggested that these studies might have significant implications for our understanding of children's internalization of attitudes and values. Yet, this work seemed to provide little evidence concerning the processes presumed to underlie such effects; it was to this general issue that our initial studies were addressed.

Cognitive Processes in the "Forbidden-Toy" Situation

In the first of these, Mark Zanna, Bob Abelson, and I (Lepper, Zanna, & Abelson, 1970) posed a relatively straightforward question. If the devaluation of the forbidden activity in these prior studies were the result of an active process of justification of one's behavior during the temptation period, should not the effects of external justification provided to induce initial compliance differ from the effects of identical justifications provided to the child only after the temptation period? Indeed, if children in the mild-threat condition were motivated to reduce the dissonance aroused by their own behavior during the temptation period, might subsequent justifications for their actions, provided only after the fact, not prove functionally irrelevant to their later attitudes and actions?

To address these issues experimentally, kindergarten children were presented with a typical forbidden-toy procedure, in which they were asked not to play with an attractive toy during the experimenter's absence under either a relatively mild or a more severe threat of punishment for transgression. Then, to provide further justification consistent with a decision not to transgress, experimental subjects were provided with "consensus" information concerning their behavior (Kelley, 1967)—that is, they were told that other children in similar situations had all complied with the experimenter's requests not to play with particular toys. For half the subjects, this consensual

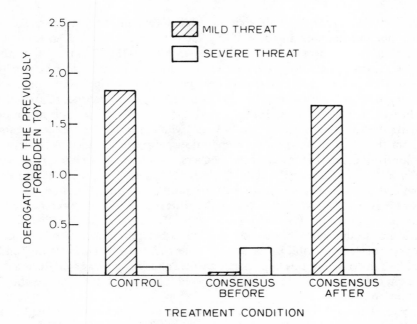

FIG. 5.1.   Mean derogation of the previously forbidden toy, by conditions.
Data from Lepper, Zanna, and Abelson (1970).

justification was provided before the temptation period; for the other half, exactly the same information was provided immediately after the temptation period. Control subjects received no such information. Subsequently, children's evaluations of the toys they had encountered were assessed by a second, "blind" experimenter.

The results of this procedure appear in Fig. 5.1 and provide relatively compelling evidence that the processes underlying derogation of the forbidden activity do indeed occur during the temptation period. The control conditions to the left of the Fig. establish a difference between mild- and severe-threat conditions in the absence of consensus information, paralleling the results of previous studies. The experimental conditions beside them indicate that when consensual justification was added to the threat manipulation prior to the temptation period, this additional justification was sufficient to prevent devaluation of the forbidden activity under mild threat; but, this same information, if provided after the temptation period, seemed to have little effect on subjects' attitudes towards the activity.

Having established that the processes underlying derogation in this setting seem to occur during the temptation interval, we were led to ask how these processes might be examined more directly. Suppose, for example, that the child's attention could be drawn explicitly to the salient ingredients of this conflictful situation—the attractive forbidden toy and the fact that the child was not playing with this toy. If, by such a procedure, children could be induced to perform more "cognitive work"—to think more about the dilemma presented—one might expect derogation of the forbidden activity to be further enhanced. In two studies designed to examine this proposition, we attempted to draw the child's attention to this basic conflict (Carlsmith, Ebbesen, Lepper, Zanna, Joncas, & Abelson, 1969). In one, this attention manipulation took the form of a "janitor" who appeared in the experimental room unexpectedly during the temptation period, ostensibly to retrieve a chair from the room for one of the teachers. As he did so, the janitor excused himself for interrupting the child and indicated causally to the child that he or she had a nice bunch of toys. In the forced-attention condition, however, the janitor also added, conversationally, the critical question: "How come you're not playing with this (i.e., the forbidden) toy?" In a conceptual replication of this first study, salience was manipulated rather differently. The forbidden toy was placed on a table by the experimenter, next to a "defective lamp," and, for half the subjects, this lamp began to buzz and flicker on and off during the temptation period, illuminating the forbidden toy and drawing the child's attention to it.

The results of these two studies were quite comparable, though not precisely in accord with out expectations, and are presented in Fig. 5.2. Whereas our expectation had been that increasing salience of the forbidden toy would enhance derogation for mild-threat subjects, who should presumably experience the situation as dissonance provoking, we had not expected that this manipulation would affect the responses of severe-threat subjects. As Fig. 5.2 clearly indicates, however, derogation of the forbidden activity was increased by this procedure in both the mild- and severe-threat conditions.

With the wisdom of hindsight, however, it seemed to us that perhaps these unanticipated results were not completely inconsistent with our basic formulation. Perhaps by making salient the forbidden toy, without at the same time reinstating the threatened punishment that would follow if the child were to transgress, we had simply magnified the dissonance produced in this situation for all subjects. By this account, the forced-attention manipulation should have differential effects as a function of the threat manipulation only if the level of initial threat were also made salient at the time the child's attention is drawn to the forbidden toy. In this case, a salience manipulation should magnify the effects of dissonance only within the mild-threat condition.

To examine this argument, one further study was conducted (Zanna, Lepper, & Abelson, 1973). As before, children were asked not to play with one of a set of attractive toys under either mild or severe threat of punishment. In this study, however, as the experimenter delivered the prohibition against

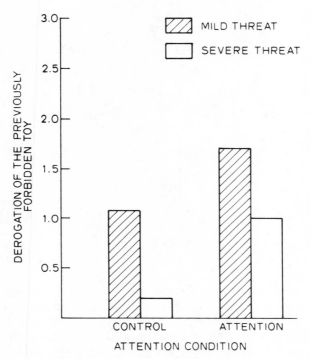

FIG. 5.2.   Mean derogation of the previously forbidden toy, by conditions, Experiments 1 and 2 combined. Data from Carlsmith et al. (1969).

playing with the forbidden toy, he placed a large sticker on the side of the toy facing the child, as a "reminder" to the child that this was the toy he or she was not to play with, and restated the critical threat manipulation. Subsequently, during the temptation period, our familiar janitor entered the room, retrieved an extra chair, and commented on the toys. For half the subjects, however, the janitor casually added the critical question: "How come this (i.e., the forbidden) toy is up here on the table?" Following the temptation period, children's relative preferences for the various toys were again assessed by a second experimenter.

The results of this experiment—in which the procedure employed to call the child's attention to the forbidden toy was explicitly designed to remind the child simultaneously of the threat delivered at the time the toy had been forbidden—appear in Fig. 5.3. In this case, our manipulation of subjects' attention had quite different effects within the two threat conditions. For subjects in the mild-threat conditions, derogation of the forbidden toy was increased; for subjects in the severe-threat conditions, a nonsignificant trend in the opposite direction was observed.

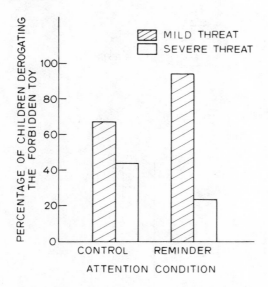

FIG. 5.3.   Percentage of children derogating the forbidden toy, by conditions. Data from Zanna, Lepper, and Abelson (1973).

Taken together, these studies suggested to us that the devaluation of a previously forbidden activity observed so consistently in this paradigm was the result of an active cognitive process that served to justify the child's own resolution not to play with the prohibited activity under conditions of minimal external pressure. Additional justification provided following the temptation period appeared to have no effects on the devaluation process, and manipulations designed to focus the child's attention during this period on either the forbidden activity itself or the activity and the threat of punishment that accompanied its prohibition appeared to influence children's responses in a systematic fashion, consistent with our basic hypotheses.

Producing Internalization of More General Values

At the same time, more informal observations over the course of these studies also suggested the possibility of an even more general effect of exposure to the "insufficient" justification provided children in the mild-threat conditions of these studies. Under mild-, but not severe-, threat conditions, a number of children spontaneously volunteered to the second experimenter, following the temptation period, comments suggesting that they had been "good" boys or girls—e.g., that they had not played with the forbidden toy, that they had done just what the other man asked, or that they had done things "just right." Such seemingly self-congratulatory responses, of course, may have many potential meanings. The possibility that interested us most, however, was that these responses represented an alternative or additional means of justifying or explaining one's resistance to temptation in the absence of salient external constraints. Clearly, the conflict involved in resisting temptation is less if one decides the forbidden activity is not very attractive. Perhaps a decision that it is really important to obey adult requests or that the ability to resist temptation reflects something good about oneself may similarly reduce the conflict the child experiences in this situation.

Such a possibility seemed reminiscent of one account offered by Freedman and Fraser (1966) to explain the unexpected cross-situational generality of what they termed the "foot-in-the-door" effect—an increase in subsequent compliance with a large request produced following prior compliance with a much smaller request. In their study, housewives were asked first to comply with a seemingly trivial request, either to place a small placard in their window or to sign a relatively innocuous petition, on one of two rather (at the time) noncontroversial issues—promoting auto safety or saving the California redwoods. Virtually all subjects complied. Several weeks later, these same subjects were contacted by a different individual and were all asked to comply with a much larger request—to place a 6' × 12' hand-painted and rather ugly billboard reading "Drive Safely" on their lawns for the next few weeks. Compared to subjects who had not been originally contacted with an initial smaller request, all of the prior-compliance conditions showed significant increases in the likelihood of agreeing to this second request. Most striking was the fact that even those subjects who had initially complied with a smaller request on a different issue showed increased compliance with this later request: Virtually half of the subjects asked to sign a petition to keep California beautiful subsequently agreed to have the safe driving billboard placed on their lawn. Perhaps, Freedman and Fraser speculated, compliance with the initial request may have led subjects to view themselves as more altruistic or public spirited or to see such campaigns as generally more significant and important.

Might not a similar process be involved in children's reactions to the forbidden-toy paradigm under conditions of mild threats of punishment? The key question, clearly, was whether exposure to this situation would have effects on their later behavior in different, though conceptually related, situations involving adherence to adult standards in the absence of salient external coercion. Such effects would have important implications for understanding the development of internalized standards and controls.

To examine these generalized consequences of initial compliance elicited under varying levels of initial justification required an experimental procedure in which children were seen in two ostensibly unrelated experimental sessions (Lepper, 1973). The first of these sessions involved the same basic paradigm as our previous studies. Second-grade children were asked not to play with particular, highly attractive toy under the threat of either a mild or a severe punishment for transgression, with predictable results. Relative to the severe-threat conditions, mild-threat subjects were significantly more likely to rate the specific previously forbidden toy as less inherently attractive following the temptation period, as in prior experiments. To permit us, in addition, to assess the later effects of both threat procedures relative to an appropriate baseline, a no-prohibition control condition was added to the design.

Several weeks later, these same children were seen in a second experimental session, conducted by a different and ostensibly unrelated experimenter in a different part of the school. In this second session, children were presented with another common, but quite distinct, test of resistance to temptation.

Specifically, children were asked to play a bowling game, presented as a test of skill, but in which their scores were actually programmed in advance. The children were asked, and shown how, to keep score for themselves and were informed that if they obtained a sufficiently high score on the game, they would be allowed to choose a reward for themselves from among a collection of attractive small prizes—e.g., dolls, flashlights, toy cars, etc.—and were then left alone to play the game in the experimenter's absence. The score each child obtained, however, fell just short of that required to win a prize; hence, children could obtain the reward only by falsifying their actual scores at the game.

In contrast to the first session, in which great care was taken to ensure that all children would be able to resist temptation, this second situation was intentionally designed, after substantial pretesting, to elicit transgression from roughly half of the children—through the use of quite attractive rewards for transgression and the creation of a setting in which children believed that the experimenter would have no possible way of knowing how they had actually performed in her absence. The prizes offered, moreover, were deliberately chosen to be quite different from the toys employed in the initial session to ensure that any differences in behavior in this second session were not some simple function of a differential attractiveness of the rewards across conditions.

This procedure, then, allowed us to examine the effects of prior compliance with an adult prohibition, in the face of either minimal or unnecessarily powerful external pressures, on subsequent resistance to temptation in a very different context in which children were confronted with the opportunity to transgress in the face of minimal external pressures with little probability of detection. The data from this second session are presented in Fig. 5.4, and provide some evidence consistent with our analysis. There is, specifically, a highly significant difference in subsequent resistance to temptation between the mild-threat and severe-threat conditions. Not only were mild-threat subjects more likely to show derogation of the particular toy that had been previously forbidden; they behaved more "honestly" in a different temptation

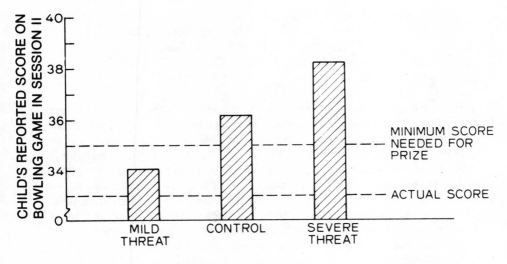

FIG. 5.4. Mean scores reported by children playing the bowling game in Session II, by condition. Data from Lepper (1973).

situation several weeks later, as well. Comparisons of both experimental conditions to the no-prohibition control condition, moreover, suggested an active effect of both treatments; children who had initially complied under mild-threat conditions proved more likely to resist temptation in this later setting, whereas children who had initially complied under severe-threat conditions tended to be less likely to resist this subsequent temptation.[1]

Prior compliance with an adult prohibition, it seemed, may breed later internalization of that specific prohibition and perhaps some more general values concerning compliance, but only when the external pressure used to promote initial compliance is relatively minimal. The same behavior elicited through the use of unnecessarily powerful external pressures, by contrast, seemed counterproductive; if anything, it produced an opposite effect.

---

[1]For purposes of presentation, these data are collapsed across a second factor—a procedure designed to minimize, for some subjects, initial derogation of the specific forbidden activity—because this variation had no effect on subsequent resistance to temptation (cf. Lepper, 1973, for further details).

INTRINSIC VERSUS EXTRINSIC MOTIVATION:
THE EFFECTS OF EXTRINSIC REWARDS
ON TASK PERFORMANCE AND
SUBSEQUENT INTRINSIC INTEREST

It is, in retrospect, a small conceptual leap from these last findings concerning the effects of variations in external pressures employed to induce initial compliance on subsequent internalization of the attitudes and values underlying the initial prohibition to the later work on extrinsic constraints and intrinsic interest that has formed the second focus of my research in this area. At the time, however, this step was not a trivial one. Two principal factors led me to consider the possibility that similar processes might be at work in these different domains: first, anecdotal observations on the use of tangible reward systems with preschool children, and second, the development of a broader theoretical framework in which both sets of findings appeared related.

That the inappropriate use of extrinsic rewards to "reinforce" activities of initial interest might have detrimental effects on subsequent intrinsic interest was first suggested to me by a set of informal observations of Project Headstart classrooms in which small-scale systematic reward programs were being used to induce children to engage, for brief periods each day, in activities deemed to be of particular academic value. Although amateurish in design, these reward programs were clearly effective in their principal aim of inducing task engagement during the designated reward periods. At the same time, however, these programs also appeared to define the actvities involved for the children as something to be done only when tangible rewards were available. Although the actvities themselves seemed to be of considerable "intrinsic" interest, in the absence of external constraints, to children in other classrooms where such reward systems were not present, children in those classes with these reward programs appeared to avoid the activities except during the specified reward periods. The potential parallel between this seeming detrimental effect of extrinsic rewards on intrinsic interest and the effects of superfluous extrinsic constraints on later internalization of adult values became clear, however, primarily as a result of shifts in the social–psychological literature that led us to reconsider the traditional "insufficient-justification" paradigm in attributional terms.

For more than a decade, Festinger's (1957) theory of cognitive dissonance had provided the dominant theoretical paradigm for interpreting the effects of compliance in the face of different sorts of external pressures on subsequent attitude change or internalization of values (cf. Lepper, in press). At the time of our own work on children's reactions to adult prohibitions, however, an alternative formulation of some of these findings within the framework of attribution or self-perception theory was beginning to obtain currency (Bem, 1967; Kelley, 1967). A person's attitudes towards an activity or entity, in this view, were seen as determined partly by the individual's prior behavior towards that entity and the reasons he or she assumed or inferred to underlie those actions.

Dissonance theory had focused on the motivational effects of behavior that was clearly at variance with one's previous attitudes or beliefs and had, therefore, implied that variations in external pressure or constraint should affect subsequent attitudes only when the behavior in question was aversive, or otherwise inconsistent with one's prior beliefs. The attribution or self-perception model, however, suggested that such effects might be considerably more general. In this reinterpretation (Bem, 1967, 1972; Kelley, 1967, 1973), to the extent that external constraints and contingencies controlling one's behavior are salient, unambiguous, and sufficient to explain one's actions, a person will be likely to attribute his or her actions to these compelling constraints. If, on the other hand, the external contingencies in a particular situation are seen as weak, unclear, or psychologically insufficient to account for one's actions, the person will be more likely to attribute those actions to his or her own dispositions, attitudes, or interests. Under low-justification conditions, therefore, subjects will be likely to view their own prior actions as reflections of their own preferences and standards; under high-justification conditions, they will be more likely to see their previous behavior as controlled and determined by the extrinsic constraints in the situation.

In many respects, the dissonance and attribution accounts of this prior literature have proved indistinguishable (cf. Greenwald, 1975), although recent data suggest that there may be reasons to prefer the dissonance interpretation of the insufficient-justification literature (e.g., Fazio, Zanna, & Cooper, 1977; Zanna & Cooper, 1976). The important contribution of the attribution account generally and its specific relevance to our own research program, however, lay in its implication that conceptually analogous effects of variations in the external justification provided to induce compliance might occur even when the actions involved were not overtly inconsistent with one's initial attitudes or beliefs.

Hence, this account provided one possible explanation for our Headstart observations suggesting a potential deleterious effect of extrinsic rewards on later intrinsic interest for children for whom the activities being reinforced were of initial inherent interest. The addition of unnecessary extrinsic constraints may have led these children to view their engagement in these activities as extrinsically, rather than intrinsically, motivated and, therefore, to see the activity as less inherently interesting in the later absence of salient extrinsic rewards.

The "Overjustification" Paradigm

More generally, this view suggested that the use of unnecessarily powerful or salient techniques of social control—even of a seemingly benign sort, such as the addition of attractive rewards contingent upon engagement in a task of inherent interest—in order to induce an individual to engage in an activity of initial interest may, in effect, undermine that individual's later interest in the activity per se, when extrinsic rewards and constraints are no longer salient. Colloquially, we were suggesting that the use of functionally superfluous extrinsic incentives may turn *play*—that is, something that is seen as enjoyable in its own right—into *work*—that is, something that is seen as worth undertaking only when it will lead to some attractive extrinsic goal.

Our basic hypothesis was the following: If a child were led to view his or her engagement in an activity of initial intrinsic interest as an explicit means to some ulterior goal, his or her subsequent interest in the activity, in the later absence of further extrinsic pressures, may be decreased. In order to emphasize the conceptual parallel between this line of work and our prior research on insufficient justification, we termed this proposition the "over-justification" hypothesis.

To examine this proposition experimentally requires several critical ingredients that we attempted to incorporate into our initial study in this area (Lepper, Greene, & Nisbett, 1973). It requires, first, an operational definition of intrinsic interest. For this purpose, we turned to the Bing Nursery School, a laboratory preschool facility, located on the Stanford University campus, that seemed to provide a nearly ideal setting for examining children's intrinsic interest in various activities. First, the structure of the program at the school was, by intention, child-centered, with large blocks of time devoted explicitly to "free-play" periods in which children were encouraged to choose freely among a wide variety of interesting and enjoyable activities. Second, it was possible in this school to ask teachers to set out, as a part of the children's regular classroom program, particular target activities without intrusion into the classroom by research personnel; we could then observe children's responses to these activities without their knowing their behavior was being monitored. Under these conditions, we were willing to infer that children's choices among activities reflected their relative intrinsic interest in those activities. Thus, on the basis of covert baseline observations of children's choices in the classroom, we selected as subjects for our study only those children who had shown initial intrinsic interest in a target activity.

To examine the hypothesis that inducing subjects to engage in an activity of initial interest as an explicit means to the attainment of an extrinsic reward should adversely affect later interest in the activity also necessitated a comparison between subjects who had engaged in the target activity in order to obtain a reward and others who had engaged in the activity and had received the same reward, but who should not perceive their behavior as having been instrumentally governed. To accomplish this, our subjects were escorted individually to a different setting in which they were asked to engage in our target activity under one of three conditions. In the Expected-Award condition, children were first shown an extrinsic reward—a "Good Player" certificate—and were asked if they wished to engage in the target activity in order to obtain this reward. Our intent, obviously, was to make salient to the children in this group the instrumentality of their actions as a means of obtaining the proffered reward. In a second, Unexpected-Award, condition, children were simply asked if they would be willing to engage in the target activity without any mention of an extrinsic reward. Unexpectedly, after having finished with the activity, these subjects were presented with the same reward and the same feedback as our Expected-Award subjects. This procedure provided a control for task engagement and receipt of reward without producing conditions likely to promote a perception of one's activity as having been directed towards obtaining the reward. Finally, in a third, Control, condition, children were simply asked to engage in the same activity without promise or receipt of a reward. These children received the same feedback as children in the other conditions, but no tangible reward.

Our hypothesis predicted decreased subsequent intrinsic interest in later situations where extrinsic constraints were no longer salient among children who had contracted to engage in the activity in order to obtain the reward, relative to the two other groups. Hence, several weeks following the individual experimental sessions, we again observed unobtrusively the amount of time each child chose to spend with the target activity in the classroom setting. The results of this procedure, presented in Fig. 5.5, appear to support our basic contention. Children in the Expected-Award condition showed significantly less interest in the activity in the classroom following the experimental sessions than they had during baseline period; indeed, they spent only half as much time during the posttest sessions as they had during baseline, whereas subjects in the remaining two conditions showed no significant change in interest from baseline levels. Corresponding between-groups comparisons of subsequent intrinsic interest revealed significant differences between the Expected-Award condition and both the Unexpected-Award and Control conditions.

Conceptually, these findings concerning the detrimental effects of "overly sufficient" justification parallel the results of our earlier work on "insufficient" justification. In contrast to these earlier findings that went largely unnoticed outside of social psychology, the reaction to this first overjustification study and comparable early results obtained with older subject populations by other investigators (Deci, 1971; Kruglanski, Friedman, & Zeevi, 1971) has been extensive and extraordinarily varied. Although in our initial presentation of these results, we noted a number of theoretical

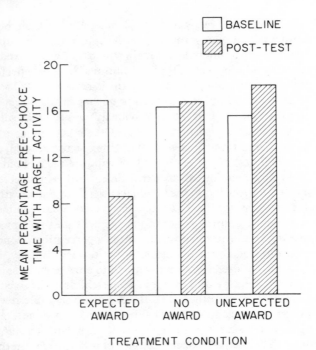

FIG. 5.5. Mean intrinsic interest in the target activity during baseline and postexperimental observations in children's classrooms, by condition. Data from Lepper, et al. (1973).

limitations of our findings and cautioned against "overgeneralization"— indicating, in fact, (Lepper et al., 1973) that "certainly there is nothing in the present line of reasoning or the present data to suggest that contracting to engage in an activity for an intrinsic reward will always, or even usually, result in a decrement in intrinsic interest in the activity [p. 135]"—extravagant claims concerning these studies have been offered on both sides of the issue. Extreme proponents of the underlying model have extrapolated far beyond the available evidence to argue, in general, against the use of systematic reward programs to modify behavior. Extreme opponents, on the other hand, have argued not only that this work is fundamentally incorrect, but also that it stands in the way of the use of effective procedures for alleviating human suffering through the application of tested behavioral principles.

Both these extreme cases are, I believe, overstated (cf. Lepper & Greene, 1978a, 1978c). There are clearly settings in which the use of tangible rewards is appropriate and commendable, and other settings in which their use may be inappropriate. To evaluate this question more fully, let us examine the research literature that has developed in this area over the last several years in some detail and consider the central issues this research has addressed. Several of these issues may be seen as the result of attempts to assess the relevance of alternative models for understanding the processes underlying the appearance of undermining effects; all deal, in one fashion or another, with the conditions under which such detrimental effects are likely to occur and the conditions under which extrinsic rewards are alternatively likely to enhance or maintain subsequent interest.

Variations in Reward Contingency

Consider first the role of the contingency imposed between the receipt of extrinsic rewards and engagement in the experimental activity. In an attributional account, decreases in subsequent intrinsic interest are hypothesized to result from the perceived instrumentality of one's behavior as a means to some extrinsic goal. There are, however, a variety of other models that imply somewhat different accounts of these effects. Perhaps these decreases are a simple function of the linking of the target activity with a reward usually associated with tasks or activities of little interest value. Alternatively, children could have found it distracting, frustrating, or otherwise aversive simply to have to wait during the experimental sessions before they would receive the proffered reward. From these accounts, one might expect comparable decreases in subsequent intrinsic interest even if the reward were not specifically contingent upon task performance. There are, by now, a number of studies that speak to these issues. They suggest, I believe, two general conclusions.

Salience of Instrumentality

There is, first, considerable evidence of the importance of perceived instrumentality to the demonstration of subsequent detrimental effects of extrinsic rewards. It is, for instance, a reasonably consistent finding that extrinsic rewards that are not anticipated at the time the activity is undertaken will not produce detrimental effects on subsequent interest (e.g., Enzle & Ross, 1978; Greene & Lepper, 1974; Lepper & Greene, 1975; Lepper, Sagotsky, & Greene, 1980; W. F. Smith, 1976). Indeed, the one study in which objectively unexpected rewards have been shown to produce subsequent decrements in interest (Kruglanski, Alon, & Lewis, 1972) is one in which an explicit attempt was made to deceive children into believing that the reward *had* been mentioned at the time they undertook the target activities, and even within this study, detrimental effects appear to have occurred only for those children who accepted this deliberate deception. Hence, these effects seem not to depend simply on the linkage of the activity with some reward typically associated with tasks of little inherent value.

Similarly, a number of other studies have examined the effects of "contingent" and "noncontingent" expected-reward procedures on subsequent intrinsic interest. These experiments suggest that it is not the salience of the reward per se, but the salience of instrumentality, that is responsible for subsequent decreases in intrinsic interest. In the two most compelling demonstrations in this area, Ross, Karniol, and Rothstein (1976) and Swann and Pittman (1977) both compared procedures in which engagement in a target activity was presented as instrumental to the attainment of an attractive reward with procedures in which the same reward was presented as contingent upon simply waiting for a fixed period of time, while incidentally engaged in the same activity. In both cases, significant decrements in later interest were observed in the former conditions, but not the latter. Some comparable results have been obtained with adult subjects (e.g., Deci, 1972a; Pinder, 1976), although both the procedures employed and the results obtained with adults have been less clear (e.g., Farr, 1976; Hamner & Foster, 1975).[2]

Finally, there is evidence to indicate that the likelihood of detrimental effects of extrinsic rewards on later intrinsic interest will vary predictably as a function of manipulations designed to focus subjects' attention on either the instrumentality of their actions, or the inherent interest value of the activity itself. Ross (1975), for example, has shown that the effects of asking children to undertake an activity of initial interest in order to obtain an extrinsic reward will differ as a function of instructions to "think about" either the reward they had been offered or a contingency-irrelevant topic. Relative to nonreward control subjects, children asked to think about the reward showed a significant decrease in interest, whereas subjects given an irrelevant distraction task showed no such decrease. Other studies with adult populations provide even stronger evidence. Pittman, Cooper, and Smith (1977) provided subjects, all of whom had been offered an extrinsic reward contingent upon task engagement, with false physiological feedback purportedly indicative of either their intrinsic interest in the task itself or their interest in the reward they would obtain by engaging in the task. Again, relative to a nonrewarded control condition, subjects whose attention had been drawn to their interest in the task itself showed no subsequent decrease in later interest, whereas subjects whose attention had been drawn to their interest in the reward did evidence later decrements in interest. Perhaps more subtly, Johnson, Greene, and Carroll (1979) attempted to manipulate directly

---

[2]The procedural ambiguity in most of this research with adult subjects involves the use of "noncontingent"-reward procedures in which subjects are told that they are bring paid for participating in the experiment, which then consists of engagement in the target activity. Whether subjects do, or should, view their engagement in the activity in instrumental terms under these conditions seems difficult to determine without further, more direct data.

subjects' perceptions of their reasons for engaging in a target activity for which they had been promised extrinsic rewards through a direct "restatement" of the subjects' agreement to engage in the activity that emphasized either their interest in the task itself or their receipt of payment as their reason for agreeing to engage in the activity. Making salient "intrinsic" reasons for engaging in the activity served to eliminate the detrimental effect of expected extrinsic rewards that was evident in both a noninstruction condition and the condition in which "extrinsic" reasons were stressed.

Together, these studies suggest a first general conclusion concerning the conditions under which detrimental effects of extrinsic rewards are likely to occur. Consistent with our initial model, detrimental effects seem more likely to occur under conditions that permit, or indeed force, subjects to view their engagement in the target activity as instrumental to the attainment of extrinsic reward, but are correspondingly less likely to occur under conditions in which their behavior is not easily viewed as instrumental or in which the instrumentality of their actions has been deemphasized.

Task-Contingent Versus Performance-Contingent Rewards

There is, however, a second general conclusion that derives from further research on the comparative effects of two basic sorts of contingencies that might be imposed between one's actions and receipt of an extrinsic reward. The first of these, and the one that characterizes most of the preceding research, involves what one might term "task-contingent" rewards—rewards that are contingent upon mere engagement in some activity under specified conditions or for a specified period of time. The second involves rewards that might be classified as "performance-contingent"—rewards that are contingent not only upon task engagement, but whose attainment also requires that the person's performance meet or exceed some specified standard of success or comparative excellence.

In our own research program, the potential significance of this distinction was a focus of early concern, and in one early study, we attempted to compare these two sorts of reward procedures directly (Greene & Lepper, 1974). Our hypothesis in doing so was quite straightforward. Receipt of a performance-contingent reward—because it should convey to the person information indicative of his or her superior competence at the activity, information that would be expected to enhance later intrinsic interest—should be less likely to produce a net decrease in later interest than receipt of a reward contingent only upon task engagement. Our method of examining this question seemed, at the time, none too subtle. In essence, we replicated our earlier procedure with one important variation: Within the reward conditions of the study, the Good Player Award was presented to half the subjects as something that could be earned by any child who wished to engage in the activity; for the remaining subjects, this same reward was presented as something that could be earned only by a normatively superior performance, by doing better than most other children in the school. After subjects had agreed to undertake the activity in order to earn the award under one condition or the other, or had been provided the same information and reward unexpectedly after their engagement in the task, we examined, as before, their later intrinsic interest in this activity in their classrooms in the absence of further salient constraints.

Our data, presented in Fig. 5.6, provided no support for our hypothesis. The Fig. reveals a replication of our previous findings, with no indication of any effect of our manipulation of the nature of the stated contingency, or performance demand, underlying receipt of the reward. Fortunately, however, other investigators were less daunted by this initial failure than we were, and have proceeded to investigate this general hypothesis further with more positive results.

In the first of the studies, Karniol and Ross (1977) compared the effects of task-contingent and performance-contingent rewards relative to a nonrewarded control procedure, using both a considerably more complex procedure and a sample of somewhat older children. Their experiment showed differential effects of this manipulation. Significant decreases in subsequent

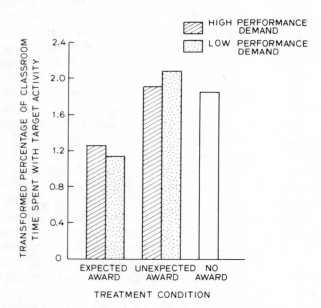

FIG. 5.6.   Mean intrinsic interest in the target activity, during postexperimental classroom observations, by condition. Data from Greene and Lepper (1974).

interest were obtained with task-contingent rewards, relative to control group levels; but, these differences did not appear when the same reward was presented as contingent upon normatively superior performance. Conceptually comparable results with adult subjects across variations in the size of the reward offered in either a task-contingent or performance-contingent fashion have been reported more recently by Enzle and Ross (1978). Most importantly, however, an elegant developmental study by Boggiano and Ruble (1979) shows directly that the difference between our earlier lack of effect and these more recent investigations lies in developmental changes in children's reactions to social–comparison feedback. Specifically, these investigators replicated both sets of results in a single paradigm, showing that although younger children were sensitive to variations in contingency, they were oblivious to information suggesting their *relative* superiority or inferiority at the task, whereas older children showed highly differential responses to variations in both contingency and normative social–comparison feedback.

In short, performance-contingent rewards seem generally less likely to produce subsequent detrimental effects on interest than task-contingent rewards. Although several processes may contribute to this effect, we have found it useful to view these effects as a function of the positive effects of increases in perceived competence on later intrinsic motivation. Hence, this variation in contingency is seen as relevant to later interest largely as a function of the information that receipt of reward conveys, under performance-contingency conditions, concerning one's competence and ability at the experimental activity (cf. Deci, 1975). Such a focus is also helpful in understanding studies that have compared the results of tangible rewards and verbal praise: With both children (Anderson, Manoogian, & Reznick, 1976; Dollinger & Thelen, 1978; Swann & Pittman, 1977) and adults (Blanck, Reis, & Jackson, 1979; Deci, 1971, 1972b; Harackiewicz, 1979; Weiner & Mander, 1978), consistent differences have been obtained, with verbal praise seeming to increase subsequent intrinsic motivation. A closer examination of these studies, however, suggests that these findings can be explained by the differential informational value of the tangible-reward and verbal-reward procedures in these studies concerning one's competence and task ability relative to others (cf. Pittman, Davey, Alafat, Wetherill, & Wirsul, in press).

Other Forms of Extrinsic Constraint

In the preceding sections, I have focused on the ways in which extrinsic reward procedures that differentially affect perceived instrumentality and perceived competence may influence subsequent intrinsic interest. It should be clear, however, that our analysis of these effects is not restricted to rewards per se, but applies more generally to the use of superfluous social-control techniques of any sort that might induce children to perceive their actions as extrinsically motivated and externally constrained. Hence, a third general issue guiding further study in this domain has concerned the potential applicability of this analysis to other forms of extrinsic constraint.

In one early study, for example, we examined the joint effects of expectation of a tangible reward and unnecessarily close adult surveillance on children's subsequent intrinsic interest (Lepper & Greene, 1975). As before, our basic paradigm involved the imposition of different experimental procedures on children's behavior in individual experimental sessions and, some weeks later, the unobtrusive observation of children's subsequent behavior in their classrooms during designated free-play periods. Different rewards and target activities were used, however, to ensure that our conclusions would not be limited to irrelevant particulars of our initial procedure. In this study, children were asked to solve a set of geometric puzzles. Half the children were offered access to a cabinet full of highly attractive toys as a reward for engaging in this activity; others received the same opportunity to play with the attractive toys unexpectedly. Within each of these conditions, half the children were asked to work on the puzzles under close and constant adult surveillance, while the remainder were allowed to work on the puzzles on their own. Subsequently, we observed children's interest in the activity in their classrooms, in the absence of further surveillance or expectation of reward. The results are presented in Fig. 5.7, which illustrates that both prior surveillance and expectation of reward had independent, detrimental effects on children's later intrinsic interest in the activity.

Other related studies provide evidence of comparable effects as a function of other sorts of extrinsic constraints. Amabile, De Jong, and Lepper (1976) demonstrated that the imposition of functionally superfluous temporal deadlines on adult subjects working on a word-manipulation game of initial interest produced significant decrements in later interest and attitudes towards that task. Similarly, Rosenhan (1969) has reported adverse effects, on subsequent charitability in a seemingly unmonitored setting, of a procedure in which children were "forced" to behave charitably in a prior experimental setting. Deci (1975) has reported data suggestive of a detrimental effect of threatened punishment on later intrinsic motivation.

Such findings suggest that our basic analysis may have considerably greater generality than is implied by the particular focus of most of this research on the effects of tangible extrinsic rewards. A variety of salient and superfluous social-control techniques, it appears, may reduce subsequent intrinsic interest. Hence, it is the consequences of salient extrinsic constraints in a more general sense—rather than the effects of rewards, or threats, or surveillance, or deadlines per se—to which this literature is properly addressed (Lepper & Greene, 1976, 1978c).

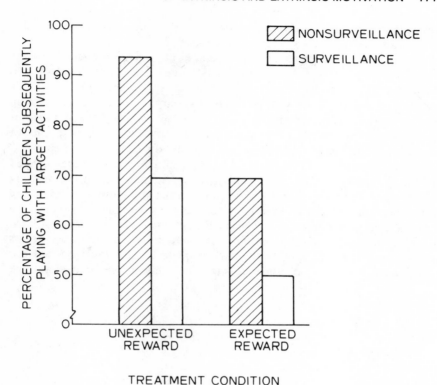

FIG. 5.7. Percentage of children showing intrinsic interest in the target activity during postexperimental classroom observations, by condition. Data from Lepper and Greene (1975).

Effects of Extrinsic Rewards on Immediate Task Performance

With these basic conclusions concerning the importance of perceived constraint and perceived competence in mind, let us turn to a second general issue concerning the relationship between the effects that extrinsic rewards have on task performance in the immediate experimental setting, in which the rewards are available, and their effects on subsequent intrinsic motivation in later settings, in which such rewards are no longer available. Again, this subsequent work derived initially from a concern with possible alternative explanations of our initial findings. Suppose subjects in expected- or contingent-reward conditions were led by the offer of a reward to perform differently at the task during the experimental sessions. Might these immediate performance differences not, in and of themselves, have adverse effects on later intrinsic interest in this activity?

Some evidence that such a process might be at work was uncovered in our first two studies (Greene & Lepper, 1974; Lepper et al., 1973). Both had employed the same drawing activity as the experimental task. For this activity, it was relatively easy to obtain two sorts of measures concerning subjects' performance during the experimental sessions—the number of pictures they had drawn, and the quality, as rated by "blind" judges, of each of these drawings. Across the two studies, we found a consistent, albeit weak, effect of expectation of reward on both measures. These results are illustrated in Fig. 5.8, which shows that children who had undertaken the drawing activity in order to obtain a reward drew significantly more pictures during the experimental sessions than their counterparts who had not expected a reward. But (as one might expect because the children's efforts were restricted to a fixed time period) these pictures were rated, on the average, as significantly lower in quality than those made by children who had not anticipated a reward for their efforts. These effects on immediate task

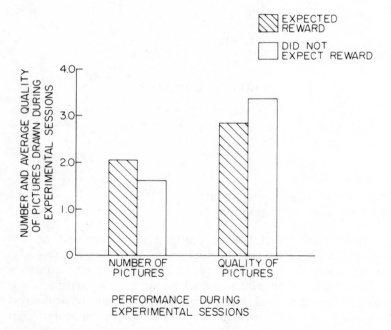

FIG. 5.8. Mean quality and quantity of children's drawings during the treatment phase, by condition, across two experiments. Data from Lepper et al. (1973) and Greene and Lepper (1974).

performance, moreover, showed a small but statistically significant positive correlation across conditions with subsequent classroom interest.

Given these suggestive early findings, further studies have investigated whether detrimental effects of extrinsic rewards on subsequent intrinsic interest in other unconstrained situations depend on prior negative effects of those rewards on immediate performance at the activity during the treatment phase in which a contingency has been imposed on one's behavior. The results of this work, in my view, can be summarized in terms of three general issues.

Detrimental Effects of Rewards on Task Performance

On the one hand, there is now an impressive array of evidence—of considerable interest in its own right—that salient extrinsic rewards can produce a wide variety of detrimental effects on immediate task performance. In different studies, these adverse effects have included selective avoidance of difficult tasks, impairments in learning or performance on task parameters incidental to reward attainment, deterioration of central task performance with tasks that are complex and of initial interest, and other qualitative deficits that seem to accompany a preoccupation with attainment of an extrinsic reward (Condry, 1977).

In studies with both children (Blackwell, 1974; Harter, 1978b; Lepper, Gilovich, & Rest, in progress) and adults (Condry & Chambers, 1978; Shapira, 1976), the offer of extrinsic rewards contingent upon "correct answers" in a context in which subjects are presented with problems that vary in their level of difficulty has resulted in subjects' choosing significantly less difficult—and presumably less challenging, and perhaps less interesting—problems than they would in the absence of extrinsic rewards. In perhaps the most elegant of these investigations, Harter (1978b) demonstrated not only that children offered rewards for task accomplishment selectively chose more simple problems, but also that both the offer of rewards itself and the resulting choice of less challenging problems appeared to decrease children's enjoyment of the activity during the experimental sessions, as indicated by data on smiling at the time of problem solution. Our first version of this study, a doctoral dissertation by Laird Blackwell (1974), also showed this effect clearly, and suggested further parallels between immediate performance effects of this sort and subsequent intrinsic interest. Blackwell's data, concerning both subjects' problem choices during the experimental session and their subsequent interest in the activity in the later absence of further rewards, appear in Fig. 5.9. Note, however, that these data also indicate that this effect does not appear if children are offered a reward contingent upon

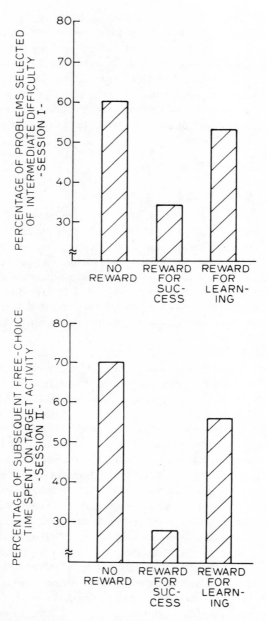

FIG. 5.9. *Top:* Percentage of problems of intermediate difficulty selected during the treatment phase, by conditions. *Bottom:* Percentage of free-choice time spent on target activity during posttreatment phase, by conditions. Data from Blackwell (1974).

their performance on a test to be given at a later time to assess the amount they learned from their engagement in this activity.[3]

Other detrimental effects of extrinsic rewards have been less extensively studied; nonetheless, the diversity of such effects remains impressive (McCullers, 1978; McGraw, 1978). For example, it has long been known that the imposition of extrinsic rewards may impair learning or performance on aspects of the task that are incidental to the attainment of reward (McGraw, 1978). Comparable effects have received further documentation in recent studies concerned with decreases in later intrinsic interest (Harackiewicz, 1979; Kruglanski et al., 1971; Kruglanski, Stein, & Riter, 1977).

Perhaps more strikingly, this recent literature also clearly documents further that extrinsic rewards may have detrimental effects even on measures of central task performance (cf. Spence, 1956), when the task is sufficiently complex that it cannot be easily solved through the simple application of well-learned algorithms and is of sufficient initial attractiveness to maintain interest among subjects not expecting a reward for task performance (McGraw, 1978). Both Kruglanski et al. (1971) and Amabile (1979) have shown contingent extrinsic constraints to reduce creativity on tasks involving, respectively, verbal fluency and artistic skills. Others (McGraw, 1978; McGraw & McCullers, 1979) have shown that subjects expecting to earn an extrinsic reward appear to perform less well on tasks that require "insight" or the ability to "break set" for their solution.

Finally, more diffuse and qualitative detrimental effects on complex task performance have also been demonstrated. For example, Garbarino (1975) asked sixth-grade children to serve as tutors for first-grade children, either with or without the promise of extrinsic reward for a successful effort. Tutors who were offered a reward exhibited a more "instrumental" orientation towards their pupils: They were more critical and demanding, made less efficient use of time, and created a more negative emotional atmosphere in the tutoring sessions. Not surprisingly, given these effects, central task performance suffered as well: The younger children taught by tutors expecting a reward learned less than those taught by tutors who did not expect a reward. Similarly, Condry and Chambers (1978) showed that adult subjects offered a tangible reward for solution of a complex concept attainment task were likely to make less efficient use of the information they obtained at the task and to approach the task in an "answer-oriented" fashion, attempting to guess the

---

[3]The reader may note some ambiguity in the appropriate interpretation of the subsequent interest measure in the rewards-for-learning condition of this study. Because these children had not yet been tested at the time of the free-choice measure, they may have felt that further practice at the activity would enable them to obtain a higher score on the later test, which would determine whether they were to receive a reward. Hence, their relatively higher level of later interest may have been as much a reflection of their perception of the continued instrumentality of further task engagement as of their intrinsic interest in the activity.

solution before sufficient evidence was available (cf. Holt, 1964). Perhaps more impressively, when subjects were later confronted with a similar task, without the offer of any reward, and under different instructions that explicitly prohibited guessing and asked subjects to respond only when they were certain of the accuracy of their answers, those subjects who had been previously rewarded continued to offer solutions earlier—before they could logically have eliminated relevant alternative hypotheses.

In short, one clear conclusion from this literature is that the use of salient extrinsic rewards may produce a variety of negative effects on task performance during the treatment period when rewards are expected. In such cases, moreover, it seems reasonable to expect that these differences in performance may themselves contribute to decrements in later intrinsic interest in an unconstrained situation.

Effects on Performance Versus Effects on Subsequent Interest

At the same time, let me hasten to add the second conclusion that I feel this literature warrants—that such detrimental effects on performance are not necessary to produce decreases in later intrinsic interest, though they may be sufficient (Lepper & Greene, 1976; 1978c). Rather, these performance effects appear to be much more highly dependent on the specific relationship between the demands imposed by a particular task and the specific contingency imposed on one's performance at the task. I began this discussion, with findings from our initial studies that indicated a negative effect of expected rewards on the quality of task performance. In later studies in which we made the task contingency more specific, by telling children that they would have to draw some particular number of pictures (Lepper, Sagotsky, Dafoe, & Greene, 1980) or would have to work on the task for a specified period of time (Lepper, Sagostky, & Greene, 1980), expectation of reward did not result in performance decrements. Nor were performance decrements observed when other tasks containing objective criteria for success, such as the solution of a set of puzzles or a series of template-matching tasks (Lepper & Greene, 1975; Lepper, Sagotsky, & Greene, in preparation), were employed as the experimental activity. Yet, in all of these studies, comparable detrimental effects on later intrinsic interest in the children's classrooms were found, whether the effects of the reward procedure on immediate performance had been negative, positive, or nonexistent. Similar results, suggesting that subsequent decreases in intrinsic interest do not depend on prior differences in task performance during the treatment phase also appear in a number of other studies reporting data on both indices (Amabile et al., 1976; Boggiano & Ruble, 1979; Calder & Staw, 1975; Dollinger & Thelen, 1978; Enzle & Ross, 1978; Harackiewicz, 1979; Ross, 1975; Ross et al., 1976; Smith & Pittman, 1978).

In a related vein, other work has shown that changes in the contingencies sufficient to reverse these negative effects of rewards on immediate performance measures do not necessarily produce corresponding increases in later intrinsic interest. In a recent doctoral dissertation on the effects of extrinsic constraints on creativity and subsequent interest, Terri Amabile (1979) was able to produce both positive and negative effects on measures of "creativity" and "technical competence" as a function of the specificity of the criteria subjects were given as the basis on which their work would be evaluated. These differences in performance, however, did not lead to corresponding increases or decreases in later intrinsic interest. Along similar lines, Tom Gilovich, Greg Rest, and I are presently involved in a study exmaining the effects on later intrinsic interest of contingency systems designed to induce children to choose either more, or less, difficult and challenging problems. In an Equal-Reward condition, as in previous research in this domain, children were offered an equivalent reward for each problem solved, regardless of its difficulty level; in this case, it is instrumentally sensible for children to select easier problems more likely to ensure their receipt of the reward. In contrast children in a Graduated Reward condition were offered considerably greater rewards for solving more difficult problems than for solving easier problems; this contingency was designed to make it instrumentally sensible for children to select considerably more challenging tasks than they would otherwise choose. Both procedures produced highly significant results on children's choice of problems during the reward phase. Relative to nonrewarded control subjects, children in the Equal-Reward condition, as in prior studies, selected much easier problems, whereas children in the Graduated-Reward condition selected significantly more difficult problems. These dramatic differences in task selection, however, did not produce differential effects on subsequent intrinsic interest when tangible rewards were no longer available.

Taken together, these data suggest the utility of distinguishing between the processes by which extrinsic rewards produce adverse effects on immediate performance measures versus subsequent interest measures. Although performance decrements may often accompany manipulations of perceived instrumentality—and, when they do occur, may contribute to later decrements in subsequent interest—their appearance does not seem to be necessary to the production of later effects. Conceptually, this distinction also seems mandated on theoretical grounds. With measures of task performance in the presence of anticipated rewards, we would assume the individual's efforts to be a simultaneous function of two distinct, and potentially competing, forces: the individual's wishing, on the one hand, to maximize enjoyment of the task per se, and, on the other, to maximize the likelihood of obtaining the proffered reward. In contrast, with later measures of intrinsic interest, task engagement or performance is no longer instrumental, and choices should be made almost entirely on the basis of the individual's relative interest in the activity itself. Hence, it is not surprising that performance decrements appear to depend much more precisely on the specific nature of the activity involved and the contingency imposed upon the activity than do subsequent decreases in intrinsic interest.

The specificity of these detrimental effects of extrinsic rewards on immediate performance measures can be viewed, in particular, as the result of three related consequences of the introduction of an instrumental contingency on subjects' goals and criteria for performance in undertaking the activity, the focus of their attention while engaged in the activity, and the possible induction of arousal or anxiety over performance (cf. Lepper & Greene, 1978c). Thus, when an activity is undertaken primarily in order to obtain some extrinsic reward, those conditions perceived as necessary to attain the reward will define the minimal sufficient criteria for performance and will determine one's manner of approach to the activity, one's goals and strategies while engaged in the activity, and the point at which one will terminate work at the activity. In such circumstances, instrumentally oriented subjects may be seen as motivated to obtain the desired reward through the least effortful and exacting means available (Condry & Chambers, 1978; Kruglanski, 1978; Lepper & Greene, 1978c). Thus, if reward attainment can be ensured by the selection of easier and less challenging versions of the task, subjects will be likely to approach the task in that manner; similarly, if the reward may possibly be obtained through guessing, cheating, or other means of circumventing further engagement with the task, such strategies will be likely to be tried. At the same time, these instrumental performance criteria will also serve to focus the subjects' attention on aspects of performance that are perceived to be instrumentally relevant, and may, therefore, result in correspondingly less attention being paid to aspects of the task that are not seen as relevant to reward attainment (cf. Easterbrook, 1959; Simon, 1967). Hence, incidental learning and performance along qualitative dimensions not affecting the probability of obtaining the reward are likely to suffer. Finally, the imposition of extrinsic incentives may increase arousal or induce performance anxiety if reward attainment is seen as problematic. This may, in turn, lead to an increased reliance on well-rehearsed and overlearned strategies and response patterns (cf. Spence, 1956). Such a focus may aid performance on simple tasks, where prepotent responses and algorithmic solutions are appropriate, but may impair performance on complex tasks that require novel and heuristic approaches for their solution (McGraw, 1978).

Reinforcement Effects and Subsequent Intrinsic and Extrinsic Motivation

Decreases in later intrinsic interest following the imposition of unnecessarily powerful extrinsic constraints, then, do not appear to depend on prior deleterious effects on performance. The current literature, however, has also raised equally compelling questions involving consideration of the other side of this coin: the extent to which decreases in subsequent intrinsic interest are precluded or minimized by reward procedures that have produced significant reinforcement effects during the prior treatment sessions. It is to these complementary issues that I now wish to turn.

The relevant empirical question is quite simple, although the underlying conceptual issues are complex. In the literature I have described, "reward procedures" are used that differ markedly from those typically employed in investigations of the application of systematic reward programs, such as token economies (Kazdin & Bootzin, 1972; O'Leary, 1978; O'Leary & Drabman, 1971), to establish and demonstrate functional control over particular responses (cf. Lepper & Greene, 1978a, 1978c; O'Leary, 1978; Vasta, in press). Generally, in the overjustification literature, subjects are rewarded on only a single trial, rather than over multiple trials. Only rarely have these studies demonstrated that the reward procedures used produced an (empirically defined) "reinforcement effect"—that is, an increase in the probability of the reinforced response during the reward phase of the study. This omission is not accidental. On the contrary, investigators in this area have intentionally sought to examine the effects of reward procedures that would not produce increased engagement in the target activity, relative to nonrewarded control conditions, in order to rule out possible alternative explanations for subsequent decreases in interest among previously rewarded subjects, in terms of satiation, fatigue, or other correlates of increased engagement in the activity. Nonetheless, the failure of these studies to demonstrate that the rewards employed were effective reinforcers raises the question of whether the detrimental effects observed in these studies are inherently limited to ineffective reward procedures that do not increase response probability.

That detrimental effects on subsequent interest will, in fact, not appear when objectively and demonstrably reinforcing reward procedures are used has been suggested by a number of authors, and for a number of reasons. Some have argued that these detrimental effects are simply the consequence of transitory processes involving distraction or frustration that might habituate with continued exposure to the rewards over trials. Others have suggested that these adverse effects will occur only when the presumed "rewards" are not actually sufficiently attractive for the subject population studied to provide a true incentive. Similarly one might argue that only with repeated pairings of the response and the reward will the conditioned incentive value of the activity increase. All of these possibilities suggest a fundamental reinterpretation of previous findings. Alternatively, one could argue that the use of demonstrably effective reinforcers introduces additional factors that, along with perceptions of constraint and competence, affect later interest. Thus, increases in engagement in the activity per se may lead to increases in task-relevant skills or may allow the subject to discover elements of the activity that are not apparent on limited contact or until some level of practice or proficiency has been achieved. These consequences of increased task engagement themselves, or the simple increase in mere exposure to the activity (Zajonc, 1968, in press), might lead to increased interest in the activity. The outcome of the application of a particular reinforcement procedure, then, would depend on the joint effects of a number of potentially competing factors.

Evidence consistent with the general hypothesis that demonstrably reinforcing, multiple-trial reward procedures will not produce decreases in later interest comes from a number of recent studies in the functional analysis tradition (Davidson & Bucher, 1978; Feingold & Mahoney, 1975; Reiss & Sushinsky, 1975; Vasta, Andrews, McLaughlin, Stirpe, & Comfort, 1978; Vasta & Stirpe, 1979). None of these studies, however, attempts to distinguish among possible explanations of these effects. Because the issue is important, let us consider these studies in a bit more detail. Despite potentially relevant differences, these studies share a basic set of common features, characteristic of good operant research. In an initial baseline phase, children's choices among a set of two to four activities of initial interest are observed in the absence of explicit extrinsic contingencies. During a following treatment phase, children are provided with systematic token reinforcement, contingent upon their engagement in a particular one of these several activities. This procedure is continued until powerful and dramatic increases in task engagement as a function of the introduction of this reward system have been demonstrated. Subsequently, children are placed on an extinction schedule— the same array of activities remains available, but they are told that the tokens and back-up reinforcers are no longer available and that they may choose any of the activities. Typically, with some variation across studies, all of the experimental sessions take place in the same or a similar setting, are conducted by the same experimenter, and involve observations made by individuals who remain in the room with the children. The results of these procedures are clear, and at odds with prior research using only single-trial reward procedures: During extinction, children continue to select the previously rewarded activity more often than they did during baseline observations (and, in some cases, more than nonreinforced control subjects).

Should one conclude from these results that extrinsic rewards will have detrimental effects on subsequent intrinsic interest only when single-trial or objectively nonreinforcing reward procedures are used? Certainly, these data, and the variety of processes that might produce such effects, should lead to considerable caution in generalizing from previous work to conclusions concerning the likely effects of long-term reward programs that produce dramatic increases in response probability (Lepper & Greene, 1978a; O'Leary, 1978; Vasta, in press). At the same time, I believe that the appropriate interpretation of these effects, and hence the implication of these studies, is not yet clear and that more research is needed to elucidate the conditions under which reward programs of this sort will produce either positive or negative effects.

My grounds for this assertion are twofold. First, although they are atypical of the literature in general, several studies have demonstrated detrimental effects on later intrinsic interest of multiple-trial or demonstrably effective reward procedures (Brownell, Colletti, Ersner-Hershfield, Hershfield, & Wilson, 1977; Colvin, 1972; Greene, Sternberg, & Lepper, 1976; Lepper, Sagotsky & Greene, 1980; Smith & Pittman, 1978). Moreover, because none of these studies (with one exception) has produced both positive and negative effects in the same paradigm, it is difficult to specify clearly the differences in procedure that have led to these divergent findings. Second, there is a knotty, but important, conceptual issue raised by these studies demonstrating positive effects of multiple-trial reinforcement concerning the comparability of dependent measures across these different studies—questions concerning the conditions under which one can legitimately draw inferences from an individual's choices concerning *intrinsic* interest (Lepper & Greene, 1976, 1978c).

Thus, within an attributional framework in which one wishes to distinguish between intrinsic and extrinsic motivation, inferences concerning the person's later intrinsic interest can be made only when that person's behavior is subsequently observed in a setting in which neither tangible nor social rewards are expected to be contingent upon one's choices. In our own research, we have taken great pains to observe children's choice behavior in a setting in which they have no expectation that their behavior is even a source of interest to others in that environment. Suppose, instead, that we had observed children's behavior in a setting in which they expected to receive further tangible rewards, or in which tangible rewards had been removed but the children had been told that it would please the person who set out the choices for the day very much if they would play with the activity that had been previously rewarded. Were the children then to play more with the previously rewarded activity, would one infer that they did so because the found the activity more intrinsically interesting? I would submit not. Suppose, however, that the experimenter had told the children that they were free to choose any of the activities, but they—on the basis of their previous experience in this same setting, where they had received contingent rewards for only one of the activities, perhaps from this same experimenter—inferred that the experimenter would prefer that they play with the previously rewarded activity. From an attributional perspective again, one would like to distinguish behavior motivated by a desire to please or elicit approval from the experimenter, for example, from behavior motivated by some internalized set of preferences for some activities over others.

A central theoretical issue in interpreting these previous studies in which differential rewards for engagement in one of a small set of activities produced later increases in engagement in that activity is whether the children in these studies believe there to be a "right answer" or a proper thing to do in the test situation—whether they believe that the person posing the choice, despite the absence of further tangible rewards, would be more pleased if the child were to continue to select the previously rewarded activity—or whether their behavior reflects an increased interest in the activity for its own sake. The relevant empirical test is how these same children would act if confronted with the activity in a very different setting in which they had no expectation that anyone would care about, or even be aware of, their choices.

To examine this question, Jerry Sagotsky, David Greene, and I performed an experiment in which we explicitly compared children's choices in these two sorts of situations (Lepper, Sagotsky, & Greene, 1980). In this study, children selected for an initial interest in a target activity were exposed to a multiple-trial, contingent-reward procedure, or one of several control prcedures. In one set of conditions, children were differentially rewarded on a fixed-interval schedule over multiple trials, with tokens that could be redeemed for attractive rewards for playing with one of four alternative activities. Noncontingent-reward subjects, by contrast, received tokens for engaging in any of the four activities. Thus, a comparison of the behavior of these groups during the experimental sessions allowed us to demonstrate a highly significant "reinforcement" effect of the differential reward procedure. In a second set of conditions, contingent-reward subjects were given tokens for engagement in the target activity, but were not offered any alternative choices; noncontingent-reward subjects in these conditions simply received the same reward, unexpectedly, at the end of the session. These conditions, then, provided a multiple-trial analog to our previous studies in which the reward is functionally superfluous, relative to appropriate control procedures. They furnished, as well, a control for the possible consequences of increased task engagement per se. A final, control condition, in which children were not presented with the target activity, provided a baseline for comparison.

Several weeks after these experimental sessions, children's engagement in the target activity was observed in two very different settings. Subsequent intrinsic interest in the activity was assessed, as in our earlier studies, through dissociated, unobtrusive observations of subjects' behavior during free-play periods in their regular classrooms. Subsequent task engagement was also observed, however, when children were returned to the setting in which they had previously received tangible rewards and were again confronted with the four activities previously presented in that setting. These sessions were conducted by a different experimenter, who informed the children that there were no tangible rewards available, but the children remained aware of their behavior was being monitored. A comparison of children's choices in these two settings, then, provided a means of examining the possibility that previous conflicting results may have been a function of differences in the dependent measures employed in these studies—measures involving, on the one hand, unobtrusive observations of later intrinsic interest in a setting in which perceived extrinsic constraints had been minimized, and, on the other, more intrusive observations of subsequent behavior in settings in which a variety of social demand characteristics might lead children, regardless of their own preferences, to continue to select the activity that had been previously rewarded.

This study demonstrated two basic effects. First, when children's subsequent interest in the activity was covertly observed in their classrooms, detrimental effects of a demonstrably effective, multiple-trial reinforcement procedure on later intrinsic interest, relative to control and noncontingent reinforcement procedures, were apparent, as illustrated in the top half of Fig. 5.10. In contrast, when children's subsequent engagement in the activity was assessed in further experimental sessions in which the child was presented with the same set of activities as before and was aware that his or her behavior was being observed by the experimenter, the same contingent-reward procedure resulted in significantly greater engagement in the previously rewarded activity. The results of this more intrusive measure appear in the lower half of Fig. 5.10. As these divergent results from the same subjects indicate, the apparent effects of a particular reward procedure on later behavior depend greatly on the setting in which subsequent behavior is observed.[4]

Our analysis of the critical difference between these two dependent measures rests on the assumption that children perceived social demands to continue to select the target activity in the intrusive, experimental setting, but not in the classroom. To provide more direct evidence on this issue, we created miniature replicas of these two settings, with small dolls to illustrate the principal characters in this study. We then presented a different sample of children with a description of our experimental procedure and asked them to predict how hypothetical subjects would feel later on in the classroom or back in the research room. In particular, we asked these children to tell us whether they thought that either the teachers in the classroom or the new experimenter in the research room would be more or less pleased if a child chose to play with the target activity rather than other available alternatives. The results suggested that these children did, indeed, view these situations quite differently. When asked about the research room context, children overwhelming indicated that they thought the new experimenter would be more pleased if the child were to play further with the previously rewarded activity; but when asked about the classroom situation, our subjects did not infer that

---

[4]For purposes of presentation, these data were collapsed across two different contingent and noncontingent reward procedures, because equivalent results were obtained in both cases. For additional details, see Lepper, Sagotsky, and Greene (1980).

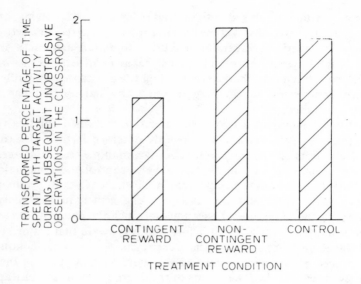

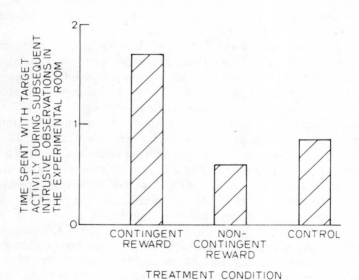

FIG. 5.10. *Top:* Mean subsequent intrinsic interest in the target activity during unobtrusive posttreatment observations in the classroom, by condition. *Bottom:* Mean subsequent task engagement during intrusive posttreatment observations in the experimental room, by condition. Data from Lepper, Sagotsky, and Greene (1980).

the teachers had any preference as to whether our hypothetical subject played with the target activity or some other activity. Indeed, many of them indicated that they thought it was a silly question, because obviously "you can do anything you want" in class.

Together, these findings suggest one possible explanation of the different results of previous research concerning the effects of multiple-trial reinforcement procedures on later interest in the target activity. Yet, without further information on children's perceptions of social demands across this diverse set of studies, it is also clear that it would be premature to assert that this is the primary or critical difference between studies that have shown positive versus negative effects on subsequent task engagement.[5] Very possibly, as indicated earlier, it is not. What these data demonstrate clearly, however, is that further attention needs to be paid to the conditions under which children's behavior will reflect an interest in the activity per se, rather than a desire to obtain further tangible rewards or adult social approval in the subsequent test situation.

The Multiple Functions of Extrinsic Rewards

Implicit in the foregoing review of research concerning the potential detrimental effects of extrinsic rewards are the elements of a more general model concerning the processes by which extrinsic rewards may influence later behavior. I wish now to make this more general analysis explicit, in order to place this research in a larger context.

The basic premise of this more general analysis is that rewards can, and often do, serve multiple functions simultaneously. Correspondingly, the

---

[5]It is important, in this context, to be clear on the difficulties inherent in attempts to draw inferences across studies concerning the likelihood that children will continue to view the previously rewarded activity as the appropriate or socially desired response during postexperimental sessions. Presumably, children's perceptions of social demands in such contexts will be multiply determined and will depend not on the most obvious factors, such as the designation of the decision as a "free choice" or the presence of observers who are monitoring the child's behavior, but also on the other broader contextual factors, such as the continuity of the experimental sessions, the use of differential contingencies, the availability of other options not available during the treatment phase, and so forth. What is clearly needed, therefore, are data obtained independently concerning the expectations that children do have concerning the social instrumentality of their actions in particular contexts, and evidence concerning potential differences in their behavior in different measurement contexts. Certainly, however, procedural controls embodied in at least some of the relevant multiple-trial reward studies (e.g., Davidson & Bucher, 1978) would seem to make the alternative account suggested by the results of this present study less likely. Additional research concerning the conditions under which multiple-trial reward programs will either increase or decrease subsequent intrinsic interest, therefore, remains an important focus for continued research.

receipt of rewards may convey information to the individual along a number of dimensions that may affect his or her subsequent behavior—information that may affect, for example, the individual's perceptions of constraint and competence or expectations concerning the future instrumental value of the activity in particular settings. Predictions of the subsequent effects of any given reward program, therefore, will depend on the interaction of these different, and often competing, processes. Let us examine, then, the functions of reward implicated in the preceding analysis.

Certainly, the most obvious function rewards may serve is an *instrumental* or *incentive function*. Thus, when the child is provided a tangible reward contingent upon some particular behavior, receipt of that reward is likely to imply that the same behavior will be likely to lead to further rewards in the future, at least in the same or functionally similar situations. Depending on the manner in which the reward has been presented, the child may come to expect further tangible rewards in later situations, or, in the absence of tangible rewards, continued adult social approval. If, in either case, the behavior is expected to have continued instrumental value in a particular situation, prior receipt of rewards should increase the child's motivation to engage in that same behavior as a variety of theoretical models would suggest (Bandura, 1977; Estes, 1972; Lepper & Greene, 1978c; Weiner, 1972). However, when one attempts to predict the effects of prior rewards on behavior in a situation in which the child clearly no longer expects the behavior to have any instrumental value, attention to the other functions rewards may serve seems required.

A second principal function of rewards is an *evaluative* or *feedback function*. That is, the receipt of rewards contingent upon task performance may signal success or failure at the task, or may convey to the child specific comparative feedback concerning the adequacy of his or her performance relative to others. The specific effects of this information on children's later behavior should depend on the attributions the child makes concerning the extent to which his or her performance was a function of ability, effort, or other factors (Bar-Tal, 1978; Weiner, 1974, 1979). In general, however, rewards that enhance perceived competence at the task and lead the child to expect continued success at the task in the future (unless the task is seen as overly simple) will enhance subsequent intrinsic interest (Harter, 1978a).

Finally, rewards may also serve a *social-control function* and may lead the child to consider his or her reasons for engaging in the activity. If the child is led to view his or her actions as extrinsically constrained, the child may come to view the activity as one that is worth undertaking only when further extrinsic rewards or constraints are present. When both perceptions of continued instrumentality and personal competence are controlled—through the use of appropriate unobtrusive measures of later intrinsic interest in the first case, and the use of rewards that do not convey salient information to the child concerning his or her capabilities in the second—the result of increases in perceived constraint will be a decrease in later intrinsic interest in the activity, as previously documented.

Thus, to predict the net effects of a particular reward program will, minimally, require attention to each of these processes and their potential effects on subsequent behavior, as illustrated in Fig. 5.11. Nor, as Fig. 5.11 also indicates, is the question even that simple; for, in addition to these primary effects of extrinsic rewards, any comprehensive analysis must also consider potential secondary effects that may result from differences in task engagement or performance in the presence of the reward and the interactions of these effects with children's existing skills and interests. Hence, if powerful extrinsic incentives are used to increase engagement with the activity during the period when rewards are present, one would need to consider the ways in which that additional practice and familiarity with the activity may itself influence later behavior. Conversely, if extrinsic rewards are employed in an appropriate fashion such that immediate task performance during the period when rewards are present is adversely affected, these detrimental perform- ance effects may themselves influence later responses to the activity.

Finally, it seems clear that the effects of any particular program of extrinsic rewards on subsequent behavior will depend partly on the initial skills, interests, and perceptions of the children to whom it is applied (Lepper & Dafoe, 1979; Lepper & Greene, 1978c). A single contingency system, for example, may prove the necessary prod for children with little initial interest and few relevant skills to produce engagement in a task that may subsequently prove enjoyable, but at the same time, it may be a superfluous constraint on the behavior of others who might have found the activity of higher initial interest—hence, its effects on subsequent intrinsic interest should differ for different children (cf. Calder & Staw, 1975; Lepper & Dafoe, 1979; Loveland & Olley, 1979; McLoyd, 1979).

Understanding the effects that rewards may have on subsequent behavior, outside of the immediate setting in which those rewards remain available, is obviously a complex task, though not, I believe, hopelessly so. This complexity makes it very tempting to avoid such questions altogether and focus exclusively on the more tractable issues of functional control in environments in which the experimenters can control and manipulate the contingencies to which our subjects are exposed. In the long run, however, I believe the measure of our understanding of social-control processes will lie precisely in our ability to understand and predict the effects of experimental procedures on subjects' behavior in posttreatment settings in which we cannot control the contingencies to which they are exposed—issues, in short, of intrinsic motivation and internalization.

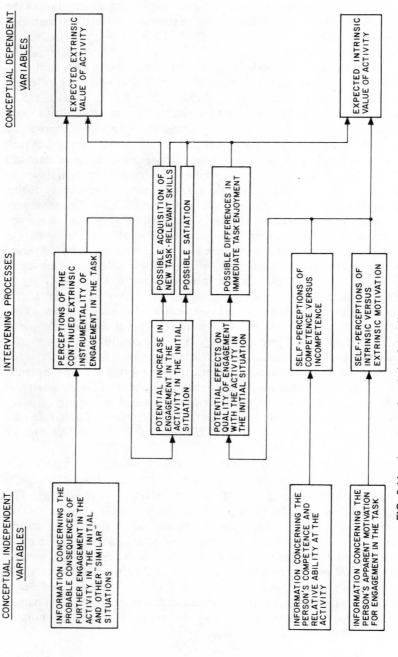

FIG. 5.11. A conceptual analysis of the effects of reinforcement procedures on subsequent expected extrinsic and intrinsic incentive values associated with an activity. From Lepper and Greene (1978c).

UNDERSTANDING SOCIAL CONSTRAINTS:
SOME DEVELOPMENTAL ISSUES

Before turning to my final concern with an integration of these two experimental literatures on the effects of superfluous extrinsic constraints on internalization and later intrinsic interest, let me turn briefly to the question of how children come to understand the implicit meaning of social-control attempts. Obviously, I am asserting that children as young as 4 and 5 seem to respond to manipulations of perceived constraint in ways that parallel the responses of much older children and even adult subjects faced with comparable situations. This assumption raises some obvious questions about how children come to understand the social meaning of offers of rewards or threats of punishment.

Indeed, one can phrase the question as a paradox. Implicit in the attributional analysis of these findings is the presumed use of a "discounting" principle (cf. Kelley, 1973)—the notion that the imposition of salient extrinsic constraints on one's actions typically implies that the action in question is one that would not be performed in the absence of such constraints. In abstract terms, this principle can be shown to govern the inferences adult subjects and older children will make when asked to infer the motivational state of another person undertaking an activity either in the face of or the absence of external constraints; they will infer that the other is less intrisically motivated if the activity is undertaken in order to obtain a reward than if the activity is undertaken seemingly for its own sake. Several studies, however, suggest that young children typically do not employ such an inferential principle in drawing conclusions about the motives of others (Karniol & Ross, 1976; Shultz, Butkowsky, Pearce, & Shanfield, 1975; M. C. Smith, 1975); in fact, they may sometimes employ an opposite, "additive" principle.

In part, the young child's lack of sophistication in the use of attributional principles in these person-perception tasks may stem from methodological difficulties inherent in the use of hypothetical and verbal materials. Children confronted with identical social situations presented in a more concrete and vivid fashion will typically respond in a more sophisticated fashion (e.g., Chandler, Greenspan, & Barenboim, 1973; Shultz & Butkowsky, 1977). More importantly, however, I suspect that these studies and the traditional self-perception analysis have put the cart before the horse. Thus, it is from their own experiences with social control and constraint that children eventually develop inferential principles that permit them to make systematic inferences about the motives of others, rather than the reverse. Hence, as in other work on social cognition (cf. Hoffman, 1976; Piaget, 1932; Wells & Shultz, 1978), we might expect children to behave in a more adult fashion when they are themselves involved in a concrete situation than when they are asked to take the role of another and make inferences about the motives or intentions of that other person.

How, then, might children come to understand the social meaning of extrinsic constraints? Let me sketch out a speculative analysis of this process (cf. Lepper & Greene, 1978c). Soon after children acquire the capacity to "get into mischief," they become the target of an increasing variety of constraints placed on their actions by adult socializing agents (cf. Minton, Kagan, & Levine, 1971). To prevent children from injuring themselves or others or doing damage to property, parents quickly begin to apply extrinsic contingencies designed to control and modify children's behavior. The child is, at various times, begged, threatened, cajoled, or bribed to induce compliance with adult demands (Carlsmith, Lepper, & Landauer, 1974). As particular interaction patterns are repeated, the child begins to abstract not only the common elements that define "approved" versus "disapproved" behavior patterns, but also the elements that signal social-control attempts. Presumably, at first, children's understanding of social-control techniques will vary in sophistication as a function of their familiarity with particular social situations and the ease with which new situations can be assimilated to more familiar social schemas. Only as the child's inventory of social experiences is expanded will he or she begin to employ more abstract distinctions (e.g., between work and play or bribes and bonuses) that adults may use to describe experiences of social constraint.

That children's social reasoning abilities and the meaning they extract from social interactions may develop as successively more abstract generalizations from initially concrete social schemas seems intuitively reasonable. It is also consistent with recent theoretical formulations concerning the representation of social knowledge (Abelson, 1976, 1978; Schank & Abelson, 1977) in terms of "scripts"—that is, organized and coherent event sequences anticipated in the presence of particular situational cues, reflecting an individual's expectations concerning apparent regularities in his or her social environment. In this model (Lepper & Greene, 1978c), relatively hypothetical or categorical scripts (e.g., "When someone offers me an extrinsic reward for doing something, the chances are that that something is boring or unpleasant.") are derived by abstraction of common features from sets of relatively more concrete "episodic" scripts (e.g., "When mom tells me I can't have my dessert until I clean my plate, what's left on my plate is usually yuckky."). Assimilation of novel situations to familiar social scripts on the basis of a small number of salient cues, moreover, has been shown to have profound effects on subjects' interpretations of and reactions to social influence attempts (Abelson, 1976; Carlsmith et al., 1974; Langer, 1978; Langer & Abelson, 1972).

This line of reasoning is consistent, as well, with our preliminary attempts to interview preschool children about their perceptions of social constraints. When asked to make inferences about their own behavior or that of others in a variety of social situations, these children did not appear to judge the motivational state of others (or, usually, themselves) in terms of any generalized "discounting" principle; there were, however, some familiar situations in which children's social inferences appeared to follow such an inferential script. To examine one of the more pervasive of these situations, 16 preschoolers were asked to imagine that Johnny's mother had brought home two new foods for dinner. When these subjects were told that Johnny's mother had said that he had to eat his "hule" in order to have his "hupe", or vice versa, every subject appeared to understand the social message implied by the imposition of this contingency. All but four confidently asserted that Johnny would prefer the second food; the remaining four each gave reasons for the opposite choice that nevertheless indicated an understanding of the underlying script. One child, for example, indicated that Johnny would prefer the first food because the second food "probably has refined sugar in it, and that's real bad for you." Control subjects told simply that Johnny's mother had given Johnny first one and then the other food showed no systematic preferences.

These results encouraged us to examine children's reactions to the imposition of a more general means–end script on their own actions, and their inferences about the attitudes of others placed in a similar setting (Lepper, Sagotsky, Dafoe, & Greene, 1980). In the self-perception version of this study, then, children were presented with two initially, and equally, attractive activities. Subjects in the means–end condition were asked if they would like to play with the "end" and, when they had assented, were told that they could win a chance to do so only by first playing with the "means." Control subjects were simply shown the two activities and asked to engage in one of the activities first and the other second, but without the imposition of any contingency between the two. Subsequently, we obtained independent, unobtrusive measures of children's intrinsic interest in each of these activities in their classrooms in the absence of further constraints. The results are presented in Fig. 5.12, which illustrates that the imposition of this nominal contingency led to decreased interest in the activity presented as a means of obtaining a chance to play with the other activity.

In the corresponding social-perception version of this study, different children were presented with narrated slide show presentations of versions of the two conditions of the preceding study and were asked to make predictions concerning how much the child in the slide show would subsequently like each of the two activities. The results on children's inferences about the protagonist's attitudes towards the two activities, as a function of their presentation in either a means–end or first–second relationship, are illustrated in Fig. 5.13. These findings, clearly, parallel those reported in Fig. 5.12, and suggest that children in this situation are employing some principle that reflects at least a rudimentary understanding of the social meaning of the imposition of a contingency on one's choices. Despite their systematic responses to specific questions about the protagonist's preferences, however,

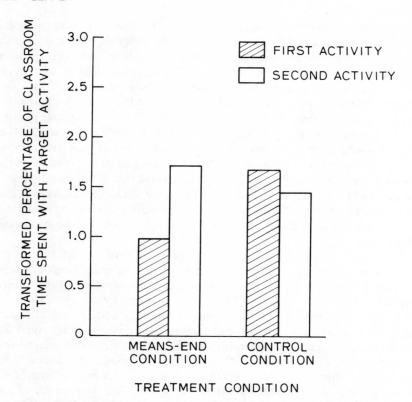

FIG. 5.12. Mean intrinsic interest in the two experimental activities, during postexperimental classroom observations, by condition. Data from Lepper, Sagotsky, Dafoe, and Greene (1980).

very few subjects seemed able to give a cogent explanation of their answers. Their inferences, in short, appeared to reflect an intuitive understanding of the social meaning of this situation, rather than some systematic analysis of social-control processes.

These findings, then, give us reason to suspect that children may have some knowledge, even at a relatively early age, of the implicit message of constraint that the imposition of a contingency may convey. However, it seems likely that there may be important developmental changes in children's responses to social-control attempts resulting from an increased ability to distinguish among the social contexts in which rewards may be employed. I have already noted the data suggesting that young children seem not to be responsive to information that rewards may convey concerning their competence or incompetence at an activity, relative to other children (Boggiano & Ruble

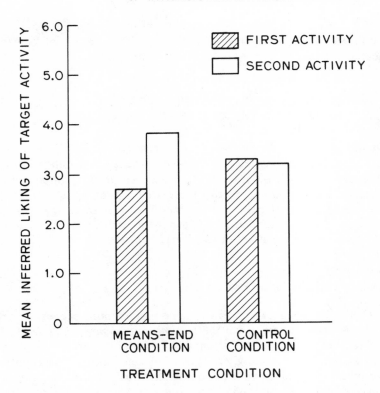

FIG. 5.13.   Mean inferred liking by the protagonist of the two experimental activities, by condition. Data from Lepper, Sagotsky, Dafoe, and Greene (1980).

1979). Other changes in our perceptions of the appropriateness of rewards as a function of the context in which they are offered may also vary with age. As one example, adults frequently appear to employ a "lesser-of-several-evils" principle in cases in which one is committed by external forces to some general goal, but is permitted a choice among several means for achieving that common end. If, under such circumstances, we believe ourselves to have had the luxury of choosing the most attractive, or least noxious, means of attaining that goal, we are, I suspect, less likely to show decreases in subsequent interest in that activity. With children, precisely the opposite effect seems to occur. In one study (Greene et al., 1976), children choosing the activities for which they were to receive rewards showed greater decreases in later interest than those for whom the activities were simply assigned. Perhaps more generally, one might expect our reactions to external social controls to come to depend, with increased experience and cognitive maturity, in a much more differentiated fashion on our perceptions of the relevant social norms, potential alternatives, or presumed motives of the agent of control in particular settings (cf. Lepper & Gilovich, in press).

THE EFFECTS OF SUPERFLUOUS SOCIAL CONTROLS: IMPLICATIONS AND SPECULATIONS

I have now summarized two basic lines of research involving the effects of threats of punishment on the subsequent internalization of adult prohibitions and the effects of extrinsic rewards on subsequent intrinsic interest. In this final section, I wish to bring together these two trains of thought, to consider some of the salient similarities and differences between these two paradigms, and to speculate a bit on the relationship of this research program to traditional issues in the study of socialization processes.

Parallels and Contrasts: The Minimal-Sufficiency Principle

Let me begin with a naive statement of the common ground between these two literatures—what we might call the *minimal-sufficiency principle* of social control (cf. Lepper, in press). Presumably, by now, the parallels are clear. In both cases, the use of seemingly less powerful techniques of social control to induce initial compliance with a request has proved more effective, under certain conditions, in producing subsequent behavior in accord with the presumed intent of the initial attempt at social control, in the later absence of further controls and the agent who administered them. Conversely, the use of unnecessarily powerful, functionally superfluous social-control procedures in both cases appears to decrease later internal controls when external constraints are subsequently minimized. In the forbidden-toy paradigm, unnecessarily powerful threats of punishment are less likely to produce subsequent adherence to the previous prohibition, or related but more implicit prohibitions, in the later absence of further explicit threats. In the overjustification paradigm, unnecessarily powerful extrinsic rewards are less likely to produce subsequent engagement in the previously rewarded activity in the later absence of further explicit rewards. Both sorts of effects are amenable to similar theoretical interpretations; both appear to respond in similar fashion to comparable manipulations involving attentional focus, timing of justification, and so forth.

Obviously, however, there are some contrasts between these two research programs. Perhaps the most salient, as should be apparent from the preceding reviews, involves the relative complexity of the processes that appear to define the limiting conditions under which each of these phenomena will occur. An analysis of the reasons underlying the greater complexity involved in the study of the effects of extrinsic rewards on subsequent intrinsic interest may prove informative and deserves further attention.

There are two obvious sources of potential divergence between the two paradigms. The first involves the historically significant theoretical distinction between social-influence attempts employed to induce the child to engage in explicitly counterattitudinal, and presumably dissonance-arousing, behavior, as in the forbidden-toy situation, and those employed to produce behavior that is not overtly inconsistent with one's previous attitudes, as in the overjustification case. The second involves two more procedural sorts of distinctions between these two paradigms: differences in the nature of the social-control technique employed—that is, promise of reward versus threat of punishment—and differences in the behavior that is the target of control— that is, producing active engagement in some activity versus inhibiting a tendency to engage in some activity.

Taking into account both sets of factors leads to a threefold classification of the circumstances in which social-control processes may take place: involving (1) the use of either promise of reward or threat of punishment; (2) either inducing an overt action or inhibiting that action; and (3) a target action that is initially either "attractive" or "unattractive" to the subject. In this schematic categorization, the two paradigms considered here represent only two of eight possible sets of conditions to which a minimal sufficiency principle might be applied.[6]

Space limitations preclude extended consideration of this classification scheme, but two salient features of this categorization deserve mention. On the one hand, this analysis provides one way of looking at the contexts in which rewards and punishments may be employed that illustrates clearly the limitations of the current literature. Although there is no necessary reason for the association, for example, some cells in this table seem quite unlikely in everyday life. We are much more likely, for instance, to threaten children with punishment than to offer them rewards to induce them to refrain from engaging in attractive, but socially undesirable, activities. Other combinations, including the overjustification case (i.e., promising a child a reward to induce engagement in an activity he or she would undertake anyway), seem to represent cases that are more likely to be created unintentionally than intentionally (Lepper & Dafoe, 1979; Lepper & Greene, 1978a). Still other

---

[6]I am indebted to Merrill Carlsmith, Gregory Northcraft, and Richard Nisbett for suggesting, independently, the utility of considering various parts of this classification scheme systematically. I should also note that even this categorization is itself an oversimplification. In any more comprehensive analysis, as one example, one would probably wish to distinguish—within the cells in which active task engagement is the goal—between the use of task-contingent versus performance-contingent incentives.

cases that seem more highly representative of the situations in which promises of rewards and threats of punishment are commonly used—e.g., to induce children to engage in activities of little initial interest or activities that are inherently aversive—have received virtually no experimental attention. A very specialized version of this case, involving the effects of payments offered for espousing a counterattitudinal position on subsequent attitudes, has received extensive study (e.g., Calder, Ross, & Insko, 1973; Collins & Hoyt, 1972; Zanna & Cooper, 1976). But, the effects of variations in the coerciveness of contingencies for inducing children to comply with adult requests to perform particular tasks (Landauer, Carlsmith, & Lepper, 1970) on their later compliance with related requests when incentive conditions are constant has not been studied. Looking at the literature in this way may serve to clarify some of the directions in which further research might be profitably pursued in contexts that have clearer implications for the socialization process (cf. Lepper, in press).

A second heuristic function of this analysis is that it provides a tool for examining the features of our two basic paradigms that may contribute to their differential conceptual complexity. In this sense, each of the dimensions of this classification suggests distinctions that may determine the range of additional factors—beyond perceptions of instrumentality and constraint common to all cases—that may influence subsequent behavior. Thus, issues concerning the possible effects of constraint on the quality of performance, the potential acquisition of additional skills or knowledge through increased task engagement, or the role of perceived competence seem particularly relevant when the target behavior in question involves active engagement in an activity. However, these same factors seem largely irrelevant to social-control attempts that involve the inhibition of activity. In the forbidden-toy paradigm, for instance, once compliance has been obtained, it is hard to imagine what measures of quality of performance of skill acquisition might look like. Indeed, the role of increased task engagement, even within those cells where active compliance is sought, should vary considerably as a function of the nature of the activity involved—whether the task is of high initial interest, is of potential intrinsic interest once certain proficiency levels have been attained, or is inherently dull and boring. Perhaps less obviously, even within otherwise comparable conditions, there seem to be some interesting assymetries inherent in the ways in which we typically use rewards and punishments, although there is, again, no necessary reason why this should be the case. Threats of punishment seem much less frequently tied to performance criteria than promises of reward; hence, variations in perceived competence may be relatively unimportant in the former case, but potentially critical in the latter. Attention to differences of this sort, and more generally to the phenomenologically distinct situations created by our typical uses of rewards and punishments (Lewin, 1935), may help clarify the relative complexity of different cases within this larger matrix of possibilities.[7]

Implications for the Socialization Process

Much research, then, is still needed to examine the more general applicability of the minimal sufficiency principle and its relevance to the socialization process. Nonetheless, I wish to speculate for a moment on the possible relevance of this analysis to broader questions concerning the conditions that promote internalization of adult values that have been a source of continuing interest to students of the socialization process.

Is there any evidence within the socialization literature to suggest that seemingly less powerful techniques of social control may prove ultimately more effective in promoting subsequent internalization of the behaviors that were the target of these controls? Let us consider, first, the area in developmental psychology in which the study of internalization has its longest legacy—the study of the development of moral values and behavior. For many years, investigators in this area have been interested in the subsequent effects of variations in the child-rearing techniques that parents use at home to teach moral values and the inhibition of "immoral" behaviors on children's later behavior in other settings in which they are no longer under their parents' surveillance or direct control. The results of this search for the antecedents of subsequent internalized controls, as illustrated most recently in the elegant work of Hoffman and his colleagues (Hoffman, 1970, 1975; Hoffman & Saltzstein, 1967; cf. also Sears, Maccoby, & Levin, 1957), suggest an inverse relationship between salience of external control and later internalization that parallels our earlier speculations.

Distinguishing between three types of disciplinary techniques that parents might employ—power assertion, love withdrawal, and induction—Hoffman finds that those techniques one would expect to be most likely to lead the child to view compliance with the parents' requests at home as extrinsically motivated are the least effective in producing subsequent internalization of parental values. Parents' use of overt power-assertive techniques, involving the heavy-handed use of physical punishment, withdrawal of tangible rewards and privileges, and so on, correlates negatively with subsequent

---

[7]Thus, it is worth noting that there may be other important differences between the use of rewards and punishments that are not included in the foregoing analysis. Clearly, in socialization contexts, the two procedures provide quite different social models to the child, and may thereby have different effects on specific classes of behaviors such as interpersonal aggression. It may also be the case, although the scaling problems are considerable, that punishment will generally produce more intense emotional responses and feelings of coercion than equivalently powerful reward procedures.

moral behavior in situations outside the home, whereas the use of induction and reasoning, the least clearly coercive of Hoffman's categories, shows consistent positive corelations with subsequent internalization of moral standards and behavior.

Other related findings in different contexts suggest a similar set of conclusions. For example, Baumrind's informative studies (e.g., 1971, 1973) on patterns of child-rearing practices and their association with indices of social responsibility and social competence outside the home provide a similar picture. In these studies, children of authoritarian parents who favor the use of highly "forceful" and "punitive" measures to elicit compliance from the child at home appear less well socialized outside of the home on a variety of measures than children of authoritative parents who were, in turn, more likely to use less power-oriented means of control and more reasoning with their children. Findings on the effects of power-oriented techniques of punishment for aggression in the home on later aggressive behavior in other settings provide analogous results (cf. Dienstbier, Hillman, Lehnhoff, Hillman, & Valkenaar, 1975).

In addition to these large-scale correlational projects, other experimental research has shown that the overt labeling of a child's compliance with an adult request as either intrinsically or extrinsically motivated may have substantial effects on the child's later behavior in settings in which he or she is no longer under the direct control of the person administering the initial request (Dienstbier et al., 1975; Grusec, in press; Grusec, Kuczynski, Rushton, & Simutis, 1978; Miller, Brickman, & Bolen, 1975). Inducing the child to think of his or her behavior—whether resistance to temptation (Dienstbier et al., 1975), altrusim (Grusec, in press; Grusec et al., 1978), or cleaning up the schoolyard (Miller et al., 1975)—in internal, rather than external terms, made it more likely that the child would show subsequent behavior in accord with the intent of the initial request in the later absence of further explicit controls.

Obviously, there are many factors that contribute to the differential effectiveness of various parental practices, and the correlational findings reported in this area are overdetermined (Dienstbier et al., 1975; Hoffman, 1970, 1975). The convergence of results obtained in these studies, the labeling literature, and the research I have reviewed, however, suggests that the minimal sufficiency principle may be implicated in the socialization process (cf. Lepper, in press). To close this chapter, let us consider two more general implications of this analysis.

Successful Versus Unsuccessful Social-Control Attempts

The first point to be made about the minimal sufficiency principle is that it suggests an active positive effect of the use of social-control techniques that are successful at producing compliance—when compliance would not otherwise be obtained—if those techniques are not so overly salient or patently coercive as to lead the child to view his or her behavior entirely as a response to those external pressures (e.g., Lepper,, 1973). Hence, this proposition is not an argument for "permissiveness" or a lack of social controls by parents and is not inconsistent with data indicating that children of parents favoring a completely permissive approach to child-rearing fare less well than those reared by authoritative parents employing firm, but not extreme, control techniques (Baumrind, 1971, 1973).

At the same time, this analysis also suggests that a complementary negative effect on later internalization or intrinsic motivation should be the result of social-control attempts that are unsuccessful (i.e., that fail to produce initial compliance). Thus, the child who feels under external pressure to behave in a particular way but resists that pressure would be predicted to view his or her failure to comply in internal terms, and should be more likely to do so the greater the pressure applied, unsuccessfully, to induce initial compliance. The child in the forbidden-toy situation, for example, who yields to temptation despite a threat of punishment for transgression should be likely to find the previously forbidden activity more attractive and should be less likely to resist temptation in future situations than a child never exposed to a request not to engage in the activity. The more powerful the threat of punishment the child has chosen to disregard in this setting, the greater this effect should be (Lepper, in press; Mills, 1958).

This formulation, therefore, implies that parents and other socializing agents must frequently walk a fine line. The difference between a barely sufficient, successful attempt at social control and a barely insufficient and unsuccessful attempt is, in terms of the parent's behavior, a small one. The difference between these two cases in terms of their subsequent effects on the child's behavior, by contrast, is theoretically enormous. Whereas the former case may result in enhanced internalization and responsiveness to further requests, the latter case may produce decreased internalization and increased resistance to further social-influence attempts. To the extent that the behavior of permissive parents may involve as much the use of insufficiently powerful and ineffective social-control techniques as a complete absence of attempts at control, the potentially detrimental effects of such practices may be increased.

Salience Versus Subtlety of
Social-Control Attempts

Second, within the domain of successful social-control procedures, sufficient to elicit initial compliance from the child, an attributional account suggests that there may be important differences in the general salience and coerciveness of different sorts of social-control techniques. These differences, and the consequent differences in the likelihood that particular techniques will produce perceptions of one's actions as extrinsically motivated, ought then to determine the effects of these procedures on subsequent internalization and later behavior in unconstrained settings.

Most of the literature I have discussed, for example, deals with the subsequent effects of tangible rewards and threats of punishment presented in an explicit contingent, and typically contractual, fashion. In this research, these procedures were chosen because they represent the case in which children are most likely to view their behavior as extrinsically governed. Both in other traditions of laboratory research and in everyday life, however, we are often exposed to social-influence techniques that may be equally effective in modifying our behavior, but do not produce the same perceptions of external constraint. Consider, for example, the large literatures documenting the effectiveness of various modeling techniques (Bandura, 1971, 1977) or the use of contingent social reinforcement or approval (Kazdin, 1975) as means of producing dramatic changes in children's behavior. My suspicion is that, despite their demonstrable effectiveness in producing functional control over behavior, both these techniques would be less likely to lead children to view their behavior as extrinsically constrained than the use of tangible rewards and punishments. I believe that we learn early on to think about immediate palpable rewards and punishments as reasons for our actions (e.g., "I did it for the money," or "I did it to avoid a spanking."), but that we are less likely to view our actions in comparable instrumental terms when the stimulus to our actions is some prior model or even diffuse social approval. Control in the former case seems to demand a response; in the latter case, the control technique seems more suggestive than demanding. If this were so, one might predict that less phenomenologically coercive techniques of this sort would be less likely to produce subsequent negative effects and more likely to produce positive effects on subsequent behavior in the later absence of further constraint (cf. Grusec, in press; Lepper, Sagotsky, & Mailer, 1975; Rosenhan, 1969).

Similar considerations may also apply in the case of more delayed and diffuse, as opposed to immediate and highly palpable, goals or incentives. Often, we encourage children to engage in particular activities because they will be ultimately instrumental to long-term goals that may be many years away. The power of such distant goals to provoke continuing perceptions of one's actions as instrumentally directed is, I suspect, much less than the power of more immediate goals to do so. There may be a world of difference between doing your schoolwork in order to win the $5.00 Dad pays for each "A" on your report card and doing the same work because success will eventually enable you to go to the college or pursue the career of your choice.

Finally, there may be similar elements involved in the difference between self-imposed versus externally imposed standards and contingency systems. In recent years, we have seen the growth of a large literature investigating the use of techniques for training children to impose contingencies on their own actions (Bandura, 1976; Mahoney, 1974, 1977)—a trend that seems based in part on the assumption that changes in behavior produced through techniques that involve the subject as an active participant in the social-control process will be more likely to produce generalization of those changes in behavior to other settings in which salient extrinsic constraints are absent. Although good comparative evidence is lacking, the existing data in support of this argument (e.g., Brownell et al., 1977; Drabman, Spitalnik, & O'Leary, 1973; Turkewitz, O'Leary, & Ironsmith, 1975; Weiner & Dubanoski, 1975) can be viewed in attributional terms, as a function of the relative likelihood of perceptions of external constraint generated by these two techniques (cf. Lepper, Sagosky, & Greene, in preparation). For most of these speculations, there is no compelling comparative evidence at the moment; my goal in presenting them is to raise issues that deserve further study.

In closing, I should note that these ideas are not entirely without precedent. Nearly 300 years ago, John Locke proposed a similar thesis in his book of advice to parents and teachers (Locke, 1693):

> *Rewards,* I grant, and *Punishments* must be proposed to Children if we intend to work upon them. The Mistake, I imagine, is that those that are generally made use of, are *ill chosen.* The Pains and Pleasures of the Body are, I think, of ill consequence, when made the Rewards and Punishments, whereby Men would prevail on their Children: For as I said before, they serve but to increase and strengthen those Inclinations which 'tis our business to subdue and master. [p. 55].

The principal alternatives Locke proposed to the use of immediate tangible rewards and punishments involved teaching the child to be responsive to the model and social approval of the parent and to view his or her actions in terms of long-term goals that extend beyond particular current situations. Perhaps, at this point, it is time to investigate the utility of his admonitions experimentally.

ACKNOWLEDGMENTS

Preparation of this chapter was supported, in part, by Research Grant HD–MH–09814 from the National Institute of Child Health and Human Development. The report was written during the author's term as a Fellow at the Center for Advanced Study in the Behavioral Sciences, Stanford, California, and financial support for this fellowship from National Science Foundation Grant BNS 78–24671 and the Spencer Foundation is gratefully acknowledged. John Condry and Thomas Gilovich also deserve thanks for their helpful comments on an earlier draft of this chapter.

REFERENCES

Abelson, R. P. Script processing in attitude formation and decision-making. In J. S. Carroll & J. W. Payne (Eds.), *Cognition and social behavior.* Hillsdale, N.J: Lawrence Erlbaum Associates, 1976.

Abelson, R. P. *Scripts.* Unpublished manuscript, Yale University, 1978.

Amabile, T. M. Effects of external evaluation on artistic creativity. *Journal of Personality and Social Psychology,* 1979, *37,* 221–233.

Amabile, T. M., DeJong, W., & Lepper, M. R. Effects of externally-imposed deadlines on subsequent intrinsic motivation. *Journal of Personality and Social Psychology,* 1976, *34,* 92–98.

Anderson, R., Manoogian, S. T., & Reznick, J. S. The undermining and enhancing of intrinsic motivation in preschool children. *Journal of Personality and Social Psychology,* 1976, *34,* 915–922.

Aronson, E. The theory of cognitive dissonance: A current perspective. In L. Berkowitz (Ed.), *Advances in experimental social psychology* (Vol. 4). New York: Academic Press, 1969.

Aronson, E., & Carlsmith, J. M. The effect of the severity of threat on the devaluation of forbidden behavior. *Journal of Abnormal and Social Psychology,* 1963, *66,* 584–588.

Bandura, A. Vicarious and self-reinforcement processes. In R. Glaser (Ed.), *The nature of reinforcement.* New York: Academic Press, 1971.

Bandura, A. Self-reinforcement: Theoretical and methodological considerations. *Behaviorism,* 1976, *4,* 135–155.

Bandura, A. *Social learning theory.* Englewood Cliffs, N.J.: Prentice-Hall, 1977.

Bar-Tal, D. Attributional analysis of achievement related behavior. *Review of Educational Research,* 1978, *48,* 259–271.

Baumrind, D. Current patterns of parental authority. *Developmental Psychology Monographs,* 1971, *4*(Whole No. 1).

Baumrind, D. The development of instrumental competence through socialization. In A. Pick (Ed.), *Minnesota symposium on child psychology* (Vol. 7). Minneapolis: University of Minnesota Press, 1973.

Bem, D. J. Self-perception: An alternative interpretation of cognitive dissonance phenomena. *Psychological Review,* 1967, *74,* 183–200.

Bem, D. J. Self-perception theory. In L. Berkowitz (Ed.), *Advances in experimental social psychology* (Vol. 6). New York: Academic Pres, 1972.

Blackwell, L. *Student choice in curriculum, feelings of control and causality, and academic motivation and performance.* Unpublished doctoral dissertation, Stanford University, 1974.

Blanck, P. D., Reis, H. T., & Jackson, L. *The effects of verbal reinforcement on intrinsic motivation.* Unpublished manuscript, University of Rochester, 1979.

Boggiano, A. K., & Ruble, D. N. Perception of competence and the overjustification effect: A developmental study. *Journal of Personality and Social Psychology,* 1979, *37,* 1462–1468.

Brownell, K., Colletti, G., Ernser-Hershfield, R., Hershfield, S. M., & Wilson, G. T. Self-control in school children: Stringency and leniency in self-determined and externally-imposed performance standards. *Behavior Therapy,* 1977, *8,* 442–455.

Calder, B. J., Ross, M., & Insko, C. A. Attitude change and attitude attribution: Effects of incentive, choice, and consequences. *Journal of Personality and Social Psychology,* 1973, *25,* 84–89.

Calder, B. J., & Staw, B. M. Self-perception of intrinsic and extrinsic motivation. *Journal of Personality and Social Psychology,* 1975, *31,* 599–605.

Carlsmith, J. M., Ebbesen, E. B., Lepper, M. R., Zanna, M. P., Joncas, A. J., & Abelson, R. P. Dissonance reduction following forced attention to the dissonance. *Proceedings of the 77th Annual Convention of the American Psychological Association,* 1969, *4,* 321–322.

Carlsmith, J. M., Lepper, M. R., & Landauer, T. K. Children's obedience to adult requests: Interactive effects of anxiety arousal and apparent punitiveness of the adult. *Journal of Personality and Social Pscyhology,* 1974, *30,* 822–828.

Chandler, M. J., Greenspan, S., & Barenboim, C. Judgments of intentionality in response to videotaped and verbally presented moral dilemmas: The medium is the message. *Child Development,* 1973, *44,* 315–320.

Collins, B. E., & Hoyt, M. F. Personal responsibility-for-consequences: An integration and extension of the "forced compliance" literature. *Journal of Experimental Social Psychology,* 1972, *8,* 558–593.

Colvin, R. H. Imposed extrinsic reward in an elementary school setting: Effects on free-operant rates and choices. (Doctoral dissertation, Southern Illinois University, 1971.) *Dissertation Abstracts International,* 1972, *32,* 5034–A.

Condry, J. C. Enemies of exploration: Self-initiated versus other-initiated learning. *Journal of Personality and Social Psychology,* 1977, *35,* 459–477.

Condry, J., & Chambers, J. C. Intrinsic motivation and the process of learning. In M. R. Lepper & D. Greene (Eds.), *The hidden costs of reward.* Hillsdale, N.J.: Lawrence Erlbaum Associates, 1978.

Davidson, P., & Bucher, B. Intrinsic interest and extrinsic reward: The effects of a continuing token program on continuing nonconstrained preference. *Behavior Therapy,* 1978, *9,* 222–234.

Deci, E. L. Effects of externally mediated rewards on intrinsic motivation. *Journal of Personality and Social Psychology,* 1971, *18,* 105–115.

Deci, E. L. The effects of contingent and non-contingent rewards and controls on intrinsic motivation. *Organizational Behavior and Human Performance,* 1972, *8,* 217–229. (a)

Deci, E. L. Intrinsic motivation, extrinsic reinforcement, and inequity. *Journal of Personality and Social Psychology,* 1972, *22,* 113–120. (b)

Deci, E. L. *Intrinsic motivation.* New York: Plenum, 1975.

Dienstbier, R. A., Hillman, D., Lehnhoff, J., Hillman, J., & Valkenaar, M. C. An emotion-attribution approach to moral behavior: Interfacing cognitive and avoidance theories of moral development. *Psychological Review,* 1975, *82,* 299–315.

Dollinger, S. J., & Thelen, M. H. Overjustification and children's intrinsic motivation: Comparative effects of four rewards. *Journal of Personality and Social Psychology,* 1978, *36,* 1259–1269.

Drabman, R. S., Spitalnik, R., & O'Leary, K. D. Teaching self-control to disruptive children. *Journal of Abnormal Psychology,* 1973, *82,* 10–16.

Easterbrook, J. A. The effect of emotion on cue utilization and organization of behavior. *Psychological Review,* 1959, *66,* 183–201.

Enzle, M. E., & Ross, J. M. Increasing and decreasing intrinsic interest with contingent rewards: A test of cognitive evaluation theory. *Journal of Experimental Social Psychology,* 1978, *14,* 588–597.

Estes, W. K. Reinforcement in human behavior. *American Scientist,* 1972, *60,* 723–729.

Farr, J. L. Task characteristics, reward contingency, and intrinsic motivation. *Organizational Behavior and Human Performance,* 1976, *16,* 294–307.

Fazio, R. H., Zanna, M. P., & Cooper, J. Dissonance vs. self-perception: An integrative view of each theory's proper domain of application. *Journal of Experimental Social Psychology,* 1977, *5,* 464–479.

Feingold, B. D., & Mahoney, M. J. Reinforcement effects on intrinsic interest: Undermining the overjustification hypothesis. *Behavior Therapy,* 1975, *6,* 367–377.

Festinger, L. *A theory of cognitive dissonance.* Stanford, Calif.: Stanford University Press, 1957.

Freedman, J. L. Long-term behavioral effects of cognitive dissonance. *Journal of Experimental Social Psychology,* 1965, *1,* 145–155.

Freedman, J. L., & Fraser, S. C. Compliance without pressure: The foot-in-the-door technique. *Journal of Personality and Social Psychology*, 1966, *4*, 195–202.

Garbarino, J. The impact of anticipated rewards on cross-age tutoring. *Journal of Personality and Social Psychology*, 1975, *32*, 421–428.

Greene, D., & Lepper, M. R. Effects of extrinsic rewards on children's subsequent intrinsic interest. *Child Development*, 1974, *45*, 1141–1145.

Greene, D., Sternberg, B., & Lepper, M. R. Overjustification in a token economy. *Journal of Personality and Social Psychology*, 1976, *34*, 1219–1234.

Greenwald, A. G. On the inconclusiveness of "crucial" cognitive tests of dissonance versus self-perception theories. *Journal of Experimental Social Psychology*, 1975, *11*, 490–499.

Grusec, J. E. Training altruistic dispositions: A cognitive analysis. To appear in T. E. Higgins, D. N. Ruble, & W. W. Hartup (Eds.) *Social cognition and social behavior: A developmental perspective*. San Francisco: Jossey-Bass, in press.

Grusec, J. E., Kuczynski, L., Rushton, J. P., & Simutis, Z. M. Modeling, direct instruction, and attributions: Effects on altruism. *Developmental Psychology*, 1978, *14*, 51–57.

Hamner, W. C., & Foster, L. W. Are intrinsic and extrinsic rewards additive: A test of Deci's cognitive evaluation theory of task motivation. *Organizational Behavior and Human Performance*, 1975, *14*, 398–415.

Harackiewicz, J. M. The effects of reward contingency and performance feedback on intrinsic motivation. *Journal of Personality and Social Pscyhology*, 1979, *37*, 1352–1361.

Harter, S. Effectance motivation reconsidered: Toward a developmental model. *Human Development*, 1978, *21*, 34–64. (a)

Harter, S. Pleasure derived from challenge and the effects of receiving grades on children's difficulty level choices. *Child Development*, 1978, *49*, 788–799. (b)

Hoffman, M. L. Moral development. In P. Mussen (Ed.), *Carmichael's handbook of child psychology* (Vol. 2). New York: Wiley, 1970.

Hoffman, M. L. Moral internalization, parental power, and the nature of parent–child interaction. *Developmental Psychology*, 1975, *11*, 228–239.

Hoffman, M. L. Empathy, role-taking, guilt, and the development of altruistic motives. In T. Lickona (Ed.), *Moral development and behavior*. New York: Holt, Rinehart, & Winston, 1976.

Hoffman, M. L., & Saltzstein, H. D. Parent discipline and the child's moral development. *Journal of Personality and Social Psychology*, 1967, *5*, 45–57.

Holt, J. *How children fail*. New York: Dell, 1964.

Hovland, C. I., Janis, I. L., & Kelley, H. H. *Communcation and persuasion*. New Haven: Yale University Press, 1953.

Johnson, E. J., Greene, D., & Carroll, J. S. *Overjustification and reasons: A test of the means–ends analysis*. Unpublished manuscript, Carnegie–Mellon University, 1979.

Karniol, R., & Ross, M. The development of causal attributions in social perception. *Journal of Personality and Social Psychology*, 1976, *34*, 455–464.

Karniol, R., & Ross, M. The effect of performance-relevant and performance-irrelevant rewards on children's intrinsic motivation. *Child Development*, 1977, *48*, 482–487.

Kazdin, A. E. *Behavior modification in applied settings*. Homewood, Ill.: Dorsey Press, 1975.

Kazdin, A. E., & Bootzin, R. R. The token economy: An evaluative review. *Journal of Applied Behavior Analysis*, 1972, *5*, 343–372.

Kelley, H. H. Attribution theory in social psychology. In D. Levine (Ed.), *Nebraska symposium on motivation* (Vol. 15). Lincoln: University of Nebraska Press, 1967.

Kelley, H. H. The processes of causal attribution. *American Psychologist*, 1973, *28*, 107–128.

Kelman, H. C. Compliance, identification, and internalization: Three processes of opinion change. *Journal of Conflict Resolution*, 1958, *2*, 51–60.

Kelman, H. C. Processes of attitude change. *Public Opinion Quarterly*, 1961, *25*, 57–78.

Kruglanski, A. W. Endogenous attribution and intrinsic motivation. In M. R. Lepper & D. Greene (Eds.), *The hidden costs of reward.* Hillsdale, N.J.: Lawrence Erlbaum Associates, 1978.

Kruglanski, A. W., Alon, S., & Lewis, T. Retrospective misattribution and task enjoyment. *Journal of Experimental Social Psychology,* 1972, *8,* 493–501.

Kruglanski, A. W., Friedman, I., & Zeevi, G. The effects of extrinsic incentives on some qualitative aspects of task performance. *Journal of Personality,*1971, *39,* 606–617.

Kruglanski, A. W., Stein, C., & Riter, A. Contingencies of exogenous reward and task performance: On the "minimax" principle in instrumental behavior. *Journal of Applied Social Psychology,* 1977, *7,* 141–148.

Landauer, T. K., Carlsmith, J. M., & Lepper, M. R. Experimental analysis of the factors determining obedience of four-year-old children to adult females. *Child Development,* 1970, *41,* 601–611.

Langer, E. J. Rethinking the role of thought in social interaction. In J. H. Harvey, W. J. Ickes, & R. F. Kidd (Eds.), *New directions in attribution research* (Vol. 2). Hillsdale, N.J.: Lawrence Erlbaum Associates, 1978.

Langer, E. J., & Abelson, R. P. The semantics of asking a favor: How to succeed in getting help without really dying. *Journal of Personality and Social Psychology,* 1972, *24,* 26–32.

Lepper, M. R. Dissonance, self-perception, and honesty in children. *Journal of Personality and Social Psychology,* 1973, *25,* 65–74.

Lepper, M. R. Social control processes, attributions of motivation, and the internalization of social values. To appear in T. E. Higgins, D. N. Ruble, & W. W. Hartup (Eds.), *Social cognition and social behavior: A developmental perspective.* San Francisco: Jossey-Bass, in press.

Lepper, M. R., & Dafoe, J. Incentives, constraints, and motivation in the classroom: An attributional analysis. In I. Frieze, D. Bar-Tal, & J. Carroll (Eds.), *Attribution theory: Applications to social problems.* San Francisco: Jossey-Bass, 1979.

Lepper, M. R., & Gilovich, T. J. The multiple functions of reward: A social-developmental perspective. To appear in S. S. Brehm, S. M. Kassin, & F. X. Gibbons (Eds.), *Developmental social psychology.* New York: Oxford University Press, in press.

Lepper, M. R., Gilovich, T., & Rest, G. Detrimental effects of extrinsic rewards on immediate task performance vs. subsequent intrinsic interest. Research in progress, 1980.

Lepper, M. R., & Greene, D. Turning play into work: Effects of adult surveillance and extrinsic rewards on children's intrinsic motivation. *Journal of Personality and Social Psychology,* 1975, *31,* 479–486.

Lepper, M. R., & Greene, D. On understanding "overjustification": A reply to Reiss and Sushinsky. *Journal of Personality and Social Psychology,* 1976, *33,* 23–35.

Lepper, M. R., & Greene, D. Divergent approaches to the study of rewards. In M. R. Lepper & D. Greene (Eds.), *The hidden costs of reward.* Hillsdale, N.J.: Lawrence Erlbaum Associates, 1978. (a)

Lepper, M. R., & Greene, D. (Eds.), *The hidden costs of reward.* Hillsdale, N.J.: Lawrence Erlbaum Associates, 1978. (b)

Lepper, M. R., & Greene, D. Overjustification research and beyond: Toward a means–ends analysis of intrinsic and extrinsic motivation. In M. R. Lepper & D. Greene (Eds.), *The hidden costs of reward.* Hillsdale, N.J: Lawrence Erlbaum Associates, 1978. (c)

Lepper, M. R., Greene, D., & Nisbett, R. E. Undermining children's intrinsic interest with extrinsic rewards: A test of the overjustification hypothesis. *Journal of Personality and Social Psychology,* 1973, *28,* 129–137.

Lepper, M. R., Sagotsky, G., Dafoe, J., & Greene, D. *Consequences of superfluous social constraints: Effects on young children's social inferences and subsequent intrinsic interest.* Unpublished manuscript, Stanford University, 1980.

Lepper, M. R., Sagotsky, G., & Greene, D. *Overjustification effects following multiple-trial reinforcement procedures: Experimental evidence concerning the assessment of intrinsic interest.* Unpublished manuscript, Stanford University, 1980.

Lepper, M. R., Sagotsky, G., & Greene, D. *Effects of choice and self-imposed vs. externally-imposed contingencies on children's subsequent intrinsic motivation.* In preparation, 1980.

Lepper, M. R., Sagotsky, G., & Mailer, J. Generalization and persistence of effects of exposure to self-reinforcement models. *Child Development,* 1975, *46,* 618–630.

Lepper, M. R., Zanna, M. P., & Abelson, R. P. Cognitive irreversibility in a dissonance-reduction situation. *Journal of Personality and Social Psychology,* 1970, *16,* 191–198.

Lewin, K. The psychological situations of reward and punishment. In K. Lewin (Ed.), *A dynamic theory of personality.* New York: McGraw-Hill, 1935.

Lewin, K., Lipsitt, R., & White, R. Patterns of aggressive behavior in experimentally created "social climates." *Journal of Social Psychology,* 1939, *10,* 271–299.

Locke, J. *Some thoughts concerning education.* London: A. & J. Churchill 1693.

Loveland, K. K., & Olley, J. G. The effect of external reward on interest and quality of task performance in children of high and low intrinsic motivation. *Child Development,* 1979, *50,* 1207–1210.

McCullers, J. C. Issues in learning and motivation. In M. R. Lepper & D. Greene (Eds.), *The hidden costs of reward.* Hillsdale, N.J.: Lawrence Erlbaum Associates, 1978.

McGraw, K. O. The detrimental effects of reward on performance: A literature review and a prediction model. In M. R. Lepper & D. Greene (Eds.), *The hidden costs of reward.* Hillsdale, N.J.: Lawrence Erlbaum Associates, 1978.

McGraw, K. O., & McCullers, J. C. Evidence of a detrimental effect of extrinsic incentives on breaking a mental set. *Journal of Experimental Social Psychology,* 1979, *15,* 285–294.

McLoyd, V. C. The effects of extrinsic rewards of differential value on high and low intrinsic interest. *Child Development,* 1979, *50,* 1010–1019.

Mahoney, M. J. *Cognition and behavior modification.* Cambridge: Ballinger, 1974.

Mahoney, M. J. Reflections on the cognitive-learning trend in psychotherapy. *American Psychologist,* 1977, *32,* 5–13.

Miller, R. L., Brickman, P., & Bolen, D. Attribution versus persuasion as a means for modifying behavior. *Journal of Personality and Social Psychology,* 1975, *31,* 430–441.

Mills, J. Changes in moral attitudes following temptation. *Journal of Personality,* 1958, *26,* 517–531.

Minton, C., Kagan, J., & Levine, J. A. Maternal control and obedience in the two-year-old. *Child Development,* 1971, *42,* 1873–1894.

O'Leary, K. D. The operant and social psychology of token systems. In A. C. Catania & T. A. Brigham (Eds.), *Handbook of applied behavior analysis.* New York: Irvington, 1978.

O'Leary, K. D., & Drabman, R. Token reinforcement programs in the classroom: A review. *Psychological Bulletin,* 1971, *75,* 379–398.

Pepitone, A., McCauley, C., & Hammond, P. Change in attractiveness of forbidden toys as a function of severity of threat. *Journal of Experimental Social Psychology,* 1967, *3,* 221–229.

Piaget, J. *The moral judgment of the child.* London: Kegan Paul, 1932.

Pinder, C. C. Additivity versus nonadditivity of intrinsic and extrinsic incentives: Implications for work motivation, performance, and attitudes. *Journal of Applied Psychology,* 1976, *61,* 693–700.

Pittman, T. S., Cooper, E. E., & Smith, T. W. Attribution of causality and the overjustification effect. *Personality and Social Psychology Bulletin,* 1977, *3,* 280–283.

Pittman, T. S., Davey, M. E., Alafat, K. A., Wetherill, K. V., & Wirsul, N. A. Informational vs. controlling verbal rewards, levels of surveillance, and intrinsic motivation. *Personality and Social Psychology Bulletin,* in press.

Reiss, S., & Sushinsky, L. W. Overjustification, competing responses, and the acquisition of intrinsic interest. *Journal of Personality and Social Psychology,* 1975, *31,* 1116–1125.

Rosenhan, D. Some origins of concern for others. In P. A. Mussen, J. Langer, & M. Covington (Eds.), *Trends and issues in developmental psychology.* New York: Holt, Rinehart, & Winston, 1969.

Ross, M. Salience of reward and intrinsic motivation. *Journal of Personality and Social Psychology,* 1975, *32,* 245–254.

Ross, M., Karniol, R., & Rothstein, M. Reward contingency and intrinsic motivation in children: A test of the delay of gratification hypothesis. *Journal of Personality and Social Psychology,* 1976, *33,* 442–447.

Schank, R., & Abelson, R. P. *Scripts, plans, goals, and understanding.* Hillsdale, N.J.: Lawrence Erlbaum Associates, 1977.

Sears, R. R., Maccoby, E. E., & Levin, H. *Patterns of child rearing.* Evanston, Ill.: Row, Peterson & Co., 1957.

Sears, R. R., Whiting, J. W. M., Nowlis, V., & Sears, P. S. Some childrearing antecedents of aggression and dependency in young children. *Genetic Psychology Monographs,* 1953, *47,* 135–234.

Shapira, Z. Expectancy determinants of intrinsically motivated behavior. *Journal of Personality and Social Psychology,* 1976, *34,* 1235–1244.

Shultz, T. R., & Butkowsky, I. Young children's use of the scheme for multiple sufficient causes in the attribution of real and hypothetical behavior. *Child Development,* 1977, *48,* 464–469.

Shultz, T. R., Butkowsky, I., Pearce, J. W., & Shanfield, H. Development of schemes for the attribution of multiple psychological causes. *Developmental Psychology,* 1975, *11,* 502–510.

Simon, H. A. Motivational and emotional controls of cognition. *Psychological Review,* 1967, *74,* 29–39.

Smith, M. C. Children's use of the multiple sufficient cause schema in social perception. *Journal of Personality and Social Psychology,* 1975, *32,* 737–747.

Smith, W. F. *The effects of social and monetary rewards on intrinsic motivation.* Unpublished doctoral dissertation, Cornell University, 1976.

Smith, T. W., & Pittman, T. S. Reward, distraction, and the overjustification effect. *Journal of Personality and Social Psychology,* 1978, *36,* 565–572.

Spence, K. W. *Behavior theory and conditioning.* New Haven, Yale University Press, 1956.

Staub, E. *Positive social behavior and morality* (Vol. 1). New York: Academic Press, 1978.

Staub, E. *Positive social behavior and morality* (Vol. 2). New York: Academic Press, 1979.

Swann, W. B., Jr., & Pittman, T. S. Initiating play activity of children: The moderating influence of verbal cues on intrinsic motivation. *Child Development,* 1977, *48,* 1125–1132.

Turkewitz, H., O'Leary, K. D., & Ironsmith, M. Producing generalization of appropriate behavior through self-control. *Journal of Consulting and Clinical Psychology,* 1975, *43,* 577–583.

Turner, E. A., & Wright, J. Effects of severity of threat and perceived availability on the attractiveness of objects. *Journal of Personality and Social Psychology,* 1965, *2,* 128–132.

Vasta, R. On token rewards and real dangers: A look at the data. *Behavior Modification,* in press.

Vasta, R., Andrews, D. E., McLaughlin, A. M., Stirpe, L. A., & Comfort, C. Reinforcement effects on intrinsic interest: A classroom analog. *Journal of School Psychology,* 1978, *16,* 161–166.

Vasta, R., & Stirpe, L. A. Reinforcement effects on three measures of children's interest in math. *Behavior Modification,* 1979, *3,* 223–244.

Weiner, B. *Theories of motivation: From mechanism to cognition.* Chicago: Markham, 1972.

Weiner, B. (Ed.). *Achievement motivation and attribution theory.* Morristown, N.J.: General Learning Press, 1974.

Weiner, B. A theory of motivation for some classroom experiences. *Journal of Educational Psychology*, 1979, *71*, 3–25.

Weiner, H. R., & Dubanoski, R. A. Resistance to extinction as a function of self- or externally determined schedules of reinforcement. *Journal of Personality and Social Psychology*, 1975, *31*, 905–910.

Weiner, M. J., & Mander, A. M. The effects of reward and perception of competency upon intrinsic motivation. *Motivation and Emotion*. 1978, *2*, 67–73.

Wells, D., & Schultz, T. R. *Factors affecting young children's use of the scheme for multiple sufficient causes.* Unpublished manuscript, McGill University, 1978.

Zajonc, R. B. The effects of mere exposure. *Journal of Personality and Social Psychology*, 1968, *9*(2), 127. (Monograph Supplements).

Zajonc, R. B. Feeling and thinking: Preferences need no inferences. *American Psychologist*, in press.

Zanna, M. P., & Cooper, J. Dissonance and the attribution process. In J. H. Harvey, W. J. Ickes, & R. F. Kidd (Eds.), *New directions in attribution research* (Vol. 1). Hillsdale, N.J.: Lawrence Erlbaum Associates, 1976.

Zanna, M. P., Lepper, M. R., & Abelson, R. P. Attentional mechanisms in children's devaluation of a forbidden activity in a forced-compliance situation. *Journal of Personality and Social Psychology*, 1973, *28*, 355–359.

6

A Model of Mastery Motivation in Children: Individual Differences and Developmental Change

Susan Harter
University of Denver

Motivational constructs have perennially been at the heart of our theorizing about human behavior. Most recently, the concept of intrinsic motivation has come into vogue. Two general approaches to this topic can be identified. Within the social–psychological camp, experimentalists such as Lepper (this volume) and Deci (1975) and their proponents as well as opponents have focused on a programmatic effort to examine the conditions under which extrinsic rewards undermine intrinsic motivation. In these attributional models, closely wed to a growing data base, a number of parameters that govern the relationship between extrinsic rewards and one's motivation to perform a given behavior have been identified.

One also finds the concept of intrinsic motivation in broad theoretical formulations that have focused on mastery and competence (see Deci's review of these positions in his book *Intrinsic Motivation,* 1975). Robert White's (1959) classic paper, "Motivation Reconsidered: The Concept of Competence" represented a very provocative, scholarly attempt to reorient our thinking to include the concept of intrinsically motivated behavior. White did not merely urge us to find a niche for this construct, but to consider it as the very cornerstone of our theorizing about what motivated an organism to act.

White's thesis was that the traditional drive theories, as well as Freud's psychoanalytic instinct theory, were incomplete or inadequate models of both human and animal behavior. To support this contention, White culled data from such seemingly diverse sources as animal laboratory studies, Piaget's observations of infant and child development, and psychoanalytic ego psychology. In voicing his discontent with traditional drive theories of motivation, White marshaled a compelling array of evidence suggesting that

215

behaviors such as exploration, curiosity, mastery, play, and one's general attempt to deal competently with one's environment could not adequately be explained by the reduction of deficit motives, nor by the operation of either secondary reinforcement or anxiety reduction.

Although White's challenge to drive theory is impressive, his solution was less than satisfactory to the rigorous at heart. White boldy proposed a new motivational construct, which he labeled "effectance" motivation, as the explanation for this class of behaviors. Effectance or competence motivation impelled the organism towards competent performance and was satisfied by a feeling of efficacy. He considered this need to deal effectively with the environment as intrinsic, a need that when gratified, produced inherent pleasure.

A MODEL OF EFFECTANCE MOTIVATION

As I have discussed elsewhere (Harter, 1978a), the concept of effectance motivation has obvious heuristic appeal, particularly for the study of the developing child in whom striving towards mastery and competence are universally evident. Indeed, because White's formulation (1959) was proposed 20 years ago, it has become common for investigators in virtually every domain to invoke this construct, and to interpret their results as consistent with White's general thesis. I myself found the construct conceptually very comforting in some of my early research in which I was attempting to characterize the differences between retarded and normal children in their approach to problem-solving tasks. However, it soon become apparent that effectance motivation, as presented in the broad brush strokes of White, had little explanatory value, little predictive power. It did not lend itself to operational definitions, and, thus, it was not readily apparent how one might put this general formulation to an empirical test.

Nevertheless, the appeal of a motive that impels the organism towards competence is obvious and compelling. Thus, a major thrust of my own efforts has been to refine and extend White's initial formulation, such that one can put specific hypotheses to an empirical test.

As a starting point, I conceptualized White's basic model as follows: Effectance motivation impels the child to engage in mastery attempts. If these attempts are successful—that is, if they result in competent performance—the child experiences feelings of efficacy or inherent pleasure. This, in turn, should maintain, if not increase, the child's effectance motivation. Two years ago (Harter, 1978a), I proposed a general framework, a working conceptual model, in which I argued that the refinement of White's formulation would require a consideration of the following issues:

1. We must not be content to view effectance motivation as a global or unitary construct, but we must move to a consideration of the possible *components* of this motive system. Furthermore, we must examine these components within a *developmental* framework, charting ontogenetic change. Such a procedure will dictate a description of changes in both the *structure* and the *content* of this motive system, as well as an examination of the actual process through which developmental change is brought about.

2. Although White focused primarily on the implications of *success* in dealing with one's environment, we must also examine the effects of *failure* experiences on the components of effectance motivation.

3. The conceptualization of intrinsic pleasure derived from success is also in need of refinement, because it is unlikely that success per se will result in a feeling of efficacy. Rather, it would seem plausible to expect that those successful mastery attempts that provide an *optimal degree of challenge* would produce the greatest sense of satisfaction.

4. It is also essential that we carefully consider the *role of the socializing agents* in one's environment, and their effect in maintaining, enhancing, or attenuating the components of effectance motivation. Such a search for the antecedents and/or determinants of this motive system will also elucidate changes in its strength and structure. Furthermore, in considering the effects of the reinforcing agents in one's socialization history, we should direct our attention to the various *functions of reward,* and how they affect this motive system.

5. A developmental consideration of the effects of reinforcement over time will also elucidate the process by which children internalize both a *self-reward* system and a set of mastery goals. In addition, this will have bearing on the ultimate strength of one's intrinsic motivation to be effective or competent.

6. Although White's major emphasis was on the intrinsic properties of this motive system, we must also address ourselves to the issue of *extrinsic* motivation, and examine the *relative strength* of intrinsic versus extrinsic motivational orientations. Within this framework, one can examine developmental, individual, and group differences in the strength of these orientations, and search for the antecedents of these differences.

7. Finally, we need to give thoughtful attention to certain correlates of these motivational constructs. In particular, such constructs as one's *perceived competence* or self esteem and one's *perception of control* would appear to be important consequences as well as mediators of one's motivational orientation.

The initial model was presented in diagrammatic form, as can be seen in Fig. 6.1. A complete description of this model can be found in an earlier paper (Harter, 1978a). I merely summarize the major feature of the model here, and

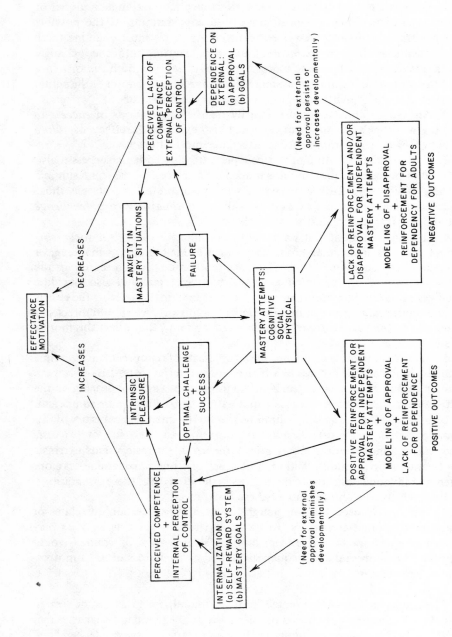

FIG. 6.1. Initial extension of White's (1959) effectance motivation formulation.

218

then proceed to describe how our empirical efforts to test certain aspects of the model have resulted in considerable subsequent refinement. Events on the left-hand side of Fig. 6.1 describe the ontogenesis of a relatively intrinsically motivated individual, whereas the right-hand side depicts the developmental path towards an extrinsic orientation.

White's general formulation is embedded in the diagram, as the inner loop on the left, with some modifications. Although he viewed effectance motivation as a global construct impelling the organism towards mastery, the schematic of the refined model suggests the fruitfulness of examining separately mastery attempts for each of several skill areas in the child's life— the cognitive, social, and physical domains. These areas were defined as school performance, peer relationships, and athletic prowess, respectively.

White's initial model weighed success very heavily in the effectance motivation equation, implying that success generally leads to feelings of efficacy or intrinsic pleasure. An additional component was added in the earlier refinement—namely, the concept of optimal challenge. It was argued that the maximum pleasure would be derived from successes that were optimally challenging for the child. A series of studies demonstrating a positive relationship between pleasure and task difficulty for successfully solved problems now documents this hypothesis (Harter, 1974 ,1977, 1978b).

In White's description of the effectance-motivation process, he placed most of his emphasis on successful mastery attempts, on the positive outcomes of one's behavior. The implications of failure were not elucidated. Clearly, any model of the consequences of one's mastery attempts must include an analysis of the effects of failure, as well as the interaction, the relative importance of success and failure experiences. Thus, failure was included as part of the inner loop on the right, although this depiction was oversimplified and, to some extent, misleading. The implication of placing success on the left and failure on the right is that success is sufficient as the only prerequisite for the happy outcomes and clusters of characteristics displayed on the left. Conversely, Fig. 6.1 implies that the only consequences of failure are the negative outcome and attributes on the right. The picture is undoubtedly much more complex. Ultimately, we need to direct our attention to the issue of the relative balance of success and failure responsible for producing either an intrinsically motivated or an extrinsically motivated individual.

In fleshing out the earlier refinement, I was interested in the affective consequences of one's failure experiences. Thus, I postulated that anxiety in mastery situations would result from a pattern or history characterized by failure, which would, in turn, attenuate one's effectance motivation.

The most critical addition to White's (1959) formulation involved the effects of the child's socialization history. Any comprehensive model must address the role that child-rearing agents play in influencing the developmental course of the components of effectance motivation. These effects are diagrammed in the outer loops of Fig. 6.1. It was hypothesized that, for the child to develop and maintain his or her effectance motivation, a sufficient degree of positive reinforcement for his or her mastery attempts would be required; sufficient implies that the balance of positive to negative is high. It was also hypothesized that this reinforcement must occur very early in the ontogenetic sequence and that it was especially critical in the first several years of life. The argument was advanced that such reinforcement should be provided for independent mastery *attempts,* not merely for a successful product.

In the model, we went on to postulate that with sufficient positive reinforcement for independent mastery attempts during early childhood, the child gradually internalizes two critical systems, a self-reward system and a system of standards or mastery goals. The self-reward system allows one to praise or reinforce one's self for mastery attempts and successes. The child also internalizes the mastery goals of the socializing agents who have rewarded or punished him or her. That is, through a history of differential reinforcement and observational learning, these standards become increasingly salient. As this internalization process occurs, however, the need for, and dependency on, external social reinforcement diminishes. This ontogenetic change with regard to positive outcomes, which results in a relatively intrinsically motivated individual, is depicted in the left outer circle of Fig. 6.1. The entire left side of Fig. 6.1 represents a positive picture of optimal development in which the child's social environment cooperated with his or her natural desires towards mastery, such that the net result is a child for whom intrinsic motivation becomes a major determinant of behavior.

On the right-hand side of Fig. 6.1, the *negative* outcomes are depicted— namely, those that should ultimately produce an extrinsically oriented individual. If such consequences are typical or occur with sufficient frequency, the child's intrinsic motivation and resulting mastery will eventually be attenuated, and other motives will predominate. With regard to the response of the child's socializing agents, three possible reactions are depicted: (1) lack of reinforcement and/or disapproval for independent mastery attempts; (2) modeling of such disapproval; and (3) reinforcement for dependency on adults. In many cases, it is likely that all three possibilities will cooccur, although the relative importance of each remains an empirical question.

The predicted outcome of such a socialization history during the early years is precisely the opposite of that described for the left-hand side of Fig. 6.1, where the antecedents of an intrinsically motivated individual were outlined. Those children who experience the cluster of negative consequences just described should, during middle childhood, increasingly display a need for external appproval as well as a dependence on externally defined goals for behavior.

Finally, the earlier extension of the effectance model postulated that one's reinforcement history will have implications not only for one's motivational orientation, but for one's perceived competence as well as one's sense of control over the outcomes in one's life. Very generally, the schematic suggests that the outcomes on the left, which result in a relatively intrinsically motivated individual, will, in turn, mediate feelings of perceived competence as well as control in those mastery domains that were positively reinforced. These perceptions should influence the child's sense of intrinsic pleasure and serve to enhance or maintain one's motivation to engage in subsequent mastery behaviors.

Conversely, the child who has experienced a history of relative failure and disapproval, resulting in a relatively extrinsic motivational orientation, should experience related feelings of low competence and the perception that external agents and events control what happens to them. These perceptions, in turn, should serve to create anxiety in mastery situation and to attenuate one's motivation to be engaged in mastery behaviors.

The preceding description only sketches the highlights of the earlier working model. Howerver, rather than review it in its most minute detail, I prefer to address the question: "In what sense is it working?" What empirical efforts did it dictate? And how have these efforts caused considerable refinement in the model? Three years, and some 4000 children, have taught us a great deal.

CONSTRUCTS IN SEARCH OF MEASURES:
AN INTERLUDE

At the outset, we focused on child variables, deferring the more difficult questions involving parenting and socialization history. Thus, we set out to examine the relationships among those constructs we have labeled as motivational orientation (intrinsic or extrinsic), perceptions of competence, perceptions of control, anxiety in mastery situations, and optimal challenge. In charting our empirical attack, we returned to the literature, reexamining the theoretical models that addressed these constructs and searching through the various compendia of tests and measurements for possible instruments to assess them. Our enthusiasm was decidedly dampened.

Although we were enamored with White's (1959) formulation, his constructs were too global and, therefore, too vague in that they did not lend themselves to obvious operational definitions. Conversely, we felt that the very precise attempts of experimental social psychologists to define conditions under which extrinsic rewards would underline intrinsic motivation were inadequate for our needs in that they defined a very narrow band of behaviors, whereas we were interested in a broader spectrum of constructs that could be examined developmentally. The model we were constructing posed a challenge: as developmentalists, we wanted to understand ontogenetic change, but not at the expense of ignoring individual differences at any given developmental level. Historically, those who have espoused developmental frames of reference, models, and theories have typically not been concerned with individual differences. Conversely, those who have focused on individual differences have not devoted sufficient attention to development level. And, those employing experimental paradigms typically eschew both developmental and individual differences. Thus, the literature povided little direction in our search for an empirical approach that would attend to both develpmental level and the individual differences manifest within a given age or stage.

Our search of the assessment literature was also disappointing, given the constructs we wished to examine. This literature is replete with instruments that tap constructs in the cogntive–intellectual domain. There, we found numerous measures of IQ, achievement, cognitive–developmental level, problem solving, information processing, perceptual motor functioning, and so on. However, assessment efforts have lagged far behind in the nonintellectual sphere. There is a paucity of adequate measuring instruments for use with children in the general domain of attitudes, motivation, and personality.

One might take issue with this conclusion, pointing to the variety of projective measures available in our clinical assessment battery. Or, some might support Wechsler's (1950) argument that his intelligence scales also assess nonintellective, or what he terms "conative," factors. Furthermore, one can point to the numerous self-report measures and questionnaires that are concerned with various facets of the "self"—namely, scales that are purported to tap self concept, self esteem, etc.

Based on considerable experience with each type of measure, however, my response is that there are a number of problems that cause these instruments to be inadequate for testing the constructs under consideration. The more projective measures require too much inference on the part of the test interpreter, such that a respectable level of interrater agreement is difficult to obtain. In part, this is related to the lack of scoring systems and standardized norms and, particularly, data analytic procedures that are sensitive to developmental level. Furthermore, many of the more clinically oriented instruments in our diagnostic armamentarium are, from a practical point of view, rather cumbersome and time consuming to administer and interpret.

What can be said about the more objective questionnaires and scales available? We have reviewed many of these measures, and have utilized them in our own research. Although a detailed review of these measures is beyond the scope of this chapter, one can point to a number of general problems that have caused us to question the usefulness of these scales (see Wylie, 1974, for a comprehensive critique). The *content* of the items is often questionable. On certain scales, the strategy has been to take an existing adult scale designed to tap the construct of interest and refashion it for children, rather than initially taking a more child-centered approach. Thus, one substitutes the word "penny" for "dollar" or "Cub Scout troop" for the "Teamsters' Union" and assumes that the items are comparable and that the same construct is being tapped. We cannot make these assumptions. An adult's reaction to the stock market plummeting is, in all probability, not analogous to the reaction of the 10-year-old who gets grounded and loses a week's allowance.

The *reliability* of certain scales is questionable, particularly where indices of internal consistency are employed. One popular self-concept scale requires that a child respond to more than 90 items in order to achieve a reliability in the .70's. As one member of our research team pointed out, if you had 90 yes–no choices, with no items as such, merely a list of 90 yeses and noes, and asked subjects to circle either yes or no 90 times, there would be enough systematicity in their responses to guarantee a cumulative reliability of .70 or better! In this context, questions of validity are also of concern.

We have been particularly troubled by the lack of what may be viewed as the *factorial validity* of many existing scales. On several of the more widely used instruments, the test constructors specify subscales designed to tap separate or discrete areas of the child's life. For example, one may hypothetically distinguish between self esteem with regard to school and self esteem with regard to family. Although we feel that it is commendable to make differentiations in one's constructs, in fact, this is the conceptual cornerstone of our own approach, it is imperative that the distinctions imposed by the scale constructor correspond to distinctions perceived by the child. That is, if we are going to slice the behavioral pie into domains that result in separate subscales, any meaningful interpretation of these subscales is contingent upon the demonstration that the child is utilizing the same frame of reference, is segmenting his or her life in a similar fashion.

We have repeatedly found, however, in examining the factor patterns of scales that include separate subscales, that the divisions that the test constructor superimposes on the child's life do not emerge in the data. Children do not segment their worlds in the manner dictated by the scale. Certain investigators are aware of this outcome and typically opt for one of two alternatives. They either acknowledge that the scale is not perfect and continue to treat the subscale scores as interpretable, or they conclude that a child simply is not making differentiations about the domains in his or her life and, therefore, one should calculate a total score that reflects the child's global feelings about one's self, feelings that can then be generalized to any domain.

Neither of these alternatives is defensible. A test constructor's failure to demonstrate the existence of separate and meaningful subscales may, in all likelihood, be due to that person's own erroneous impression of the domains relevant to children's lives, or to that person's inability to devise items that adequately tap these domains. The empirical effort to sort out these possible interpretations is considerable; in the absence of such efforts, however, we will not have instruments that are psychologically meaningful or psychometrically sound.

We have also found that the typical *item format*, either True–False or Like me–Unlike me, poses problems. Self-concept items such as "I am easy to like," when cast into this response format, tend to pull for the socially desirable response. This tendency seems to be enhanced by the presence of only two choices. Our own pilot studies with such self-concept scales has documented this tendency; the data show that one's score on self-concept items is positively related to scores on lie scales embedded within the measure, as well as to scores on the Children's Social Desirability Scale (Crandall, Crandall, & Katkovsky, 1965).

Finally, for the most part, scales within the domain of attitudes and self concept have not been sufficiently sensitive to *develomental level*. As I have discussed in an earlier paper (Harter, 1978a), this is an omnipresent issue for the developmental researcher who chooses to assess the same construct at different ages or stages. Does one employ the same measure at each developmental level, or does one need to employ a different measure at different levels to tap the same construct? And, how does one determine whether one is indeed assessing the same construct, given either strategy? These issues have not been thoughtfully addressed in the assessment literature on self-concept and related constructs. Our own attempts to grapple with this problem are discussed in subsequent sections of this chapter that deal with the specific measures we have devised.

At this point, we entertained three possible alternatives for empirically examining the relationship postulated by our working model: (1) to utilize existing measures despite their inadequacies; (2) to invent what we could not discover—namely, to devise scales of our own; or (3) to remain content to sit in our armchairs flaunting our flow diagram and mumbling pedantically.

We chose the second strategy, to invent what we could not discover, and embarked on a venture with the appropriate balance of knowledge and ignorance. I say ignorance, because if we had known back then what is required to construct adequate instruments that met the previously raised objections, we might well have opted to pedantically mumble! Instead, we adopted five criteria that guided our measurement efforts, each of which corresponds to one of the considerations just discussed. In addressing ourselves to the issue of item content, we have placed heavy emphasis on the ecological validity of our scales. Although our measurement efforts have been guided by obvious theoretical considerations, we have become increasingly interested in the real-life concerns of the children about whose attitudes and behaviors we are speculating. Thus, in each of our scales, items are very directly worded to tap issues relevant to the everyday lives and experiences of children.

Perhaps the most important criterion we adopted was based on our view that one should take a more differentiated approach to the constructs in question, to isolate the components that seem meaningful. This, in turn, dictated scale structures in which each component defined a separate subscale, yielding its own score. A critical feature of our data-analytic strategy, therefore, was to determine whether the structure that we imposed on the various scales emerged in the children's responses. To answer this question, we relied heavily on factor-analytic procedures.

The question of reliability was addressed within the context of the subscale structure. We placed heavy emphasis on the internal consistency of a given subscale, employing a minimum of items, typically six. Test–retest data have been a secondary consideration. We have also spent considerable energy devising a new question format that is very effective in offsetting the child's tendency to give a socially desirable response.

Finally, we have approached the problem of how to best tap the same construct at different developmental levels in several ways. We targeted the grade school years as the initial age range. Item appropriateness was in part determined by individual interviews and discussions with children. Once scales were constructed, a major criterion was that the factor structure remained stable across grade level. As the subsequent discussion of each measure indicates, however, our attempts to tap the same constructs in younger children as well as in high school students have required somewhat different items and/or item formats.

My approach in this chapter falls somewhere between the presentation of an elegant polished product and a description of the sordid details that, cast as a soap opera, might be entitled "As the Lab Turns." I would like to assure the reader that we are headed in the right direction in our attempts to develop a model of mastery motivation in children. However, in so doing, I would like to share some of the process involved. In particular, I hope to alert the reader to the importance of sound measurement construction in the area of attitudinal, affective, and motivational constructs. The field is in its infancy, and yet it is already replete with congenital defects and developmental disabilities. We need efforts at early detection, psychometric remediation, as well as new methodological conceptions. In our own group, we are discovering that traditional psychometricians and neodevelopmentalists do not make for such strange conceptual bedfellows after all!

Thus, I'd like to share some of our own methodological baby steps, accompanied by the inevitable bumps and bruises resulting from our falls. In many such instances, these minor empirical injuries have led to some major rethinking at the level of our constructs and our model. This has not been a singular effort on my part. My colleagues, or toddlers, to pursue the metaphor, have been an outstanding group of graduate students whose names you encounter throughout this chapter. They have enriched my thinking immensely, and often it is difficult to determine where one person's thought left off and another's began. What follows is a description of various pieces of this collective process. I hope to describe how our measurement construction efforts have not only resulted in a battery of promising measures, but have altered our conceptualization of the constructs themselves, thereby more clearly defining their contribution to the model.

SCALE CONSTRUCTION AND THE VICISSITUDES OF SINGLE CONSTRUCTS

Perceived Competence

Our measurment efforts began with two central constructs in the model, the child's motivational orientation, which we conceptualized along a dimension of intrinsic or extrinsic, and the child's feelings of competence. Because the construction of the perceived-competence scale has served as the prototype of our measurement attempts and has given us fewer methodological growing pains, I describe how we set out to assess this particular construct in keeping with the criteria just outlined. It should be noted that the construct of perceived competence was not assumed to be synonymous with, or equivalent to, the term "self concept" or "self esteem." There are undoubtedly other factors influencing a child's sense of self. However, given the conceptual model from which this scale evolved, the focus was primarily on perceived competence, as reflected in the title of the measure, *The Perceived Competence Scale for Children*.

We began with the assumption that perceived competence is not a global trait or unitary construct. It seemed more fruitful to adopt a differentiated approach whereby one could assess a child's feelings of competence in the different domains of his or her life. This viewpoint then led us to specify those major competence domains considered to be relevant in the lives of elementary school children, in keeping with our emphasis on the ecological validity of our measures. Three general areas were identified: (1) *cognitive* competence, with an emphasis on academic performance; (2) *social* competence, vis-a-vis one's peer relationships; and (3) *physical* competence, with a focus on sports and outdoor games. The scale structure reflects these distinctions in that it includes a separate subscale for each competence domain.

In addition to these specific competence domains, it seemed desirable to assess a child's *general sense of worth*, independent of a particular skill domain. Thus, a fourth subscale was included, one that was qualitatively different from the three preceding subscales in that the items contained no reference to competence per se.

Our next hurdle was more challenging—namely, the choice of question format. A number of problems were raised in the preceding section concerning true–false type formats, the most critical of which is their susceptibility to social-desirability response tendencies. After considerable pilot work, we finally found a format that offsets this tendency. In this "structured alternative format," the child is presented with the following type of question:

Really true for me	Sort of true for me				Sort of true for me	Really true for me
☐	☐	Some kids often forget what they learn.	BUT	Other kids can remember things easily.	☐	☐

The child is first asked to decide "which kind of kid you are most like, the kids described on the right or on the left?" Having made this decision, the child then decides whether the description on that side is "sort of true" or "really true" for him or her. The effectiveness of this format lies in the implication that half of the children in the world (or in one's reference group) view themselves in one way, whereas the other half view themselves in the opposite manner; this type of question legitimizes either choice. The fact that all choices refer to "true" may also facilitate responding. Our confidence in this question format is bolstered by several sources of evidence, which are described in detail elsewhere (Harter, in press). Items are scored on a four-point ordinal scale where a score of 1 indicates low perceived competence and a score of 4 reflects high perceived competence. Each of the four subscales contains seven items, constituting a total of 28 items.

Our most important goal was to demonstrate that children make distinctions between these four areas, such that the subscales can be meaningfully interpreted. We have relied primarily on factor-analytic procedures, which we have now performed on numerous samples, totaling approximately 4000 children, from four states; Colorado, California, New York, and Connecticut. The factor pattern for all samples is consistently clean, with high item loadings on the designated factor, and no replicable cross-loadings of interpretable magnitude. A sample factor pattern is presented in Table 6.1. This factor structure is extremely stable for all grades tested, namely third through ninth. Thus, we have successfully met the criterion of factorial validity for the entire grade span sampled and have proceeded to examine the relationship of perceived competence to other constructs in the model. Our criterion of acceptable reliability, in the form of subscale internal consistency, was also met, with values in the high .70's and .80's.

Although it was critical that the subscale structure be identical across this age range, in order to make meaningful developmental comparisons, there were no a priori constraints on the absolute values of subscale scores.

TABLE 6.1
Perceived Competence Scale[a]

Item Abbreviation	I Cognition	II Social	III Physical	IV General	Item Mean	Item S.D.
Cognitive Competence						
1. Good at schoolwork	.64				2.7	.93
2. Like school, doing well	.63				2.8	1.02
3. Just as smart as others	.67				2.9	1.00
4. Can figure out answers	.45				2.8	.93
5. Finish schoolwork quickly	.50				3.1	.80
6. Remember things easily	.42				2.9	1.01
7. Understand what read	.69				2.8	.92
Social Competence						
1. Have a lot of friends		.61			3.0	.93
2. Popular with kids		.66			3.2	1.00
3. Easy to like		.40			2.5	.99
4. Do things with kids		.60			2.9	1.06
5. Easy to make friends		.42		(.43)	2.7	1.07
6. Important to classmates		.43			2.8	.98
7. Most kids like me		.49			2.9	.89

	Factor Loading	M	SD
Physical Competence			
1. Do well at all sports	.79	2.9	1.06
2. Better at sports	.62	2.5	1.20
3. Do well at new activity	.45	2.8	.95
4. Good enough at sports	.75	2.7	.98
5. First chosen for games	.55	3.2	1.03
6. Play rather than watch	.60	2.8	.91
7. Good at new games	.46	2.5	1.06
General Self Worth			
1. Sure of myself	.64	2.6	1.12
2. Happy the way I am	.41	3.0	.89
3. Feel good/way I act	.55	2.8	.99
4. Sure am doing right thing	.39	3.0	.85
5. Am a good person	.69	3.0	1.00
6. Want to stay the same	.48	2.9	.93
7. Do things fine	.35	2.7	.95

[a]Factor pattern, item means, and standard deviations, for a sample of 341 pupils in the third through sixth grades. Loadings less than .27 are not present for the sake of clarity.

Nevertheless, mean scores for each of the four subscales show no significant differences across third through ninth grade, falling slightly above the midpoint of 2.5, with values ranging from 2.6 to 3.0. (The psychometric properties are presented in detail elsewhere; see Harter, in press.)

Extension for Younger Children.   Although it was possible to utilize the same instrument to tap perceived competence for grades three through nine, it was necessary to devise a different format for younger children who were not able to handle the paper-and-pencil format. We moved to as pictorial format, retaining the three competence domains present in the older children's version—cognitive, social, and physical. (Because general self worth did not lend itself to pictorial depiction, this subscale was not included.) Given our theoretical interest in parental approval and acceptance during the early years, we added a fourth subscale that basically tapped maternal acceptance, specifically, the extent to which the child perceived mother as doing enjoyable things with and for the child. Sample items involved mother cooking favorite foods, reading stories, and so on. Cognitive items involved, for example, doing puzzles well, knowing letters; physical items included running fast and climbing the jungle gym; social items referred to having a lot of friends and getting invited to parties.

A sample item is presented in Fig. 6.2. The subject child is read a brief statement about each child in the pictures—for example, this child is good at doing puzzles and this child isn't very good. The subject is first asked to pick the child who is most like him or her, and then to indicate, by pointing to the appropriate circle, whether that child is really like him or her (the big circle) or just sort of like him or her (the smaller circle). The children find this format readily understandable; furthermore, our discussions with teachers indicate that most children seem to be giving accurate judgments of their own feelings of competence in these areas.

FIG. 6.2.   Sample cognitive item from the Pictorial Perceived Competence Scale for Young Children.

Our experience with this instrument, however, was not nearly as successful, initially, as with the older children's version. We found it necessary to alter an earlier four-picture format to the current two-picture choice procedure. We also discovered that it was not possible to find activities that were appropriate across the entire 4 to 7 year age range. For example, an item such as hopping was appropriate for the younger children but not for the older, whereas the converse was true for an activity such as skipping. Thus, it was necessary to devise two forms, one for the preschool and kindergarten group, and another for first and second graders. Some items were common to both. These revisions were largely dictated by pragmatic considerations.

More conceptually interesting problems arose when we had sufficient data to factor analyze the scale. Unlike the older children's version, in which our own conception of domains corresponded to the children's, the pictorial version for young children did not yield a four-factor solution corresponding to the four subscales we had defined. Rather, we found that a two-factor solution best described the data. One factor is comprised primarily of items from the cognitive and physical subscales. The second factor is defined by items from the peer–social subscale and the mother-acceptance subscale.

After considerable examination of the items themselves, in conjunction with their pattern of loadings, we hit upon the following hypothesis about the significance of this two-factor structure for the construct of competence: Those items defining the first factor, largely items from the physical and cognitive scale, all seemed to depict or refer to "doing well" at something, performing competently—e.g., doing puzzles well, drawing well (which we conceptualized initially as cognitive), and running fast, climbing well (which we categorized as physical). Upon closer inspection of the activities included in each domain, it seemed plausible that young children might not make a distinction between the two subscales. Many of our cognitive items referred to performance on tasks that involved some fine motor skill; this may have been the salient feature accounting for their commonality with the physical items. Although it made sense, then, that the cognitive and physical subscales should merge as one factor, we still needed an explanation for the emergence of a separate and distinct factor defined by peer social acceptance and acceptance by mother. With hindsight, it made sense that the two subscales involving acceptance and likeability should correlate highly. But, what made this a second factor? Why not a one-factor solution? In scrutinizing the items loading on the second factor, something struck us as a possible explanation: There were no references in the wording to doing well or poorly. One either has friends, gets invited to parties, acknowledges that Mother takes him or her places, or does not. This was in contrast to the cognitive and physical items, which clearly depict competence and incompetence at specific activities that involve skill. Thus, it seemed that our pictorial version was tapping two dimensions: The first factor could be labeled "general competence," and the second "social acceptance."

The implication of this interpretation is that the young child does not view acceptance as involving competence. One has friends or does not; one's mother likes one or she does not; but, these are not things one does well or poorly in the same sense that one can be skillful or unskillful at cognitive and physical activities. The concept of "social skills" did not seem to be present in the repertoire of the young child.

Very recently, we have begun to pursue this hypothesis empirically. Chris Chao and I have piloted a number of tasks and discovered one that has provided some rich data that seem to bolster our interpretation. We presented our young subjects with two pictures, one in which the child *is* successful and one in which the child is not. We selected activities from scale items that showed high loadings on their designated factor. We asked children to tell us what would have to happen for the unsuccessful child to be like the successful child. (We carefully avoided wording that might suggest that the child should *do* something, or that *someone else* needed to do something for the child.)

We are currently in the process of performing a content analysis on these data. However, the most striking observation relevant to our hypothesis is that the responses to both cognitive and physical items are qualitatively different from those given for the social areas. Our 4- and 5-year-old subjects clearly told us that to be successful at the cognitive and physical activities depicted, one needed to practice at the skill, to work hard at the activity. Sample statements were: "He should practice at climbing so he'll get good"; "He should get new jogging shoes and run every day until he's fast"; "She needs to practice at her drawing". The use of the word "practice" was quite common, and the answers also typically referred to some time course over which the skill could be acquired.

The responses to items in the social domain did not have these same connotations of competence, skill, and the need for practice. Additionally, the suggestions for what children should do to obtain friends seemed very naive. For example, children told us: "You just go to the park and find them"; "You walk up to someone's house and ring the bell and ask them to be your friend"; "Maybe the policeman can get you a friend." There were no skills involved, and no time period was necessary for the acquisition of friends. Their answers implied that one can obtain instant friends. As such, they were very different from the more realistic solutions posed for the cognitive and physical domains. We are pursuing this line of inquiry, because these verbal data present a picture that is consistent with our discovery of the two-factor structure of perceived competence. Both sets of findings suggest that young children make a conceptual distinction between general competence and social acceptance.

The most important revelation of our measurement efforts with young children has been the need to alter our thinking about the meaning of the construct "perceived competence" at this developmental level. Our various converging operations strongly suggest that although young children have a clear concept of competence or skill, they restrict it to those activities that we had initially labeled as cognitive and physical and do not make a distinction between performance in what we, as test constructors, considered to be different domains. In contrast to these activities, they do not view social acceptance by peers or mother as an arena of their life that requires skill or competence. We are eager to pursue this question developmentally, because our data with older children indicate that they make finer distinctions among domains and view the social arena as one that involves competence, one over which they have some control. Empirical work is needed, however. Perhaps the most important lesson we have learned in our scale-construction efforts is that our procedures must be sensitive enough to allow the children to provide *their* definition of the construct, and we in turn must be open to accepting the manner in which they choose to define it.

Perceptions of Control

This same lesson was brought home to us again in our attempts to devise a measure of children's perceptions of control, another variable that we postulated to be a correlate of one's motivational orientation. Jim Connell came to the University of Denver with an interest in the locus of control variable and shared with me the common goal of constructing measures that permitted a more differentiated look at the constructs in question. Connell (1979) has questioned certain assumptions underlying Rotter's locus-of-control measure—namely, that people can be characterized by a single score typing them as either internal or external with regard to their perceptions of control. In so doing, he has constructed a scale that assesses the degree to which a child's perception of control is situation specific. One situational parameter involves the three competence domains incorporated in the perceived competence scale for older children: tapping cognitve, social, and physical skills. This permits one to indicate that behavioral outcomes in one competence area may be viewed as internally controlled—e.g., "I do well in school because I work hard"—whereas in the another domain they are viewed as under more external control—e.g., "The reason I don't do well at sports is because the coach won't give me a chance to play."

Another dimension that has been incorporated into Connell's scale is the nature of the outcome, whether it is a success or failure. In the example just given, the child is taking internal responsibility for success in the cognitive area, but attributing failures in the domain of physical skills to an external source. One can envisage myriad patterns or interactions among the dimensions of source of control, competence area, and nature of the outcome.

The most interesting revelation in Connell's work concerns children's conceptions of the possible sources of control over the events in their lives.

The initial version of the scale adapted Levenson's (1972) three-fold conceptualization of the sources of control: internal (I am responsible), external, powerful others (someone else is responsible), and external chance (it was luck, fate, or a chance happening). Nested within each of these three sources of control were separate subscales for each competence area, and within each competence area, half of the items referred to successes and half to failures. One final dimension Connell included was what he terms "realm of reference." Here, a distinction is made between the realm of the child's own personal experience (what happens to *me*) in contrast to one's perception of what is responsible for what happens to children in general, more maxim-like perceptions.

On the drawing board, the scale looked elegant, with the potential for providing a very sensitive multidimensional analysis of children's perceptions of control. However, when data from the earliest administrations were analyzed, there was one noteworthy problem with regard to the source of control dimension. Although the subscales assessing internal source of control and external control by powerful others emerged as interpretable subscales, the chance or luck scale accounted for virtually none of the variance. There was simply no evidence in the data that children make systematic attributions on this basis. Upon closer scrutiny of the items, Connell discovered some commonality between a small subset that did tend to form an interpretable cluster—namely, items that conveyed the notion that one does not *know* or understand the source of control over one's behavior. Following this empirical lead, Connell abandoned the initial chance subscale, and replaced it with what he has labeled "*Unknown* source of control." Data gathered from the administration of this revision clearly indicate that this is a relevant attribution among children. Thus, the scale structure now includes three meaningful sources of control: internal (I am responsible), powerful others (someone else is responsible), and unknown (I don't know what is responsible for what happens to me). This particular saga highlights the potential dangers in imposing scale dimensions revealed to be relevant to adults on our assessment procedures with children without the demonstration that they are indeed appropriate.

This particular scale allows for a multidimensional assessment of children's perceptions of control across and within the four dimensions isolated: source of control, competence area, nature of the outcome, and realm of reference. In addition, Connell has utilized a variety of contrast scores in his analysis of the data. For example, he has created one such score that assesses the child's *level* of understanding, where level is viewed as a discrepancy between the two *known* sources of control (internal and powerful others) and the *unknown* source of control. One can also examine what he has termed the *content* of a child's understanding, reflected by the different domains and outcomes included in the scale.

Developmental patterns. Developmental data on this scale are now available for a cross-sectional sample of third to ninth graders. Although numerous trends and relationships are now being explored, one striking developmental finding deserves mention here. The findings indicate that the value of the known minus unknown contrast score shows a linear increase with age until the sixth grade, followed by a dramatic decrease in the seventh grade, followed by a subsequent increase through the ninth grade. That is, children seem to gain increasing knowledge about the events that control their lives through the elementary school years, until junior high school, where there seems to be a psychological setback with regard to their understanding of the reasons for why things happen to them. One can speculate about the possible explanations for such a developmental shift. The seventh graders in this sample had all made the transition from a traditional elementary school single classroom situation to the multiple-class structure of junior high school. This particular phase of adolescence is also marked by a variety of psycho–social and sexual changes that, however predictable, must be experienced with a certain degree of personal puzzlement. The contribution of cognitive advances, the emergence of formal operations, may also be implicated in the seventh-grade shift. There are many fruitful avenues to pursue in further exploring this particular developmental phenomenon, and we are beginning to find convergences with measures of our other constructs as well.

One such convergence was revealed when we examined the correlation between children's perceptions of their *cognitive* competence, on the perceived competence scale, and their actual competence, as revealed by standard achievement test scores, for the same cross-sectional sample. This relationship increased steadily across the third to sixth grades, and then plummeted in the seventh grade, showing a subsequent increase over the eighth- and ninth-grade years. These findings lend themselves to a similar interpretation. The seventh-grade shift causes pupils to be less certain about the bases for the judgments about their cognitive competence, leading to the relatively low correlation between their perceived and their actual competence in the academic domain. The contribution of the possible events accounting for this shift is the topic of further inquiry.

Motivational Orientation in the Classroom

The primary purpose of the initial proposed model was to trace the developmental path of intrinsic motivation as well as its counterpart, an extrinsic motivational orientation. In addition to our theoretical interest in these constructs, we were committed to an exploration of their educational implications. Thus, as a starting point, we addressed the following question: To what degree is children's motivation for classroom learning determined by their intrinsic interest in learning and mastery, curiosity, preference for challenge, and to what degree is it determined by a more extrinsic orientation in which teacher approval and grades are the motivation and the children are very dependent on the teacher for guidance? Given this focus on classroom performance, we restricted our first such scale to the cognitive domain and set out to determine whether we could identify components of classroom learning that could be defined by both an intrinsic and extrinsic motivational pole. Our scale construction efforts have now revealed that children make clear distinctions between five different aspects of classroom learning, as substantiated by a replicable five-factor solution. Each of these components constitutes a separate subscale, which we have defined as follows:

1. *Preference for challenge versus preference for easy work assigned.* Is the child intrinsically motivated to perform hard, challenging work or does the child prefer to do the easier work assigned by the teacher?

2. *Incentive to work to satisfy one's own interest and curiosity versus working to please the teacher and obtain good grades.* Here, as the subscale title indicates, we were interested in the relative strength of the child's intrinsic motivation compared to a more extrinsic orientation to obtain teacher approval and grades.

3. *Independent mastery attempts versus dependence on the teacher.* This subscale taps the degree to which a child prefers to figure out problems on his or her own in contrast to a dependence on the teacher for help and guidance, particularly when it comes to figuring out problems and assignments.

4. *Independent judgment versus reliance on teacher's judgment.* This subscale assesses whether the child feels that he or she is capable of making certain judgments about what to do in the classroom in contrast to a dependence on the teacher's opinion or judgment about what to do.

5. *Internal criteria for success/failure versus external criteria for success/ failure.* Does the child have some internal sense of whether he or she has succeeded or done poorly on a test or on a school assignment or is the child dependent on external sources of evaluation such as teacher feedback, grades, and marks?

In constructing the actual scale, we utilized the forced-choice format that we designed for the perceived competence scale. A sample item follows:

Really true for me	Sort of true for me				Sort of true for me	Really true for me
☐	☐	Some kids know whether or not they're doing well in school without grades.	BUT	Other kids need to have grades to know how well they are doing.	☐	☐

Responses were scored on a scale from 4 to 1, where 4 represented the maximum intrinsic orientation and 1 the extreme extrinsic orientation.

This particular scale also underwent numerous revisions, both with regard to the scale structure as well as specific scale items. Our intuitive designation of five subscales in the first version of the scale was confirmed, but with some modifications. Two of our original subscales merged into one, which we have now labeled as curiosity/interest, and a new and distinct factor emerged, which we have now labeled independent judgment versus reliance on teacher's judgment. As with our previous scales, we have relied on factorial validity as a major criterion and have altered our conception of the construct based on the children's responses. We have now replicated the new five-subscale structure with samples of elementary children from Colorado, New York, and California. Factor loadings are high on the designated subscale with no replicable cross loadings of substantial magnitude. (See Harter, 1979, for additional data on the psychometric properties of the scale as well as data on its empirical validity.)

The most fascinating findings to emerge from this scale involve striking developmental trends, which we feel are interpretable, even though their pattern was not predicted. Two of the subscales—independent judgment versus reliance on teacher's judgment and internal criteria versus external criteria—show dramatic linear trends across the third to ninth grades. Scores for third graders are relatively extrinsic, crossing the midpoint in the later elementary school grades into the intrinsic range for the junior-high pupils. The opposite linear trend is found for the three remaining subscales, preference for challenge versus preference for easy work, curiosity/interest versus teacher approval/ grades, and independent mastery versus dependence on the teacher. For each of these dimensions, children begin with relatively intrinsic scores in the younger grades and shift towards a more extrinsic orientation.

These findings raise a number of intriguing questions. For example, what do they imply for our understanding of the construct *intrinsic motivation*? How do we need to refine our definition of this construct in view of the data? What factors are accounting for the dramatic developmental increase in two components, and the decrease for the remaining three? And what implications do these findings have for models that postulate a general development shift towards an intrinsic orientation and the internalization of a self-reward system?

At the most general level, they alert us to the importance of considering the components of intrinsic motivation, rather than viewing motivational orientation as a global or unitary construct. Had our scale construction efforts been dictated by the latter viewpoint, such that we had calculated a total scale score, the distinct developmental trends for separate subscales would have ben obscured.

How do we interpret these trends? We first asked what the independent judgment and internal criteria subscales had in common that, in turn, appeared to be different from interest and independent mastery. (These clusters were also confirmed by correlational data and higher order factoring.) It struck us that the subscales in the second cluster—challenge, curiosity, and mastery—each had a distinct *motivational* flavor in that they tapped issues involving what the child *wants* to do, *likes* to do, *prefers*. In contrast, the independent judgment and internal criteria subscales seem to tap more *cognitive-informational* structures: What does the child *know*? On what basis does he or she make decisions? How much has the child learned about the rules of the game called "school"?

From this perspective, it seemed plausible that across grades in school, children become more knowledgeable, more capable of making their own judgments, and more able to determine whether or not they were successful. The developmental decline, however, in those three subscales that seemingly tap more motivational components was open to a more complex set of interpretations. Perhaps the most value-laden interpretation is that our school systems are gradually stifling children's intrinsic interest in school learning, specifically with regard to challenge, curiosity, and independent mastery. A related view of these data is that the child is adapting to the demands of the school culture, which reinforces a relatively extrinsic orientation. It should be noted that this trend may be very domain specific; that is, although it would appear that one's motivation to perform in school is becoming less intrinsic with age, one's motivation in other domains may not show this trend. The child may be channeling intrinsic interest into other areas of his or her life. Because this particular scale allowed us to tap the cognitive domain only, we did not have data to bear on this interpretation. The construction of an additional scale, presented in a later section, allows us to test this hypothesis.

The empirical demonstration of two clusters of subscales—one motivational in nature and one more cognitive-informational—pointed to the need to refine the original model. Both the developmental data as well as individual profiles clearly indicated that a given child could be relatively intrinsic on one cluster and relatively extrinsic on the other. With regard to the internalization process postulated in the original model, then, a child may internalize knowledge about which mastery goals are important and about what criteria to employ in judgments of success and failure, but such a child may not necessarily be motivated by intrinsic goals. In fact, he or she may be very extrinsically motivated. Thus, it became apparent that the model needed to be revised to accommodate these more differentiated patterns of response.

THE FUNCTION OF REWARD:
AN ALTERNATIVE FRAME OF REFERENCE

The discussion to this point may imply an empirical boot-strapping effort whereby we relied solely on the incoming data and its responsiveness to factor-analytic procedures. Such was not the case; we did more than interpret the empirical dust that settled. While the data from the motivational-orientation measure were sorting themselves into motivational and informational clusters of subscales, I was simultaneously attacking the issue from a very theoretical perspective. Specifically, I was struggling with the literature on the functions of reward, attempting to explore the implications for the internalization process I had postulated of the development of a self-reward system. I was in general agreement with theorists (Aronfreed, 1969; Bandura, 1971) who have postulated two general functions of reward—a motivational-emotional and an information function—but made further distinctions within each of these categories, as well. Within the motivational domain, one may distinguish between an *incentive* function that impels the child to engage in particular activities in the anticipation of reward and the *affective* properties of reward that provide the child with feelings of satisfaction. With regard to the informational functions, one may also distinguish two subcategories: (1) at a *general* level, reward provides information that assists the child in determining his or her mastery goals, and information that *defines* those behavioral and outcomes that are *important;* (2) at a more *specific* level, reward conveys information about evaluative *criteria* with regard to the success or failure of one's behavior. Although a given reinforcer may serve more than one or even all of these functions simultaneously, it would seem critical to separate conceptually these various properties, because they each have implications for different constructs in the model.

In thinking about the process whereby children incorporate a self-reward system, it seemed fruitful to extend this analysis of the functions of reward to specify the intrinsic properties of the system. For example, with the incentive function, the child was initially motivated to engage in the behavior in the expectation of extrinsic reward; subsequently, this behavior should become motivated by the child's intrinsic interest in the activity itself. The affective function can be described in a similar fashion: Although the child may have initially felt happy at performing an activity because he or she received extrinsic approval, later in development, pleasure is derived from a sense of inherent satisfaction and personal efficacy.

The informational functions can also be described in terms of a shift from extrinsic to intrinsic. Although the young child knows what goals are important not only because models provide an example he or she can imitate but also because that behavior is rewarded, later in development, the child has less need for these reinforcing models because he or she has internalized the standards and goals. With regard to the evaluative function, the young child can initially evaluate his or her performance and determine whether it is successful or unsuccessful on the basis of external feedback. This function becomes intrinsic when the criteria for success and failure have become internalized.

This formulation allowed us to begin to think about the possibility of assessing the degree to which each of these reward functions is relatively extrinsic for the child, or whether he or she had undergone the internalization of a self-reward system that would result in a relatively intrinsic individual. We found that we could construct a scale, utilizing the structured alternative question format, in which a given item tapped one function and pitted an intrinsic against an extrinsic orientation—namely, self-reward against external reward.

This raised the issue of which socializing agents we should designate as the dispensers of external approval. The first model focused largely on the role of adult social feedback during the early years. It was also noted that during middle childhood and adolescence, the effects of the peer culture as a dispenser of reinforcement and a determinant of mastery goals should be considered. Furthermore, the relative importance of peer and adult approval probably also depends on the particular competence domain. For example, adult feedback may be more critical in the cognitive domain, whereas peer approval takes on considerable importance in the social sphere.

Accordingly, we designed a scale to tap these three dimensions in interaction: reward function (incentive, affective, information about goals, and evlauative criteria); source of external reinforcement to be pitted against self reward (adult and peer); and competence domain (cognitive, social, physical). A sample item from incentive function, adult versus Self Reward, in the cognitive area would be: "The reason some kids work hard in school is because they know their parents want them to, but other kids work hard because they enjoy learning new things." A parallel item for this same function in the cognitive area pitting peer against self reward would read: "Some kids try to do well in school because they want to learn a lot, but other kids try to do well in school because they think their friends will like them better."

We have now constructed such a scale and administered it to one sample of older elementary school children. This particular scale does not lend itself to factor-analytic procedures, given the large number of potential subscales that result from the crossing of the three dimensions. Nor was there any expectation that children would make distinctions between the various functions of reward. Presumably, rewards fulfill different functions simultaneously, and this psychological convergence should result in a statistical merger as well. We are currently examining the psychometric properties of the scale, including the internal consistency as defined by the correlation of item replicates for each of the 12 potential subscales. Until these data are available, it is difficult to interpret subscale scores.

Nevertheless, some interesting patterns promise to emerge. Each of the three dimensions—reward function, external agent (peer or adult) pitted against self reward, and competence area—affect the degree to which children are intrinsic or extrinsic, and there are several complex interpretations that warrant closer scrutiny. One such example was found for the evaluative function, how children know whether or not they are successful. In the cognitive domain, children were very extrinsic when the source of extrinsic reward (pitted against self reward) was an adult. In the same domain, scores were in the extreme intrinsic range when the extrinsic reward source (pitted against self reward) was a peer. This pattern was just the reverse in the social domain; children were more extrinsic when peers were pitted against self reward and rated themselves as more intrinsic when adults were the competing reward agent. In the physical domain, reward source made no difference, with children claiming to be relative intrinsically motivated in general.

Our goal, after refining the scale, will be to examine these dimensions developmentally. If our model is correct, we expect that, as development proceeds, children become increasingly intrinsic when self reward is pitted against adult reward. Conversely, we predict that children become more extrinsic in certain domains when self-reward is pitted against peer reinforcement. We have yet to speculate about the particular age at which the older child or adolescent internalizes or incorporates the peer-approval functions. This will eventually require a thoughtful life-span approach in which we extend our analysis and resulting assessment procedures into adolescence and young adulthood.

AFFECTIVE CONCOMITANTS OF ONE'S MOTIVATIONAL ORIENTATION

One dimension in the preceding analysis involved the affective function of reward. My interest in this general topic predated a consideration of a particular theoretical framework; in fact, in some of my earliest empirical work in this area, I addressed the issue of the pleasure derived from challenge. In White's (1959) model, intrinsic pleasure had been identified as the reward for competent performance, or success at mastery attempts; in my initial refinement of his model, I suggested that it might be fruitful to examine the relationship between the amount of challenge presented by the task and the degree of pleasure experienced through success. In the first study of this programmatic effort, a clear-cut positive relationship was obtained between pleasure, as reflected in smiling, and level of difficulty for those tasks that were successfully solved (Harter, 1974). The findings from this first study, in which fifth and sixth graders were asked to solve an anagram task, were replicated with first graders who were given puzzles of varying difficulty level (Harter, 1977). This second study also revealed, however, that a positive linear relationship between smiling and task difficulty was not obtained in a condition where normal children were socially reinforced for their performance. In such a condition, social smiling in response to the approving adult appears to reach a ceiling, such that effects attributable to a "mastery" smile were obscured.

Subject variables (viz. IQ and gender) were also found to be determinants of the relationship between pleasure and success at tasks of varying difficulty. For children in the retarded range, a negative relationship was obtained; maximum smiling was manifest to the easiest puzzles solved, and the least smiling to the most difficult items solved. Gender differences also emerged, suggesting the need to take a more careful look at within-gender differences, particularly for girls. In particular, given the model proposed, one needs to examine the socialization histories that may be responsible for the responses of the various subgroups we identified.

In a more recent follow-up study with elementary school children, the range of anagram task difficulty was extended from three to four difficulty levels (Harter, 1978b). The results indicated a positive linear relationship between smiling and task difficulty for the first three levels only. At the most difficult level, there was a slight attenuation of the smiling response. These findings suggested that the initial positive relationship obtained does not extend to the *most* challenging items an individual is able to master. Rather, it appears that there are certain very difficult tasks that one may eventually complete successfully; however, one attaches a somewhat negative subjective evaluation to his or her performance due to the amount of time or effort required, and thus does not experience maximum pleasure. Feelings of annoyance, embarrassment, frustration, and so on, serve to attenuate the gratification obtained.

When pleasure was examined as a function of *perceived* difficulty (which subjects rated on a four-point scale for each item), this pattern was even stronger. That is, a positive linear relationship was obtained between perceived difficulty and smiling, but it dropped off dramatically for those items judged very hard. In addition, the inquiry data strongly supported the notion that even though subjects were able to solve some of the very difficult anagrams, they enjoyed these problem-solving efforts less than their success on items that were challenging, but in their opinion, not excessively difficult. An important mediating variable here appears to be perceived solution time. Subjects were extremely sensitive to the time dimension and verbally

Buhrmester's school-concerns scale. As predicted we found that cognitive competence is significantly related to anxiety about school performance; the lower one's feeling of competence, the higher one's anxiety level. Children's perceptions of social and physical competence, as well as their feelings of general self worth, were also related to Buhrmester's peer-esteem scale; the more anxious children had lower feelings of competence and self worth. We will explore these data in more detail to see whether models other than a straightforward linear relationship better describe the interaction of these two variables.

Perceived Competence and Perceptions of Control

Our first speculations about the relationship between these two variables were very straighforward, if not simplistic, in that we expected that children with high perceived competence would have more internal perceptions of control and children with low perceived competence would display more external preceptions of control. The construction of Connell's (1978) multidimensional perceived control scale and resulting data have revealed that the picture is considerably more complex. The emergence of an entirely new construct, which Connell has labeled *unknown* source of control, has added intriguing dimension to our thinking about the relationships between perceived competence and perceived control. Recall that although earlier investigators had conceptualized control as either internal or external, Connell's findings revealed an important third type of perception whereby children acknowledge that they do not know what is responsible for the happenings in their lives.

We have now tested large samples of children from the third to the ninth grade where data from both the perceived-competence scale and the perceptions-of-control scale are available. These data constitute a rich source of information about individual differences, as well as developmental change. Rather than mindlessly correlate all of the pertinent variables, we have randomly sampled from our data pool and have performed planned correlation analyses that will initially assist us in formulating minimodels of the relationships between our variables. These will then be tested on other samples, eventually using higher-order factoring procedures, regression analyses, and path analyses.

One example gives the flavor of this strategy, and some sense of the complexity of the phenomena. Within the cognitive domain only, Connell and Harter (1979) first examined the correlations among perceived cognitive competence and internal, external, and unknown sources of control. Standard achievement test scores were also included in this initial correlational analysis. The findings revealed that perceived cognitive competence was most highly related to the unknown-source-of-control score; the more competent children perceive themselves to be, the lower their scores on the unknown-control subscale. The scores of children whose perceived competence is low indicate that they are uncertain about what controls the outcomes in their life. Interestingly, the unknown-control score was even more highly related to children's actual competence as reflected in their achievement scores. Perceived and actual competence were also significantly related to one another.

We were somewhat puzzled, however, because our prediction that perceived competence would be positively related to *internal* control scores did not find direct support. The magnitude of this correlation, although positive, was small. We were aware, however, that there were often large discrepancies between a child's internal perceptions of control over success as compared to failure. This led us to speculate that some children who were taking more internal responsibility for their failures, relative to their successes, might be attenuating the overall relationship between internality and perceived competence. Thus, through higher-order factor-analytic procedures, we are currently testing the following minimodel with regard to the relationship between perceived competence and perceptions of control in the cognitive domain: Partialing out those children who take more responsibility for their failures than successes, we are predicting a higher-order competence-control factor defined by perceived competence, unknown control, and internal control. A high scorer on this factor would be the child who feels cognitively competent, whose low unknown-control score reflects the fact that he or she is aware of what controls the events in his or her life, and who feels that he or she is internally responsible for these events. This child is saying, in effect, "I'm competent, I know what's going on, and I'm in control." Low scorers on this factor do not feel competent, admit that they do not understand who or what is in control, and acknowledge that they are not personally responsible.

Although these predictions are compelling, theoretically as well as intuitively, they represent only one small piece of the pie and delimit the relationship among a small subset of variables. Our strategy next dictates that we relate this higher-order factor to our major motivational construct. Recall here that three of the subscales on the classroom scale emerged as motivational in nature, whereas two defined a separate higher-order factor, which we interpreted as more informational. Our best prediction is that children high on the competence-control factor would also be more intrinsically motivated those first three subscales, defined by preference for challenge, curiosity, and independent mastery attempts. This constellation of characteristics, culled from three of our scales, seems to define what for now appears to be the quintessential mastery orientation. The child higher on this factor is telling us: I enjoy the mastery *process* (I'm intrinsically motivated to master), the *product* is successful (I'm competent), I know why it happened, who is in control, and that person is me, I'm primarily responsible. The child low on this factor does not enjoy the mastery process, does not feel competent, and is uncertain about who or what is responsible for this outcome.

This, then, provides an example of the direction of our minimodeling efforts. Sometimes the data follow; more often, they lead. The choreography is complex, to say the least, and at times the soure of control appears to be unknown. But we dance on, often content to allow the data the status of a powerful other. The steps are small ones. It would appear that we have abandoned some of our more daring leaps. What does all of this imply for model building? I attempt to address this question, more humbly than I would have preferred.

MUSINGS ON A MODEL OF MASTERY MOTIVATION

Initially, I had wanted this chapter to present a bigger and better model. At best, we have captured a respectable portion of the variance for a few interesting constructs. We have become much less grandiose in one sense, forsaking the diagramatic effort to depict the big picture. In abandoning that goal, we feel we have allowed a much richer understanding of the phenomena to emerge. We have taken off a number of theoretical blinders and, as a result, have been somewhat bedazzled. It has become clear that our energies should be directed towards the construction of various minimodels rather than an attempt to articulate an all-encompassing theory, as such. Our efforts do not appear piecemeal, however. There are a number of general issues and specific directions that we feel we can highlight at this point.

The Fate of Effectance Motivation as a Construct

Our empirical journeys have taken us far afield from our origin, which in turn has raised the question: Do we need this global construct at all? What does it buy us? Not much in the methodological marketplace, we have learned. Initially, we felt that this construct guided our efforts to pinpoint components that we might operationally define more precisely. As each of these constructs has seemingly taken on a conceptual life of its own, however, the role of the parent construct has become more obscure. Personally, I rather like the notion of an adaptive motive force such as effectance, viewed from an evolutionary perspective, as White proposed. However, effectance motivation appears to be a hypothetical construct very much like Santa Claus. It is rather oversized and ephemeral. We do not quite know its location, cannot quite pin it down. Yet, it is a source of goodness, and debunking the myth somehow does not destroy the construct. Yes, Virginia, somewhere there is an effectance motive.

A More Differentiated Approach

As I think we have demonstrated, however, our harvest has been much more fruitful when we have considered the components of the miniconstructs we have identified. Our biggest success, perhaps, has been the situation specificity that we have brought to bear on these constructs. For us, this translates into the competence domains on the perceived-control scale, into dimensions of classroom learning on the motivational-orientation scale, distinctions between attributions for success and failure on Connell's Control Scale, and issues or situations that elicit anxiety on Buhrmester's School-Concerns Scale. An important feature of our scale-construction efforts has been the demonstration that the children themselves are sensitive to these distinctions. The data have repeatedly highlighted the need to take such a differentiated approach. As such, they have thwarted our efforts to make the kind of sweeping generalizations that characterized the initial model.

Constructs and Operational Definitions

The specification of subscales has allowed us to be more precise in our definitions of the constructs in question. We feel this is an essential step, conceptually and methodologically. Too often, terms such as "self esteem" and "intrinsic motivation" are bandied about without any clear referents, and only becloud our thinking about these constructs.

We must also be cautious, however, not to allow the measures themselves to take on a life of their own and *become* the construct in question. For example, our motivational-orientation scale employs a forced-choice format in which intrinsic and extrinsic orientations are pitted against one another. In devising this scale, we intentionally wanted to assess the relative strength of these two orientations. This scale format implies a motivational continuum going from intrinsic to extrinsic and further suggests that the converse of an intrinsic motivational orientation is an extrinsic psychological stance. Although this measure met our initial needs, we realize that, ultimately, we will need to alter this measure such that it will be sensitive to the simultaneous operation of both intrinsic and extrinsic forces and to the relative strength of each. Thus, we hope to move to a question format that will not only allow for an independent assessment of the strength of both intrinsic and extrinsic orientations, but would also allow us to identify the relatively *unmotivated* child for whom both orientations are weak. We are certainly aware of the existence of such children from our experience in the classroom; we would do well to design measures sensitive to this pattern. Such a measure would also allow us to trace the developmental precursors of such a pattern.

Individual Differences and Developmental Change

The issue of developmental change is one that we must eventually tackle, and to date we have not devoted sufficient energy to this enterprise. We have been awed by the tremendous individual differences we consistently discover not only with regard to single variables, but to the patterns, constellations of variables, and typologies of children that some of our higher-order factoring has revealed. Historically, individual differences have been the bane of the developmentalist's existence. We have found ourselves wallowing in them to some extent. We have become preoccupied with the *demonstration* of reliable individual differences. We have yet to investigate the antecedents of these differences, however—an awesome task indeed. It is important to note that the developmental thrust of our research is not simply the typical ontogenetic study of age- or stage-related change. Rather, we must examine the historical antecedents that are responsible for the development of *differences* among children at various age levels, as well as similarities.

The Functions of Reward: A Potential New Link in the Ontogenetic Chain

The conceptualization of the various functions of reward holds particular promise. The construction of a scale that allows us to assess meaningfully the degree to which these functions have been internalized has been an important first step. We can now determine whether each function—incentive, affective, goal identification, and criteria for success/failure—is controlled primarily by external sources of reward (adult or peer approval) or by the child's self-reward system; we can make this determination separately for each competence domain.

This possibility both broadens and sharpens our thinking concerning the relatively intrinsic individual. Previously, we have confined the intrinsic-extrinsic distinction to what we believed were primarily *motivational* parameters. However, the separation into motivational and informational dimensions appears to provide a more meaningful framework for thinking about an intrinsic or extrinsic orientation. The directionality of these two functions does not necessarily covary. For example, children may be characterized as relatively intrinsic on the motivational dimension, and yet relatively extrinsic on the information dimension. Such children may be motivated to engage in an activity for its own sake, and may derive intrinsic pleasure from their performance, yet may still be dependent on external sources to define what mastery goals were important, and whether or not their efforts were successful. An inspection of individual profiles from our functions-of-reward scale indicates the existence of this type of pattern. Its converse can also be documented. In this case, children require extrinsic rewards or sanctions to motivate them to perform the behavior, but have internalized the standards, rules, and criteria to evaluate their performance. These patterns define individual children.

The motivational–information distinction also contributes to our understanding of developmental change, although we had not intended our classroom-orientation scale to tap these two dimensions. The results indicated, however, that the three motivational subscales showed a systematic shift from intrinsic to extrinsic across the elementary and junior high years, whereas the two informational subscales showed the opposite shift, from an extrinsic orientation.

The differentiation between motivational and informational functions may also aid in our understanding of our major attributional constructs, perceived competence, and perception of control. One hypothesis we can now examine is that the motivational properties—incentive and affective—have their major influence on the child's sense of competence, whereas the informational functions—knowledge of mastery goals and the criteria for success—more directly determine the child's perceptions of control. To the extent that a given child has internalized a self-reward system in which the incentive and affective functions are intrinsic, feelings of competence should be relatively high; conversely, the child whose motivation to perform is primarily extrinsic probably has relatively low feelings of competence. The informational functions, however, would not have such a direct effect on competence. We can test this hypothesis by administering our new functions-of-reward scale in conjunction with the perceived-competence scale. Evidence to support this type of prediction comes from our higher-ordering factoring of the classroom scale in conjunction with the perceived-competence measure, in which the more motivational subscales loaded on a factor with perceived-cognitive competence, whereas the two informational subscales defined their own unrelated factor.

One would expect that the informational functions of reward, as conceptualized by this formulation, would be more directly related to a child's perception of control. The child who has internalized standards of performance, mastery goals, and the criteria for success and failure would be expected to manifest a relatively internal perception of control, with low scores on those subscales tapping powerful others or an unknown source of control; the child who has not internalized these informational functions would be expected to have low scores on the internal subscale, relative to the other two sources of control. These hypotheses can be tested by examining the pattern of response on the functions of reward and perceptions of control scales.

Implications for the Internalization Process
and the Reinforcement History of the Child

The goal of our model in waiting is to understand the developmental course that predicts the pattern of individual differences that we have now begun to document with our data. In our initial analysis, we implicated the reinforcement history of the child; we looked very generally to the role of the socializing agents in the child's life. We now feel that we can conceptualize these effects more precisely in terms of the reward functions served by parental or peer responses.

In the earlier model, we singled out parental approval of independent mastery attempts as an important prerequisite for the internalization of a self-reward system; disapproval and reinforcement for dependency were seen as related to the development of a more extrinsic orientation. We can now go beyond this suggestion and begin to conceptualize the various functions that parental reward might serve, although an empirical attack may require considerable ingenuity. Consider the child who is receiving approval for mastery behaviors, within the context of the functions that extrinsic reward can serve. To what extent is this approval conveying information with regard to mastery goals and standards, with regard to the importance of being good at behaviors in domain X? To what extent does it convey information concerning the criteria by which one judges his or her success in that domain? With regard to the potential motivational functions, to what degree does this reward provide an incentive to repeat the behavior? And, what affective consequences does it have in producing pleasures?

Theoretically, we can speculate that parental approval may be more salient with regard to certain functions than to others. Consistency of parental emphasis and labeling of these functions may also be a related factor influencing the strength of the mastery goals and self-reward system internalized by the child. Admittedly, these factors constitute only a small segment of that larger domain of parental response styles and child-rearing variables. There is much to be done in charting this terrain.

Future Directions in Model Building:
Correlation Versus Cause

We have illustrated some of the possible directions in which our efforts might take us. To date, we have only discussed the empirical relationships among variables in correlational terms. Thus, for example, we are now confident in our finding that an intrinsic motivational orientation is related to a child's sense of competence as well as control. But what about the causal links among these variables? These are questions of both theoretical and practical significance. Is the child's sense of competence a precursor of his or her intrinsic orientation, or does one's intrinsic orientation lead to mastery attempts, which, if successful, enhance one's sense of competence? Where does the child's sense of control enter into this network? These are questions that we can now ask of the data. Currently, we are beginning to employ path-analytic techniques to test alternative causal models. For example, the causal implications in the original diagram were that some combination of intrinsic motivation and success would lead to perceptions of competence and control. Beyond this, however, specific predictions were not advanced. Our measures have allowed us to test much more specific predictions and to pit several seemingly reasonable models against one another in order to determine which one best characterizes our data. In addition to cross-sectional data, we are into the third year of a longitudinal study that will provide us with even greater predictive power (Connell & Harter, 1979). Thus, we are now in a position to examine causal relationships in the model.

But wait. What model? Do we or do we not have a new and more differentiated model? An earlier section of this chapter referred to "constructs in search of a measure." Perhaps we are now in a position to conclude that there are measurable constructs in search of a model. But right now, it feels a bit beyond our grasp, perhaps not unlike effectance motivation and Santa Claus. Yes, Virginia, somewhere there is a model. Just wait until next Christmas!

ACKNOWLEDGMENTS

The research reported in this chapter was supported by a grant #HD-09613 from the National Institute for Child Health and Human Development, NIH, U.S.P.H.S. Much of the research and thinking presented here has grown out of my collaboration with Jim Connell and Bob Engstrom who have constantly provided conceptual input and statistical expertise. Manuals for the instruments described can be obtained from the author. Author's address: Department of Psychology, University of Denver, 2040 South York, Denver, Colorado 80208.

REFERENCES

Aronfreed, J. The concept of internalization. In Goslin (Ed.), *Handbook of socialization theory and research.* Chicago: Rand McNally, 1969.
Bandura, A. Vicarious and self-reinforcement processes. In Glaser (Ed.), *The nature of reinforcement.* New York: Academic Press, 1971.
Connell, J. P. *A multidimensional measure of children's perceptions of control.* Unpublished manuscript, University of Denver, 1979.

Connell, J. P., & Harter, S. *The relationship between children's motivational orientation, perceived competence, and perceptions of control: A test of alternative models.* Unpublished manuscript, University of Denver, 1979.

Crandall, V. C., Crandall, V. J., & Katkovsky, W. A children's social desirability questionnaire. *Journal of Consulting Psychology,* 1965, *29,* 27–36.

Deci, E. L. *Intrinsic motivation.* New York: Plenum Press, 1975.

Harter, S. Pleasure derived from cognitive challenge and mastery. *Child Development,*1974, *45,* 661–669.

Harter, S. The effects of social reinforcement and task difficulty on the pleasure derived by normal and retarded children from cognitive challenge and master. *Journal of Experimental Child Psychology,* 1977, *24,* 476–494.

Harter, S. Effectance motivation reconsidered: Toward a developmental model. *Human Development,*1978, *1,* 34–64. (a)

Harter, S. Pleasure derived from optimal challenge and the effects of extrinsic rewards on children's difficulty level choices. *Child Development,*1978, *49,* 788–799. (b)

Harter, S. Intrinsic versus Extrinsic Orientation in the Classroom, *Developmental Psychology,* in press.

Harter S. *Perceived competence and its relationship to preference for challenging tasks.* Unpublished manuscript, University of Denver, 1980.

Harter, S. The perceived competence scale for children. *Child Development,* in press.

Levenson, H. *Distinction within the concept of internal–external control.* Paper presented at the American Psychological Association Convention, Washington, D.C., 1972.

Wechsler, D. Cognitive, conative, and non-intellective intelligence. *American Psychologist,* 1950, *5,* 78–83.

White, R. Motivation reconsidered: The concept of competence. *Psychological Review,* 1959, *66,* 297–323.

Wylie, R. C. *The self concept* (Vol. 1). Lincoln, Neb.: University of Nebraska Press, 1974.

Zigler, E., & Harter, S. The socialization of the mentally retarded. In D. A. Goslin (Ed.), *Handbook of socialization theory and research.* Chicago: Rand McNally, 1969.

List of Contributors

Marc H. Bornstein is assistant professor of psychology at New York University. A Ph.D. of Yale University, he has been a Visiting Scientist at the Max-Planck-Institut für Psychiatrie in Munich and a Visiting Fellow at University College, London.

Michael Cole is professor of psychology and director of the laboratory of Comparative Human Cognition at the University of California, San Diego. He earned a doctorate at Indiana University and has held faculty appointments at Yale, University of California at Irvine, and Rockefeller University, and has been an Exchange Scholar at Moscow University.

Kenneth Traupmann, a Ph.D in psychology from the University of Wisconsin, Milwaukee, is an assistant research pediatric psychologist at the Center for Human Information Processing, University of California, San Diego.

Frances K. Graham is professor of pediatrics and psychology at the University of Wisconsin, Madison. Her doctorate is from Yale, and she has held faculty appointments at Washington University and Barnard College.

Barbara D. Strock and *Bonnie L. Zeigler* are doctoral students in psychology at the University of Wisconsin, Madison.

Susan Harter, a Ph.D. of Yale University, is professor of psychology at the University of Denver. Her previous faculty appointments have been at Yale.

Mark Lepper is associate professor of psychology at Stanford University and, in 1979–80, a fellow at the Center for the Advanced Study in the Behavioral Sciences. He received his doctorate at Yale.

Elissa L. Newport received her Ph.D. from the University of Pennsylvania and has held faculty appointments at the University.

Author Index

Numbers in *italics* denote pages with complete bibliographic information.

Subject Index